PATRIOTS: GOING, GOING, GONE!

PATRIOTS: GOING, GOING, GONE!

C. Birch Pontius

iUniverse, Inc.
New York Lincoln Shanghai

PATRIOTS: GOING, GOING, GONE!

Copyright © 2005 by Birch Pontius

iUniverse books may be ordered through booksellers or by contacting:

iUniverse
2021 Pine Lake Road, Suite 100
Lincoln, NE 68512
www.iuniverse.com
1-800-Authors (1-800-288-4677)

ISBN-13: 978-0-595-35935-6 (pbk)
ISBN-13: 978-0-595-80389-7 (ebk)
ISBN-10: 0-595-35935-3 (pbk)
ISBN-10: 0-595-80389-X (ebk)

Printed in the United States of America

Contents

ACKNOWLEDGMENT

No author worth his salt can complete a novel without a proofreading editor who corrects his sentence structure, spelling errors, grammar, and punctuation. A writer is blessed if the editor is a patient lady who's been a newspaper reporter and publicity writer.

My sincerest thanks go to Mrs. Eleanor Lucile Meck Pontius, a graduate of Kent State University, Ohio, who completed a double major in journalism and speech. Her valuable suggestions and countless hours devoted to correcting my efforts have made me appear a better author than I truly am.

So, to my wonderful wife, Eleanor Meck Pontius, I again say, "Thank you for being my severest critic and my biggest booster."

—CBP

1

Sanitation Burial

Leith Ci Ohmstead lay semiconscious, suffocating. Plastic materials squeezed every inch of his body, and rotting, pungent odors plagued his nostrils. His hands and feet could not move, due to the close-knit packing around him. Leith struggled for oxygen. All he got was a stench of fetid air, . . air so polluted with choking gas that he knew there must be an assassin's bag tied around his throat.

Yet, while slowly and painfully twisting, he could detect no cord wrapped around his neck. But, his hands and feet were bound together, tied tightly enough to cut off circulation to his wrists and knees. In his dying condition, Leith appreciated the last few precious moments of life. Despite so little breathable air, he had regained consciousness. But, even that brief respite was slipping away.

The throbbing in his skull remained unabated. He faintly recalled how the winds whistled past his ears to remind him of his last seconds on earth. He vaguely recollected his impromptu high dive from his hotel room in the Washington, D.C., skyscraper.

Normally alert, forever watchful of anything or anyone behind his back, he was blind-sided as if he were a child. He never saw his assailant, or assailants. Exhausted from tedious hours of surveillance, combined with sleepless nights, his mind wove facts and incriminating evidence together to guarantee a grand jury indictment. He physically staggered to his hotel room balcony for a breath of fresh air as he drank a welcome nightcap before retiring.

Glancing at the turned-down bedcovers, he anticipated the cool, clean white sheets and an uninterrupted night of sleep. At that weary moment, Leith was most vulnerable.

The room lights turned off then exploded on—inside his head—accompanied by a thousand shooting stars. Agent Ohmstead felt the cold concrete of the balcony when his body crumpled against the wrought iron. Barely lucid, Leith also felt the vicious tug of ropes gouging the skin of his arms and feet, ropes that bound him like a helpless calf at a championship rodeo. Strong hands hoisted him above the balcony railing. Leith was swung to and fro like a hammock, then he heard a commanding voice intone, "One, two, three, HEAVE!"

Instantly, Leith Ohmstead experienced weightlessness as he sailed through the air. He was conscious of winds whistling past his ears while he plummeted toward the pavement many stories below. Plunging to his death, Leith observed the street rising to meet him, saw the headlights of the myriad automobiles—beams of white slashing through the blackness of night. Headlights, illuminating pathways through traffic, framed the giant truck directly beneath him, its thick steel bed beckoning.

Ohmstead, his head bloodied, actually chuckled in detached euphoria because he was watching a gangster movie. Hands tied, he mentally applauded the final judgment imposed on the evil villain—Death! Leith had no doubt his own finish would be fast...and exacting. Suddenly, for no reason, he was shouting.

Better yet, he was hollering a passable imitation of the famous yell of the Hollywood actor, Johnny "Tarzan" Weissmuller. Leith was yodeling Tarzan's cry, several times, before he crashed into the huge maw of the truck's storage, a heavily stuffed storage, a crammed storage.

Agent Ohmstead smashed through it all—to oblivion. Seconds later, through the conscious crevices of his mind, he heard a grinding whine. Machinery was struggling, the pitch of the motors rising and falling, and Leith felt himself being lifted, high, higher, when, suddenly, his world turned upside down. The tight pressures of the packing around him released—and they, and he, were tumbling downward, always downward.

The torture would not stop. Leith was falling again. The foul-smelling bags, boxes, and paper sacks which absorbed his eight-story plunge, were falling with him. But, the spaces between, still stinking, were filled with air, oxygen, and the Tarzan mimic gasped loudly, inhaling deep breaths of life-giving air. Leith's oxygen-starved brain began chuckling again. He knew he was badly injured. Despite his concussion, with each breath he fanatasized and cackled with the sick joke about the man who jumped off the Empire State Building. As the man hurtled past each story, he reassured himself with snapping fingers,

"Snap! Well, so far...so good! Snap! So far...so good!" And with each priceless breath Leith's mind gradually cleared, his numb throbbing body revived, and he kept repeating, "Well, so far, so good!"

Then, he experienced another gut wrencher. This time, Ohmstead found himself standing upright in a hydraulic-operated city sanitation truck with bags, sacks, boxes of garbage, empty cans, grass and plant cuttings, limbs, and broken lumber, all surrounding and cushioning him, but effectively pinning him against any movement. Another mess of garbage fell on him from an overturning garbage dumpster. Leith stood half-in and half-out of the refuse. With his hands bound, but positioned high above his head, he looked right into the face of the dumpster operator. The operator reached for the hydraulic actuator bar, oblivious to the "pressing engagement" threatening his victim. Automatically, maximizing each load the dumpster would hold, the operator flung in one more curbside trashbag and actuated the hydraulic ram. The grinding whine began again. This time, Leith knew that the bottom blade of the press would push, then squeeze the refuse into a small mass, making room for more loads of compacted garbage. In seconds his 6' 6" body would be reduced to a small cube. The irony struck Leith Ohmstead.

"Buddy Boy, you've run out of miracles: To survive an eight-story fall was unbelievable. But, to survive being crushed into a bloody package one foot square is too much to hope for."

Leith felt himself being forced into the crushing compartment of the truck. This accident would be fast, the pain brief. Then the agent heard,

"OH, MY GOD! WHAT THE ---?"

The bag just thrown into the presser had landed against Leith's buried waist. The garbage hauler was pulling the spring-loaded hydraulic actuator when his eyes traveled from the plastic sack…up to, then onto, the bloody, torn, and garbage-stained visage of a human being. The apparition revealed a stomach, chest, and head. A battered man stood before him, his arms held high above his head.

The truck operator's mouth flew wide open in shock. There, ready to be compressed, stood a "hit victim." A victim who was supposed to disappear without a trace.

"DEAR GOD! A MAFIA HIT! In my truck, too!" thought the hauler. The hauler let go. The hydraulic-press bar sprang back to *"off"* with a CLANG!

"JODI? GOD'S SAKE, TURN OFF THE MOTOR."

"What'd you say?"

"TURN OFF THE G-- D--- MOTOR!"

Fortunately, that impossible second miracle did occur. The powerful truck motor stopped and the dumping machinery stilled. Leith Ohmstead barely remembered being pulled from the refuse and watching a knife cut the ropes. Both city employees stood dumbfounded, looking at a living dead man.

Leith hardly heard the wailing siren as the ambulance careened toward the hospital. He vaguely recalled one of the attendants complaining,

"Where in heck did this street person sleep? He's not just one of the great unwashed, he really stinks to high heaven! PHEW!"

A mangled Leith Ohmstead barely smiled. He mumbled,

"I may stink, but I'm alive."

He was glad to accept the trade.

2

Stalking His Prey

The hypodermic needle sank carefully toward the left side of Ohmstead's stomach muscle. His blackened eyes, now mere slits because of the bruising impact when he crashed into the truck's refuse bin, blinked open just enough to notice the doctor's target area and the surprising size of his syringe. Then Leith glanced at the tube and saw the huge amount of fluid it held.

The dimensions of the hypodermic reminded him of veterinarians he had watched treating horses and cattle. The injection was going to be massive. Compared to a thimble-sized flu shot, this needle would dispense a bucketful. With each inhalation, Ohmstead experienced excruciating pain. He was convinced every bone in his body had been fractured from the fall, and he wondered how many ribs were cracked or broken.

Even now, his intuition did not fail. An alarm sounded in his brain as he realized a doctor was attempting to inject an enormous dose of something into his stomach. His stomach? Not into an arm, thigh, or even his buttocks? Without warning? With no explanation? While the patient was semi-conscious?

Leith knew there was no way the medical staff could have had time to confirm he'd contacted rabies from that garbage heap. He knew that, in the past, stomach shots were given strictly for rabies. Fortunately, such a painful procedure is now outdated. His suspicious mind demanded answers, so he looked up into the face of his benefactor.

The doctor's uniform was white; a stethoscope hung around his neck; and, Leith, staring into his eyes, expected the eyes to show the "mirrors of his soul," compassion and concern. They did not. The physician's expression made Leith's blood ran cold.

In a lifetime of criminal investigation, dealing with all levels of human beings, Leith had developed an insight and "gut intuition" about people. The eyes guiding the syringe needle were anything but doctoral. The focus on the physician's face exuded evil. The doctor's eyes were sinister—malice glimmering with murder. That "intuitive hunch" left no doubt within Ohmstead. When the medical imposter realized the patient was studying him, and saw his victim's astonished facial expression, the "doctor" gasped loudly, then jammed the hypo at Leith's stomach, meanwhile already squirting a stream of liquid through the needle.

Instinctively, Leith struck at the physician's face with a hard right fist,...following through by sitting bolt upright in the hospital bed. At the same time, Leith's left hand closed over the large syringe, pushing it away from his body. Leith was gratified to hear the cartilage of the pretender's nose crunch from the solid blow.

The "doctor" screamed in anguish—his blood spraying everywhere. Despite the unexpected resistance, the uniformed assailant was determined. Using his body weight, he drove the needle downward toward Leith's abdomen. He fell on Ohmstead who now was frantically grasping the deadly hypodermic with both his hands. Ohmstead grabbed the hand holding the syringe, and twisted backward with every ounce of his remaining strength. Fighting for his life, he could not believe what had happened to him in the past hour: A high dive into a dump truck; next, rescue from a trash compactor where he was scheduled to become the square root of a cube; then, a frantic race to the hospital for emergency surgery, where, fortunately, Leith survived the operation; and now, finally, awakening just in time to struggle with some impostor trying to terminate him in his own hospital room. That's when Leith got mad.

Cursing like a top sergeant, he wrenched the lethal needle away from his body and heaved upward in a desperate burst of frenzied energy. Suddenly, he heard the white-coated assailant cry out. "WHAT—? NO. THIS CAN'T HAPPEN. NO. Not me—no one ever bests

'Andre the Specialist'. This should be over. It only takes a second,...just a sec—so quick, so easy, so qui', . . qui', . . so...."

Whoever he was, Andre staggered away from the hospital bed, disbelief contorting his face, his whining child-like voice sick with horror and torment. He stared disbelieving; stared in shock, looking at the chrome syringe now plunged deeply through his lower rib cage.

The deadly instrument's plunger had performed its function. The bulk of the murderous serum had been injected. Already the compound had spread through Andre's insides. What symptom the chemical produced must have been insufferable. The white-coated assassin collapsed and slid slowly down the wall, paralyzed. An agonized moan, then a bloody froth, broke from his convulsing lips.

The charlatan gazed at Leith while the hollow cylinder stuck visibly from his chest, its position held tightly by the assassin's muscle spasms. Bright red foam bubbled from his lips, the stain trickling downward dyeing his blouse a deep crimson.

His eyes, glazing over, gaped at his intended quarry, but the lethal solution had done its work. Andre said nothing, saw nothing. He no longer existed in this world.

A nurse opened the door, entered, and stumbled over the outstretched feet of the corpse. She took one look, screamed, and ran, shrieking, down the corridor. Room traffic grew shockingly heavy. But, Leith Ohmstead had shot his bolt. He lay in the bed, knowing nothing, unconscious. Dashing into the room, the resident doctor on duty missed little as he viewed the scene. His diagnosis, however, would have shamed Sherlock Holmes.

"Who killed this doctor? Any of you know him? Hey. What's he doing in Ohmstead's room?" Is Ohmstead dead? Get the police in here—Stat."

An R.N. rushed down the hall to the nurse's station and its telephones. The resident was joined by a senior physician on his rounds. He watched the resident doctor examine the dead man, all the while shaking his head in disbelief.

And the victim who had only wanted a peaceful night's sleep? Two nurses confirmed that Ohmstead's vital signs showed steady breathing, a somewhat irregular pulse, and that he was comatose—unconscious. Then they said,

"We find no additional marks on Mr. Ohmstead, Doctor."

The senior physician, who had come to help, replied, "It's not because someone hasn't tried."

But the resident doctor barely heard any of them. He was now sleuthing like a homicide detective.

"Sweet Jesus. This is for the police. This dead man is no doctor."

The assisting physician asked, "Why do you say that?"

"Because, this guy's carrying a wicked toadsticker strapped to his calf. He's also got a large clip 9-millimeter Beretta automatic on his belt. Hmmmmm, the gun's stamped Model 92. Hey, don't the newspapers say that's the kind of firearm professional hit men use?

"From the looks of him, with that cattle syringe in his chest, he wasn't here to heal, but to harm. Must'a been one heck of a struggle…which he lost."

The resident physician asked his colleague, "Doctor, please help me check this Ohmstead fellow. His identification states he's a government agent—but, for whom? Nothing else refers to an agency. I wonder if these two were after each other? Better yet, I'd like to know why?"

The nattily dressed senior physician pondered, then said,

"Must be a mighty important reason for someone to attempt to bump off a G-Man. Anyone stupid enough to harm a G-Man will find out government agents never quit. Like hounds after a fox, they'll run the guilty into the ground.

"Yet, you're looking at judgment, young fellow. Look at that murder weapon—the silver syringe and thick needle sticking deep into the dead man's guts. Whatever **was** that stuff in that hypo? He really suffered as he went. One hell of a way to die.

"And as for Ohmstead here, after studying his patient's chart, along with these write-ups about his emergency admittance to ICU, all I can say is—His is a hell of a way to make a living."

◆   ◆   ◆

Jameson "Cody" Dittus was a bundle of frustrated stamina. He was 5' 9" of raw power; he weighed 181 pounds—with very little fat. Broad shouldered, slim-waisted, with light brown hair concealing a tendency toward gray, Cody was endowed with a friendly ear-to-ear grin that impressed men, and endeared him to women from ages 16 to 66.

His habit of tilting his head when listening to someone's conversation, plus a boyish look that complemented his intense blue eyes, made him a favorite with attractive ladies wherever he traveled. An excellent ballroom dancer, Cody appealed to single women…and lonely wives. Both groups fought for the chance to drag him onto the dance floor—while hoping the dance might inspire a later visit to his comfortable apartment.

Cody Dittus' endless worldwide assignments kept him busy, but never lonely. An idealistic man, a gentleman to his fingertips, he never thought of listing his female conquests in a "little black book." Frankly, his major concern was keeping his name and address out of theirs.

Few women, or men—even men involved with the Mafia underworld—ever suspected the remarkable covert abilities of this handsome, charming man. But, Cody was frustrated now because his normal drive and stamina were barely evident. Due to exhaustion, his internal batteries were reading low. He needed rest and recharging.

For days he had struck a brick wall. The police had found: A bloody balcony; a bloody carpet; a remnant of a stout cord; and his close friend of 14 years, the room's occupant, *missing.*

Leith Ohmstead was to meet Cody with vital information, and Cody had startling news for Leith. Each man's data was insufficient to unearth a trail. But, combined, their findings might lead them from a trail onto a super highway of conspirators centered among powerful interests in Washington, D.C. Cody Dittus could ferret out a rattlesnake from a prairie dog's burrow. His aptitude in linking bits of inconsequential facts into a readable mosaic were legend among his adversaries...domestic and foreign.

Several stories are told of his pursuit of fleeing foreign quarries—some of the most notorious spies and informers, identified by the International Police Force—Interpol. Whispered tales circulate about international suspects whose files reside within England's incredible New Scotland Yard, and the Prime Minister's Secret Intelligence Service—better known as MI-6.

In clandestine circles, informed authorities admit that a number of wanted fugitives quickly surrendered themselves to British or American embassies before Cody Dittus was able to confront them. Cody's signature was swift, sometimes horrible, yet it was recognized with fear.

He used a flexible wire-saw to garrote—strangle—his victim. Sometimes, depending on his rage, he pulled the tiny, razor-toothed wire so tight it cut through the neck, a beheading as effective as a guillotine.

Cody's other guaranteed method relied on a silencer. His was a unique silencer, producing an audible noise no louder than the hiss of an angry cat. Dittus always used one bullet: A hollow-nosed slug from a newly developed "super 10-millimeter" Smith & Wesson automatic. Cody was never wasteful. His gun, holding a profuse clip of cartridges, used special bullets packed with hydrocyanic acid—a paste or crystal concentrate of hydrogen cyanide—a colorless, lethal, and very poisonous syrup with a bitter almond odor. Another name for the poison was prussic acid, commonly called cyanide.

Cody's accuracy with his sidearm was phenomenal. His favorite method of execution with that gun was one lead slug drilled exactly between the eyes. That "autograph" was his international calling card. However, if a fleeing opponent caused a rare miss, Cody would aim for the body. Regardless of where he struck his foe, . . anywhere, . . death would be absolute. The hydrocyanic acid would dissolve, even in a minor wound, and mix with the victim's blood, then circulate to the his heart, lungs, and brain. Such finality comes in micro-seconds—so fast few can even utter a scream. Cody's victims, struck by his lethal bullets, become too sick to do anything but crumple—dead. And Dittus' reports confirm a score of 100 per cent terminations. He could not tolerate failure.

◆   ◆   ◆

Washington police were baffled. Leith Ohmstead's ID inside the folding wallet identified him as a government agent. That's when the key questions emerged: Agent for whom? For what? No headquarters address was listed.

Summoned by hospital administrators to the IC Unit, police were unable to interrogate the terribly bruised patient swirling between delirium and coma. They listened to his ramblings and overheard him mention the Stouffer-Mayflower Hotel.

A frustrated detective said, "Well, it's a starting point."

Detective Lieutenant Priscilla Kozac, with two investigators and a laboratory technician, entered the Stouffer-Mayflower lobby. Inquiries at the desk left the group stymied. There was no room registered in the name of Leith Ohmstead. The manager and staff members could not identify Ohmstead from his description. Lieutenant Kozac grew disgusted.

No novice to the field of crime, Lt. Kozac suspected that Leith habitually registered during the busiest part of the day, usually when there were lines of people. The preoccupied staff were honoring registrations, checking guests out, and hollering for bellboys. Ohmstead's routine effectively maintained a low profile which made his identification difficult. This ingrained habit also saved his life on many occasions because enemies attempting to trace his whereabouts discovered a task in futility.

Her irritation showing, Priscilla Kozac then instructed the manager, "Okay then, pull every card of hotel guests whose last names begin with an 'O'. Over a period of, say,.the past two weeks."

"But that would take us most of the day." protested a desk clerk.

Kozac groaned, "You DO have a computer, don't you? Print all the O's."

As an afterthought, she added, "Then, have your computer print all the 'O' names whose first name or middle initial is 'L'."

"L, Miss . . ah . . ah, . .?"

"The name is Lieutenant Kozac." She stared at the manager's surprised look.

"What's the matter? Never seen a policewoman with rank? Why some of us even make sergeant."

"Yes, Ma'am."

Several minutes passed. The Reservation Operator brought a computer print-out to the desk and the waiting police officers.

The operator pointed to several lines, "Lieutenant, Ma'am," she said. "There are two names. An L. Obermann, room 221, who checked out yesterday, and a Lawrence Osborn, room 533. He's still a guest. Shall I ring him?"

Kozac smiled, "Thank you, but no. We'd like to greet him personally." Priscilla Kozac then suggested to the manager, "Mr. Witten, bring your passkeys. We'll take a look-see, and work our way up from #221."

The hotel's executive manager cast an admiring glance at the lady lieutenant. When the elevator door closed, the executive, Tye Witten, had time to study the officer, Priscilla Kozac. Her name implied Hungarian ancestry. Weighing 125 pounds in her long pants and polished low-heel boots, Priscilla was tall for a woman, 5' 10". Her prominent feature was alabaster skin enhanced by a golden tan. Lt. Kozac had a saucy upturned nose, and a square shaped face with a firm jaw that displayed bulldog tenacity. Witten observed she had striking brown eyes and perfect teeth that sparkled when she laughed. Her smile down-played sensuous scarlet-red lips.

When wearing her policeman's billed hat, and a military blouse with collar and tie, her appearance was considered by men on the Metropolitan Police Force as "stunning." Her beauty often bothered younger policemen, although the old-timers weren't far behind. Shiny brown hair, with ends rolled under in pageboy style,framed her intriguing face. Priscilla Kozac's body was slender, with outstanding measurements of 38-26-36. Even the Mayflower's manager, Tye Witten, admiring her voluptuous endowments, recalled the old saying,

"Blow out the candle in the window, Mother. I won't be home tonight."

Yet, Lt. Kozac's commanding manner was apparent. Her male cohorts answered her "Yes, Ma'am" with respect. Her voice was soft, her orders strict. And the lawmen jumped to obey. More surprising, her suggestions, softly spoken with warmth, were also treated as commands.

Tye Witten acknowledged, "This lieutenant lady is one hell of a leader."

Exiting on the fifth floor, General Manager Witten asked, "May I ask why you chose these names when there is no Leith Ohmstead registered?"

"Fair question. No Leith Ohmstead. So, we search for all of the L.O.'s you have registered. Someone traveling incognito has a tendency to use his initials for a fake name.

Easier to remember a pseudo that way."

"What if there's no one with the correct initials?"

"How many rooms do you have?"

"We can register guests in 724 rooms and suites, plus some extras in the annex next door."

Priscilla laughed, "If we strike out, then we'll become good friends over the next few days."

Witten gasped, "You mean we would have to inspect every room and suite in the Mayflower?"

"Mr. Witten, welcome to the world of the Washington Police Department. Having no alternative, that's exactly what we would do. And we'd do it just to track down one person, Sir. If we find no one, then we might have to start over—back to square one."

Manager Witten turned pale. "Good Lord. I'm praying we hit pay dirt. I wouldn't have your job for anything. Why, checking every room in the hotel would drive me crazy."

"Ah, you're learning, Mr. Witten. This procedure is considered routine, although, in this case, quite extensive. Police work is never done. Our primary occupational hazards are sore feet and long hours."

When Lt. Kozac's contingent entered the first room, # 221, they found the housekeepers had already made up the room. It was neat and clean, with two suitcases, clothes hung correctly on the closet rack, and a shave kit left on the sink. Nothing amiss here. Mr. Witten sighed, closed and locked the door.

Room 533, however, provoked interest. The hall door was locked, and no amount of master keys or persuasion could open it. It was bolted from the inside, although no additional deadbolt was apparent. Witten's master key worked the door locks just fine…except the room door wouldn't budge. The entrance door, a fire door, was metal covered, thick, and heavy. The only way inside was to smash it open.

"Well, here comes another charge to the Operations Fund," groaned Lt. Kozac. She nodded, and the two burly detectives attacked the door, and bounced off it several times. They suffered bruised shoulders. Not until the male technician joined them to make it a threesome, did the door begin to yield. Actually, it was the door frame that buckled. With a splintering "CRUNCH" the frame and part of the interior wall shattered into kindling; the door burst open, its hinge-side striking the wall with a loud "CRASH."

Priscilla Kozac recognized a fight scene: a fight that occurred at the far end of the room. The bed covers had been ripped off the mattress, and splashes of blood saturated the carpet. The blood stains led to the balcony. Fortunately, for police investigators, hotel housekeeping had been unable to get into this corner room.

Pieces of clothesline, made of twisted nylon cord, lay on the bloody carpet alongside an open sliding door to the balcony. The bed pillows were not rumpled, therefore leading Priscilla Kozac to a correct assumption: Leith Ohmstead had not occupied the bed before he was assaulted. Nor was it logical that he would sleep alongside an open balcony when his room was air conditioned. Moreover, at night, in the middle of downtown Washington, the hotel's street often becomes congested, creating a deafening noise of roaring engines, blaring horns, and groups of shouting revelers. After all, the nation's capital is a city of tourists and conventions.

To Lt. Kozac's team, their trained eyes recognized where a body had been trussed up: otherwise, a strong cord would not have been necessary. Also, the combat between Ohmstead and his assailants had ended when he fell, or was thrown, against the ornate railing and toppled to the balcony's concrete floor. Unconscious or not, a pool of blood had coagulated which outlined the profile of his face. From the balcony there was no further evidence of what happened.

The technician spoke excitedly to Priscilla Kozac,

"Lieutenant, look here. Someone stepped into the blood, several times. We have a faint outline of his sole, and a fair print of his heel. Looks like the shoe was new. But, why would an attacker stand in the blood and leave a clue for police? Notice how the toe is pointed toward the street? Now, Boss, please tell me where in hell did Ohmstead and his assailants go?"

Priscilla echoed his concern. "If I were the attacker, I'd burn the bloody shoes and then what would the police have? Yet, where did the attackers go? How did they leave this room? There's no way to bolt and lock that steel-plated door from inside and leave the way they came in."

Lt. Kozac covered her face with her hand and swore, "BLAST. Okay Mark, take pictures, check measurements, and dust for fingerprints."

The technician snorted sarcastically, began his usual routine, and said,

"With these muggers you already know what I'll find, Lieutenant. Not a darned thing." The evidence-technician's 35-millimeter camera clicked; his calipers carefully measured the footprints; he lightly brushed silver fingerprint dust onto every possible surface the felons may have touched. The silver dust used was a product that helped the police avoid being blamed for leaving the old system's black-graphite smudges behind.

As the technician had prophesied, his results, dusting painstakingly from the balcony to the doorknob, were one fat zero. The entire room, even the ornate railing, had been wiped clean. And, there was no way to lock the inside from the outside. Somebody, definitely a pro, knew his business.

A mystified detective sergeant asked, "What do you think, Lieutenant?"

"Detective Lemons, I believe we're over our heads. This is Washington, Wishard, and I'm getting that old feeling—this is too big and too professional for a small team. It's definitely not simple robbery or drugs. My whole being tells me this reeks of cloak and dagger. We need more help."

Orders were given to close #533 until further notice. Hotel Maintenance, under police orders, attached a padlock to the broken door. Yellow warning strips were taped across the door, the door frame, and hallway from wall to wall—effectively sealing off the end of the corridor. Worried and puzzled, Priscilla Kozac and her detective team trooped back to headquarters for assistance,…if available. In her mind, Priscilla Kozac could hear an angry police commissioner and her police chief chewing her. Both had done so in the past, and she knew this case would be no different.

A leery lieutenant stood before the Police Chief. "DAMN IT, PRISCILLA. How do you know it's a serious case? You're asking for more time? You want more help? Hell, Girl, time and help mean extra department expense.

"Besides, Kozac, show me the body. Where's the corpus delicti? You have a supposed government man who's been beaten up and in the hospital. But, you can't identify him belonging to any agency. You're asking assistance for an assault and battery charge? Come on, Woman, don't waste my time or the department's. When this Ohmstead recovers, he can tell us the entire story; then he can file a complaint."

"But Chief," countered Kozac, "Consider that locked door. There's no way to get out. Whoever did this is sharp. This smacks of something big and sinister." The chief Said, "Priscilla, you've just overlooked the obvious. This is a simple assault with intent to rob. You have proof of attempted murder? If it is, Young Lady, your felons failed. Your 'corpus delicti' is in the hospital. And you say 'without his wallet?' Ohmstead may have received a vicious beating, but that still says plain and simple robbery. Now you want me to inform the D.A.? "Lord, Lieutenant, the District Attorney would laugh at us; a judge would throw you, and me, out of court. Frankly, I don't like being laughed at or being played the fool. Understand? Now, get on with your caseloads and don't worry about a well locked door. Let the hotel worry about them."

Stymied, and unable to prove her suspicious hunch—which was dead center on the bull's eye—Priscilla Kozac returned to her office, and hung her head. She had to fight her tears, her superiors, and the criminals.

Same story, same verse: Never enough money, never enough police, too much crime, too little public support. This was one of the most intriguing cases she had ever experienced, but none of her bosses had time to play hunches…certainly not in a sophisticated crime like today's case.

Throwing caution to the wind, Priscilla phoned the Police Commissioner, which would incur more wrath because she went over her chief's head, and she received the same refusal. The words by the Police Chief and Police Commissioner were identical. Thoroughly discouraged, Lieutenant Kozac never returned to the hotel. Baffled, frustrated, and broken-hearted, her discontent with the legal system grew larger each year. Yes, Priscilla would check back with the hospital. That was S.O.P. (standard operational procedure). Yes, she would question the patient (if the patient would cooperate). But, Detective Kozac already knew this case would end up among other unsolved files treated as a part of the small-time-crime now ignored and condoned in Washington. On the sidewalk outside headquarters, Lt. Priscilla Kozac spoke angrily to no one in particular.

"I wonder how the beating victim in the hospital will feel about this? Justice? The law looks at who you are. Yes, Sir, it depends on whose ox is being gored."

◆   ◆   ◆

The case was relegated to an "unsolved crime file" and classified alphabetically among the dusty stacks of old records. Called to duty elsewhere, the Washington policeman who had guarded Room 533 removed the yellow police tapes "Do Not Enter," stuffed them in the trash, and sauntered dejected from the elevator of the Stouffer-Mayflower Hotel. His lieutenant, Priscilla Kozac, was in hot water again. The debarking policeman brushed against a rude man trying to beat the closing doors. The officer growled, but said nothing. He continued walking through the lobby to the front entrance. He had done this before: Case closed.

That rude man, head down, obviously impatient, a nondescript figure who appeared to be in a hurry, interfered with the closing door of the elevator—the one just used by the departing policeman. Normally unobtrusive, the plain looking man, dressed in shabby clothes, noticed a bellboy carrying flowers. The uniformed employee punched floor 23. The seedy character had entered the same elevator with the bellhop, but for a reason. The elevator crowd grew, pushing the passengers to the rear, but the nondescript stranger held his place directly behind the bellboy. When the bellboy exited on the 23rd floor, he had company.

After watching the employee deliver the flowers to a room far down the corridor, the man stopped the young bellboy with words chosen to evoke greed.

"Say, Young Man, I'm from Vegas, and I just bet a friend of mine that I can't uncover, . . oh say, discover, . . two scandals. Or at least two unusual happenings being concealed, cloaked, by this hotel right now. If you help me win that $50.00 bill, ten of it is yours."

"Mister, let's see the money. I can name you a dozen."

"I doubt that. Your events, or happenings, have to be unusual. Such as—well, go ahead, I'll bet you can't even name me three. Tell you what. Name me three and this twenty is yours."

"Mister, the Hollywood starlet, Sheera Valleigh is shacked up with a prominent U.S. Senator right down on the 15th floor."

"Okay, that's one for you. I didn't think you knew that."

"You don't want to know who the Senator is?"

"Naw, I already know who. I just didn't think you did. That gets you a third of the way. What else?"

"We have a famous televangelist on ninth floor who's been letting off torrid steam. Man, he's got a big suite and two lady parishioners staying with him. You should see the booze and partying they've done all week. We've had so many complaints that the management would sure kick him out if he wasn't so rich and famous. I'll say one thing for him: He tips BIG."

"That's news? Hey, I partied with him in Vegas earlier this year. You're right. He can sure spend the dough."

"You know HIM?"

"Told you I was from Vegas. EVERYBODY ends up there sooner or later. I'll give you a third and final try; but if you can't find anything really exciting—and new—you can kiss this twenty 'goodbye'."

"Hey, Man. Just what do you call exciting?"

"Something like murder, robbery, fights among the Washington bigwigs...all done on these premises. For instance, what upsets the management? What might harm the hotel's reputation? Could cause a lawsuit?"

"Ahhhhh, gotcha Mister. This just happened on the fifth floor. A whole bunch of cops, guns drawn, and nobody home; busted down the door, even part of the wall; looks like a tank hit the room entrance. The front desk is going bonkers...crazy sick, understand? Why, there's blood all over; everything's locked from the inside, and not a soul there. Nobody. The cops are asking "How did 'whoever-they-are' get out?'"

"Aw, come on."

"No kiddin'. The only way out is the balcony…straight down. You can prove it to yourself by going to the fifth floor. The south wing, end of the corridor. The hotel padlocked it. Police have it sealed—they taped it off and the area is 'verboten'. Strange, the police left, but they haven't returned. Management is plenty anxious about bad publicity. Honest. The occupant is gone; like I said, lots of blood; door was bolted from the inside—and cops say no fingerprints in the entire room."

"Sonny, what garbage are you giving me? That's too much to swallow."

"Listen, Mister. The desk manager is my cousin. He's almost sick with worry. Told me the whole story. You want proof? Just go to room 533. You'll see a padlock on the broken door; police ribbons all over the hallway. That's got to win you your $50.00 bill. Do I get my twenty now?"

"Hmmmmmm, okay. There's more of this if you keep your eyes and ears open. My friend loves to wager. Makes dumb bets…and I love to clean his plow. But, you lie to me and you won't get another dime."

"I'll take you to floor five, Mister. I can show you exactly where."

"No, I'll decide if you're in the know. Here's the twenty. You go about your business and I'll check out your story. Make sure you keep your mouth shut, but your eyes open. With that Vegas sucker staying here, we can make a killing the next two weeks. Comprendo, Señor?"

"YES, SIR." The bellhop saluted with a grin and jogged off, whistling. His greed guaranteed locked lips, even to the police. The bellhop was already spending the dollars to be made in the next two weeks playing, "I tell you; you pay me."

The nondescript man was smirking while he walked down the exit stairs to the fifth floor. "Well, if you ever quit your line of endeavor, you can always go into blackmail. Brother. This place is a Sodom and Gomorrah."

Walking briskly, he easily spotted the shattered, padlocked, door at the end of the south wing. He walked over one torn "Keep Out" tape lying on the hall carpet. Studying the corridor, he saw no one. He also noticed that a number of nearby rooms were empty. Although removed, the police warning ribbons had left their influence. No guests occupied any room near the crime site. Complaining guests asked for other rooms. The hotel was losing money and occupants.

By now it was twilight, and the stranger surveyed the soft hall lights. Obviously, he could be seen. Also, unexpectedly, he heard voices coming down the hallway, drawing closer. Time and seclusion were what he needed. From a leg holster beneath his pant cuff, he drew a small gunmetal-blue automatic. He quickly screwed an unusual cylinder onto the barrel. Sprinting down the corridor, he pointed the gun at the ceiling. The weapon hissed several times. Immediately, one by one, the overhead hall lights disintegrated, and showered shards of glass onto the hall carpet. Within moments, the far end of the south wing was dark.

Retreating to room 533, the cheaply dressed man waited, standing in front of the shattered room door with a padlock on it. Several hotel patrons turned the corner, looked briefly down the inky unlit corridor, and kept walking toward the elevators. The shooter sighed with relief. He could not be seen.

A thin-needled instrument appeared in his hand. But, not before skin-tight gloves were put on. Gloves leave no fingerprints. Grimacing, his tongue superstitiously pressing the corner of his lips while he picked the lock, the quiet intruder was rewarded with the click of internal pin-tumblers releasing. Within seconds the neutralized padlock was open, removed, and in his pocket. Gloved hands silently pushed the door open and, slipping inside, the trespasser quickly closed it once more. To anyone patrolling the corridor, this end of the wing was vacant.

Now he had the time, carried the necessary equipment, and could use his analytical mind; a mind almost supernaturally trained that could discern, step by step, every incident that happened to Leith Ohmstead. The stranger whispered to himself while he scrutinized the room: "There are always clues, regardless how inconsequential. Mysteries arise when there's a lack of shrewd observation; not comprehending what you are seeing." And, the intruder, a remarkable individual, was master of both.

Seething with anger because his partner lay critical in hospital, the unkempt man eagerly seized the torch that had fallen from the hand of his greatest friend; a torch that proclaimed: Duty, Honor, Country.

Vowing vengeance, the steely-eyed agent swore a solemn oath:

"I, Cody Dittus, from this time forward, renounce all civilized rules."

3

Elementary, My Dear Cody

Cody Dittus closed the room door with difficulty. In fact, he had to brace it with a stuffed chair. Only the police padlock held the door upright. Cody thought aloud, lecturing himself. He flipped on the inner room lights.

"When the police broke in the door they almost obliterated the wall beside the latch. Why? Something certainly stopped the police from getting in—must have used several strong-shouldered men. The push-button latch on the doorknob, and the deadbolt itself, both had been torn from the metal door frame and the 2' X 4" wood studs in the wall. Yet, this push-button lock on the doorknob was popped out. Undoubtedly, the hotel manager had the key. And this deadbolt itself is unlocked—maybe they thought the deadbolt wouldn't unlock. The bolt is returned back into the mechanism. It's definitely unlocked. O.K., Smart Guy, so what stopped the police from getting in? The way things are demolished, they must have used a battering ram. Hotel Manager's keys definitely worked—he had nullified both locks. Still, getting in required strong men, or a tank, to break down this solid two-inch door with metal-capped framing. Funny. The bellboy's "manager cousin" never told him about problems getting in. Why?

"We know the Washington police are downright good. Something else interrupted—something focused their attention elsewhere. What was so important that they overlooked the entryway?

"Ah. Torn-off bed covers and quilt? What the heck was Leith doing? Wait. That's what caught the eyes of the police. Blood spots on the sheets. It was night. Room lights off? Probably. And, there's where he got it. Blood spatters radiating outward from right here. Somebody zapped him from behind the exact moment Leith was pulling down the sheet. And, there's where it ended—Leith fought and staggered, step by step, across the carpet to the balcony—leaving a trail of blood. Lord, they must have been slugging him with an iron bar—only a ripped, or smashed scalp bleeds like that.

"Well, looky here, Cody. Someone dropped change. There's a quarter by the track of the sliding glass door. There's another in the corner under the writing desk. By God, there's enough clues here to keep the Washington Police mighty busy. Still, that female lieutenant stopped investigating. She sure was cute; also looked like a trooper who wouldn't quit. But she did. WHY?"

Dittus slowly stepped back toward the entryway, scanning every inch of furniture and carpeting until he reached the broken door. After studying the fragmented frame, wall, broken wood fragments, torn metal and splintered studs, he guardedly bent down and retrieved a child's toy wheel and axle.

"What's this? A piece from a Tonka Toy car? Hold on—this is a 3/8th-inch metal axle, obviously from a sturdy kid's auto. Yet, having a narrow wheel in the exact center? That doesn't make sense. Something like this shouldn't come from a child's toy. Doggone, this axle shaft telescopes. Why—it's spring loaded and this little axle telescopes in four sections. If I squeeze, it compresses to only a quarter-inch length. Say, Cody, would this be the culprit?"

Excited, Cody Dittus jumped to the door and torn metal framing. He examined the framing close to the deadbolt. There it was: A hole drilled into the edge of the door; another hole drilled through the metal framing into a 2-x-4 wall stud.

"Ah, soooo, Cody San. Clever people, these intruders. Whoever did this came equipped. Undoubtedly used an electric drill with rechargeable batteries. Brilliant. After they knocked Ohmstead unconscious and tied him up, they drilled two holes; one in the door, one in the frame, and compressed the telescoping axle, placing the skinny wheel between the door and frame. Then let the door slam shut. The little wheel jammed the door and, by slamming it, the compressed axle was forced into both drilled holes. The closed door aligned both holes side by side, and the little axle sprang open, extending the 3/8ths-inch shaft to a length exceeding one inch.

"That gimmick became a steel bar through the door and the frame. The only way to open the room door was to destroy the entrance. This is no haphazard robbery. This was well planned. What they really wanted was Leith Ohmstead."

Cody replaced the wheel among the debris where the police would find it. When the police returned they would see a child's toy wheel. It would require an astute officer to notice that the toy axle was made of precision-steel.

The agent's hands traveled briskly through the Washington phone book and stopped on a page beginning with KOZ. There, inconspicuous among so many other names, was one registered to a "Lt. P. Kozac." Since the nation's capital is full of generals and admirals, people rarely notice a mere lieutenant. Dittus jotted down the address and phone number. Holding the note pad, he walked onto the outside balcony where there would be better radio reception. He removed a small transmitter from his pocket and pressed a button. Within seconds a voice responded.

"Ozzie here. May I help you?"

"CD here. Take this name and number." He repeated them twice.

"And?"

"Call Lt. Priscilla Kozac at home and find out WHY the police have not returned to the Stouffer-Mayflower. Tell her you're the night manager. Your name is Lester Ohmsbud; that you need to know when to repair the damaged room; that the General Manager, Tye Witten, is quite concerned. It's bad for business. Call me back, immediately. Got it?"

"I got it. Just why am I Lester Ohmsbud? I can think up a better name than that. By the way, where are you? If it's the Mayflower, what room do I reach you at?"

"I believe I'm in trouble, that's where I am…and up to my neck. Listen, damn you, don't you call any room. Use that little gadget you're holding. It's called a radio. There's a record made of all phone calls, in or out, from this hotel. Worse yet, if the police should come now, I'm going to need a parachute to get the hell out of here. Now get humping."

A disgusted Cody Dittus replaced the radio in his pocket. Highly disciplined, he put everything else out of his mind and again focused on his investigation. He was crawling around on his knees. For an instant he stopped, chuckled, and whispered, "Watson, bring me my magnifying glass."

Cody grew serious as he scrutinized the ceiling, walls, and floor. Once again, the events as they happened, became apparent.

"O.K., we know the barred door gave the hoods plenty of time to escape. Whoever attacked Leith had to leave by way of the balcony. Using ropes? All the way down into heavy traffic below? Think again, Dittus, even at night the hotel spotlights would illuminate wall climbers."

Cody peered over the balcony. City refuse trucks were parked five stories below and the employees, looking like midgets, were hustling tons of trash from the Stouffer-Mayflower Hotel. He marveled at the unbelievable amounts of garbage one day's collection brought from this huge hotel.

"All right, let's examine the 25-cent coins and find the escape route." Cody Dittus knelt by the track of the sliding balcony door and carefully studied the quarters. Logic told him that, during the scuffle, somebody's pants pocket was accidentally torn and the quarters had fallen to the floor and scattered. He was about to stand, when his heart jumped, causing an audible, sharp inhalation of breath.

This quarter was unusually shiny. Shiny pocket change in circulation today? NO WAY! Cody crawled on his knees, gaping at the edge of the coin, and concluded that this was no clad—sandwich coin. He knew clad coins, a sandwich of three cheap metals, were issued after 1964 when the government removed silver from every coin except half-dollars and quarters. Soon after, Uncle Sam stopped circulating silver in any coin. This particular quarter was a collector's item—stamped with an earlier date which verified it was 90% silver.

Cody crawled under the desk. The second quarter was shiny...90% silver, also. Moreover, lying unnoticed in the corner near the coin, was a shredded piece of cloth.

"I say, Watson, what have we here? Ah, sooooo, canvas cloth with its stitching ripped open, and this swatch is a portion of something larger."

Placing the torn stitches together, Cody Dittus discovered the fragment had been a sewn tube. Coins and a canvas tube? Cody laughed, enjoying the hunt.

"What in the world would a canvas tube be doing here? Housekeeping would never allow a remnant of cloth to remain under a four-legged desk. How shaddy and unprofessional for the Mayflower Hotel. Hmmmm, why would silver quarters be involved in the abduction of Ohmstead? Somehow, this tube has something to do with it."

Leaving the coins behind, Cody slipped the canvas into his pocket. Carefully sidestepping, to avoid congealed bloodstains on the balcony's cement floor, he strode to the railing and looked over. Its height accentuated the five-story drop.

The hotel wing, facing a busy Connecticut Avenue, was well maintained. The ironwork had been recently painted, and that chore was a lucky break for the master sleuth. Again crawling, Cody inspected one of the wrought iron braces bolted to the concrete and steel balcony. He whistled in appreciation.

"Whoopeee. There it is. Paint scraped off down to the metal. The iron itself was exposed to the elements. Yes, Sir, no doubt. A steel cable did that,...perhaps a 1/8th or 3/16th-inch cable—its diameter just matches the width of the missing paint. The street side of the railing and brace are untouched.

"Looks like the cable was looped around the far side of the brace because the other three sides at the balcony door are smooth through the fresh paint. Conclusion? Somebody had rappelled downward, like a mountain climber, but down to which floor? "Uh huh. If he carried Leith's body—jeez, he'd get rid of a large man's weight at the first chance. That means the first available floor, the fourth. Besides, just how long can a killer rappel down the front side of a busy hotel, carrying a body, with all that traffic below and not be observed? If Ohmstead was dumped on 4 and still alive, his heart would pump blood stains over the room below. Cody, my boy, let's vacate this room for the police, and trust no one's home on the fourth floor."

Cody jumped a foot. A startling blaring beep sounded from his coat pocket. It came from the emergency channel on his personal transceiver.

In the silent room the radio's frantic beeping made a clamor like a brass band. Cody yanked the high-tech communicator from his pocket. "CD here. Speak to me."

"Got that lieutenant dame. She sounded like her chin was resting on the soles of her shoes. She wouldn't talk until I mentioned Witten, the hotel's General Manager."

"And…"

"The investigation's over."

Cody Dittus choked with surprise. After coughing, he said, "IT'S OVER?"

"Police don't think it's that important. Obviously a robbery."

"Like hell. There's blood all over the place. I saw her leave this hotel. That woman would never quit. A room locked from the inside and no body? What's her reason?"

"She was told to 'lay off'."

"I don't believe that. She's a lieutenant. Only her captain can give her orders…and she'd make his life miserable."

"It came from higher up."

"How high?"

"The Police Chief himself."

"By God, she should go over his head. Something's awful wrong here."

"She did. The Commissioner himself. HE told her to stop immediately, mark the file as an unsolved robbery, and hand it over to Records Department."

Had the agent on the other radio seen Cody Dittus, he would have seen a man standing with his mouth open. Cody was incredulous. But now he understood. This reached into Washington politics. Leith Ohmstead had stumbled into something sinister—sinister enough to get him killed. Dittus simply replied, "Thanks."

"Hey, one other thing, CD. I had to hang up on her."

"You WHAT? WHY?"

"She jumped ME—suddenly said, 'You say you're Lester Ohmsbud? Initials, L.O.? You know something stinks, don't you? Just who are you, Buster? Now I know I was right. Someone else is investigating what I believe to be murder. You're not the police, SO HOW DID YOU LEARN....?' THAT was when I hung up. So, what the heck is L. O.? I hope I did right for you."

"You did. L. O. stands for my partner. He's missing."

"Leith? Oh, NO. What can I do to help?"

"You already did. You let a discouraged Lt. Kozac learn that her suspicions were correct. She'll also be exploring just who it is that is giving her backup? That's the least I can do for her.

"As for you, do nothing more, for now. Keep this under your hat. I'll find out why the high-ups squashed this case. Tell the superintendents I won't be around for a while. I'll contact them when I have something. I can tell you one thing, though. That woman, Lt. Priscilla Kozac, is smarter than the Police Chief and Commissioner combined. And they know it. She's turning the screw from below; they're being squeezed from above. There's the stench of a big power—play here—right in this nation's capital. OUT."

Agent Dittus switched his transceiver to "off." Now he had to continue. His thoughts raced, "Leith Ohmstead knew something; if only I had gotten here in time to help. There's danger here in Washington. Enough to have Leith murdered. Right now I'm on the inside track where Priscilla Kozac was derailed. So, I'd better check that fourth floor."

Quietly descending the exit stairs, Cody Dittus reached the corner suite, room 433, directly below #533. No occupant answered his knocking. Out came his "Sing-Sing Special," a burglar's little lock-picking kit. In moments the only sounds were "push-pull, click-click" and the room door swung open. Dittus' dialogue with himself continued,

"You should try wall safes next time, Cody. Well, no luck here—so far, no blood. Carpet's clean. No evidence of a body dumped here. So, let's examine the glass door.

Dittus performed the same routine: Ceiling, Walls, Floor. This time it was not necessary to indulge in his painful exercise, "the sore knee crawl."

"Well, well, looky here. The sliding door hook-latch is broken and the glass seal split. Aluminum frame is bent. A small crowbar pried open this balcony door in seconds. But, there's no blood on the balcony.

"What happened to Leith? The criminals apparently swung in on their cable, landed on the balcony, broke in, and walked right to the exit stairs. Probably descended a few floors, then took an elevator to the ground floor.

"So, where is Leith? They wouldn't dare carry a body through the lobby. Suddenly, Cody knew fear. Fear for his friend.

Dittus contemplated the alternatives. The few possible answers made him cringe. Cody headed for the door, only to be startled by the appearance of a middle-aged lady, obviously the room occupant.

"WHAT are you doing in my room? Just who are you?"

Cody Dittus was a fast thinker and an excellent actor. He answered

"Ma'am, I'm the house detective, and we received a report of a burglar."

The lady was aghast, "Burglar? My door is double locked; my jewels are stored in the hotel's security safe. Just HOW would a burglar get into my room on the fourth floor?"

"We have reason to believe he flew, Ma'am.

"Flew? You're saying a burglar flew to my balcony?"

"He landed on your balcony, Ma'am. We suspect he is an aviator."

A look of incredulity spread over the woman's face. Her jaw dropped. Her mouth barely whispered, "This house detective comes from an idiot farm!"

Cody Dittus recognized a cue when he saw one. He exited stage right, arms extended like wings, making noises with his mouth like a high-powered aircraft engine. Dumbfounded, the lady watched him hedge-hop down the hallway. For a moment she was speechless. Then she dashed to her telephone and called the front desk. While the manager and his assistant rushed to meet her, the lady carefully inventoried her luggage. Nothing was missing, and, praise be, her jewels were in the hotel's safe.

"An aviator flew to my balcony?" Such asinine reasoning left her astounded. Fortuitously, her bottle of peppermint schnapps was on the table. She made a beeline for the nectar. She made a dent in the contents.

Agent Dittus walked out the front entrance of the Mayflower into the starlight. He looked up at the fifth floor—and then looked at the sidewalk, parked cabs, and the loading zone packed with city trucks. The bellhop had mentioned no suicide, no murder, nothing. Listening to cabbies and private trash haulers only disclosed small talk. Now it was question and answer time.

"Any of you cab men here two nights ago between 8:00 and 11:00 p.m.?

Cody received shrugs, blank stares, and a few hostile glances. Remembering the bellboy episode, Cody decided that he would appeal to their finer instincts: Greed.

"Fellows, my wife's playing around with a guy who works at the hotel here. There's a twenty spot for the guy who saw anything unusual or different that night. And I mean either a man or woman. You tell and I'll sort out what's important. O.K.?"

There was silence. A few cabbies, apparently who had been on duty that night, were frowning, trying to remember something. After all, "Twenty bucks is twenty bucks." One driver only shook his head.

"I'd like to help you, buddy, but I didn't see a thing. But, I sure heard the Ape Man."

"Ape Man? What do you mean you heard? Heard what?"

Now look. I wasn't drinkin'. I only had a few nips afore comin' on duty, but I heard Tarzan swinging down the avenue."

"Tarzan? What time this Tarzan?"

"Mister, I heard a guy making like Tarzan two or three times. And I mean loud. He echoed from way up to way down by this hotel. I was so scared some `suicider' was a'fallin' on me that I crawled under the cab's dash."

Cody Dittus was suddenly wide awake. "Did you hear him hit?"

No, Sir. Never did find out who it was. Probably some drunk just yellin' from his hotel balcony."

"You said he hollered several Tarzan yells; that he echoed from high up clear down to your cab? Didn't you hear anything land with a crash?"

"That's why what I'm tellin' ya sounds so crazy. I can't answer. Them dump trucks were makin' so much racket I never heard a thing. Honest."

Cody was nodding. He had an idea—an impossible idea. Without a word he handed the cab driver a $ 20.00 bill. Cody didn't even wait to hear the cabby's startled, "Thank you." He was already running down the street.

Trash crews were collecting barrels and barrels of refuse. Cody couldn't get them to stop for a meeting. As before, he would appeal to their basic needs and finer instincts.

"HEY. I've got TWO twenty dollar bills for a beer party. The guy that handles this money can keep what he doesn't spend. What say?"

Like hungry squirrels gathering around a pecan tree, a sizeable group of thirsty men surrounded Cody. He said,

"The cabbies tell me that two nights ago, about 11:00 p.m., some guy dived from this hotel. A few of them heard him making like Tarzan all the way down, but no one ever saw or heard what happened to him. This may be the guy that's been running around with my old lady. I want to know what happened and where he is, 'cause I aim to bust him up some. Any takers?"

And Cody was waving a couple of fresh 20's. He was surprised to hear two men laugh uproariously.

"Boy. Chris and Jodi will be mad when they find out they missed tonight's party…and the money."

Cody said, "You mind explaining that?"

"Sure can, Mister. I know about it 'cause they're friends of mine, but they was Johnny-on-the-spot when it happened." Cody displayed a warm grin,

"I'm curious. How come you men work so late? City pay that well?"

The group hooted and hollered. One man said, "We collect during the day, but three nights a week we pick up 'special' for the Mayflower Hotel. They have over a thousand people registered, and that means a lot of garbage. So, we work nights and the hotel pays us extra. Chris and Jodi was here that Wednesday night."

The speaker for the group, eyeing the crisp bills, continued.

"Mister, Chris and Jodi were shook up. They almost crushed a man into a small cube with the truck's hydraulic ram. This 'Tarzan fellow' was tied hand and feet. Believe it or not, he was shoutin' all the way down. Chris never did find where he fell from, but we figure at least the fifth floor or higher. Mister, this guy landed smack-dab in the middle of the last full load of trash Chris was packin', and this here Tarzan dived clear to the bottom. That takes some doin' to dive through a dumpster to the bottom. Tarzan must'a plunged right in the middle of the trash, but it saved his life…until Chris almost hydraulic-rammed him into minced dog food."

Cody asked, "What happened to this Tarzan, my friend?"

"Mister, when Jodi, who was drivin', dumped that container, all the garbage **and** the man is turned over so the whole mess can tumble out toward the press bin. What was bottom is now top, . . and here is this guy, all bloody and beaten, standing up, buried in garbage up to his waist. And after that high dive, this Ape Man is still alive.

"Well, Sir, Chris and Jodi got so sick they barely got back to the barn. They've been off since, under doctor's treatment, and both think it was the Mafia tryin' to reduce this guy to a grease spot."

Cody asked, "Answer me another question and the money is yours. What hospital did they take him to?"

"Emergency Ambulance told Chris they were headed for the nearest one, District of Columbia General Hospital, on 19th and Massachusetts."

Cody smiled the first time in two days. He added a ten-spot to the fistful of bills and handed them to the speaker.

"You boys have a good one on me. Here's a little extra, too. Not even Chris could have told me more than you have. Oh, one more question, please?"

"Yes, Sir?"

"You boys see this piece of canvas? It makes into a tube. You wouldn't have seen the rest of it anywhere around here, would you? There's another twenty waitin' for someone." Interest among the other men perked up. A young worker looked at the torn swatch, "Looks to me like the cover for a cue stick. You know, pool."

Another said, "Maybe. It also could be a case for a rifle barrel. You going to kill this guy who's cattin' round with your old lady, Mister?"

Cody laughed. "Nope, believe it or not, I'm going to inform him that I'm getting a divorce, and he has to marry the old lady. I hope he does."

The work crews roared. An older dump operator said, "Serves him right. Your problem is solved, but his is just beginnin'."

Cody asked, "What about this canvas tube? Could the rest of it be around the square? It may have been thrown out when Tarzan jumped. I know you don't care, but there's a reason it's important. I'll give another bonus to the man who finds it; and I'll give another to the man who figures just what the heck the thing is used for."

The entire group's undivided attention centered on Cody Dittus. An older worker shook his head and said, "I've never seen Santa Claus in May. Boys, we've got to prove to him it is better to give than receive."

"Spread out, Boys," said the leader. "Police the area, try to recall if you picked up anything resembling a cloth cylinder, and look in the bushes and even in the trees. Now, spread out. Next stop, Paul Revere's Ride."

Before Cody could ask, the leader said, "Paul Revere is the best roadhouse bar on the edge of town. We'll unload, go park our trucks at the barn; we'll shower, and then, . . a real wing-ding, thanks to your generosity. After all, it is Friday night."

Jameson "Cody" Dittus was pleased, yet disheartened. Pleased, because for a block in four directions, the men carefully searched; really searched, over the grounds and shrubs. Bynow, the time was near midnight, and the hotel's refuse had been collected. Although the work crews used powerful flashlights and lanterns, Cody wondered if the crew might have done better in the daytime. He cursed his slow progress. He refused to accept the fact that no other agent could have performed better. Such bustling traffic, hotel guests coming and going, were enough activities to disrupt any investigation. After all, Stouffer-Mayflower was only five blocks from the White House.

Agent Dittus was disheartened because the exploration was drawing a blank. Walking back from the perimeter's edge, the last search party possessed only weak lantern beams flickering into the trees. Any success was a long shot. Abruptly, a voice shouted, "HEY, I'VE FOUND SOMETHING HERE!"

One of the young employees among the haulers scampered up a tree like a homesick chimpanzee. Flashlight beams followed him while the alert discoverer kept his own lantern directed to a cloth object hanging from a budding cherry tree. From many stories, the object had drifted and fluttered across the avenue into one of the beautiful Japanese trees. Had the tree been in bloom, the cloth sock would never be seen. Cody was so pleased he handed the group spokesman an extra fin (a ten-spot).

"Give this to the finder, our young and agile ape. Thanks, fellows."

Everyone chuckled. But, no one moved on. They, too, studied their find.

The sock, or tube, was less than 20 inches long, with a diameter fitted more for a shotgun barrel than a rifle. Yet, the sock would encase a short barrel only. A cue stick was far too long. The canvas tube was torn at the open end where a small adjustable belt was located. The belt, apparently, was meant to tighten on whatever object it covered.

The opposite end of the tube was ripped apart. For some unexplained miracle, another **silver** quarter still rested inside the case where the leather belt reinforced the canvas. Cody began thinking out loud. He might as well speak truthfully, because he was not fooling the group spokesman, nor many of the other refuse collectors.

"Gentlemen, why, in God's name, would anyone use this canvas tube to store a batch of silver quarters? This cover underwent great strain and busted wide open. To shatter this canvas tube, he would have to put it through a meat grinder."

"Or use a roll of quarters, Boss."

Cody flinched, "What was that, Man?"

"You're talking about coins. Whoever used that probably meant it as a sapper—you know, a blackjack. A heavy roll of quarters, swung inside that, would knock a man's brains out."

FLASH. The man's answer was a revelation to Cody's mind. He knew he was tired, but this was exactly what it was. A cudgel. A roll of coins would send a man into a deep sleep, perhaps forever. But, why silver coins? Never mind. He'd figure that one out later.

"Okay, Fellows, now I understand why Chris said their Tarzan was all bloody. Obviously, he had been blackjacked. But, why not use a good strong sock? Why a long tube complete with adjustable belt and leather reinforcement? What else would this be used for? I can't figure it."

The older man with the explanation shyly stepped forward. He could joke, but he was uncomfortable in front of a superior. He appeared ready to run. His brow was creased as he looked at the narrow sock. His eyes didn't even meet Cody's when he stammered, "Mi-, Mi-, Mister? We had a si-, si-, similar piece of equipment when I was gunner on a B-25 during World War II. It use ta' fit single engine and twin engines planes. Probably fits some ci-, ci-, civilian planes, too."

Cody put a friendly hand on the elderly man's shoulder in appreciation. He softly asked,

"What do you mean, `it fits B-25's and civilian aircraft'?"

"Cap'n, this here thing might fit a Pitot tube. The Pitot's a pipe that sticks out in front of the wing and measures air pressure. Ya' can measure airspeed, and operate several other instruments with a Pitot tube."

Cody didn't even realize he was speaking out loud.

"Why would anyone use a Pitot tube cover for a sapper—a blackjack?"

The shy hauler, far more intelligent than he appeared, barely smiled as his mind returned to his exciting war of yesteryear. He answered softly,

"Probably 'cause, usin' a roll of quarters, makes it a hell of a weapon. Better'n a sock. It broke 'cause, just like ours did, it had gotten rotten from being too long in the sun on a parked aeroplane. He'll have to buy a new one to protect the Pitot."

Cody was amused at the man's thinking. The gunner was illogical.

"Why do you say, `He'll have to buy a new one'? To protect what?"

"For his plane, Mister, his plane. Easiest, and quickest, thing for him to grab—a Pitot tube cover for a sapper. This man who's been playing around with your wife, . . probably owns a plane. I'll bet he's a pilot."

Cody Dittus expressed exhilaration. He had harvested more vital information walking the street, talking to the everyday working people, than a Washington investigation squad could ever have learned studying room #533. And Cody acknowledged the police were no slouches.

Because it came to him naturally, Cody was unaware of his inborn ability to work with, and bring out the surprising capabilities of common working people around him. They did not disappoint him.

With a sincere handshake, Cody produced another twenty-spot and gave it to the ex-gunner.

"Here. Party tonight, or get something special for your wife. Thanks so much for your help."

Cody withdrew. Every hauler waved goodbye. Tonight would be a great end-of-the-week thrill for them at Paul Revere's Ride roadhouse. But, Cody Dittus enjoyed a real thrill, too.

He was headed for General Hospital and his friend, Leith Ohmstead. After that? A good night's sleep and a dangerous tomorrow—deadly, but not for Cody. He had found a fresh trail; a trail deadly for Ohmstead's assassin.

◆   ◆   ◆

Leith Ci Ohmstead lay comatose on his bed in a private room at D. C. General Hospital, now unguarded by any Washington policeman. The resident physician softly whispered to his associates,

"Concussion. Two hematomas on his skull; hemorrhaging inside. We would have drilled into his head had it not been for the new anti-swelling, anti-coagulants now available. Somebody really smashed him with a solid object, probably an iron bar. Yet, I believe he fought well. With his skull almost cracked, he must have hurt someone. His fists are swollen, the skin almost peeled off his knuckle bones. His assailants' faces probably look a sight."

Cody Dittus asked, "Doctor, you say plural, `his assailants'. Why?"

"Mr. Dittus, such head wounds could not have been administered by one man while Mr. Ohmstead was putting up such a brawl. The skull markings show small parallel impressions as if he were hit by the teeth of a heavy saw."

"Doctor, could such parallel indentations come from a stacked roll of coins,...say, a blackjack stuffed with old quarters?"

"You mean the old quarters that used to weigh more than the new ones?"

"Exactly. Used in a strong sock and swung like a club?"

The resident thought a moment before he said, "Yes—it could. Swung hard enough, those narrow coin edges would leave quite a mark. Even in bone."

Cody Dittus digested that information. So far, he was on track. "Have the police identified the fellow who tried to murder Leith? They probably haven't had time to get the imposter's ID back from FBI records."

"Oh, yes, they have. In fact, his prints were on file with the Federal Aviation Authority (FAA) because he was a licensed, senior certified, Aircraft and Engine (A&E) technician. He worked at one of the better, smaller city airports 30 miles from Washington, the Frederick Municipal Airport over the line in Maryland. Has two concrete runways, one a mile, the other 7/10ths.

"His name was Cash Delway. He contracted with the FAA for maintaining government aircraft and private aircraft owned by U.S. Senators and Congressmen. We haven't verified his close friends. Might be interesting."

The trash hauler, ex-Army gunner, had hit the nail on the head. Except for a manufacturer, where in the world would anyone find a better source of Pitot tube covers than an A&E technician at Frederick Municipal Airport where he worked on the airplanes of prominent politicians?

Cody asked, "How about Ohmstead? Will he pull through?"

The doctor said, "Doing surprisingly well. His head blows are serious, but swelling is down and he's healing fast. The multi-story fall cracked his ribs and sprained nearly every joint in his body. Garbage and other trash bags definitely saved his life. He'll be up and walking in several weeks, but he's going to hurt in places he never knew existed."

Cody marveled. Had he told the resident physician that Leith had actually dived from the fifth floor, with hands and feet bound, the doctor would have scoffed. Cody kept that fact to himself. But, his investigation left no doubt in his mind: Leith Ohmstead had been thrown to his death from the fifth floor. A truck, its garbage bin filled to the brim, had parked exactly where the rubbish heap would intercept Leith's plunge from that height. And Leith lived through it. The entire episode was inconceivable.

Cody, left alone to sit by his old friend, squeezed Leith's hand.

"Hey, you ornery cuss, I finally found you. Leith, you got the guy who tried to do you in. He's deader'n a mackerel. He went mighty hard, too. So, wake up and talk to me. I need you. I've stumbled into something."

Leith Ohmstead's eyes blinked open. There was no evidence he was seeing anything, but he stared at Cody Dittus for a while, blinked and struggled to focus his eyes, and mumbled hoarsely, "Thanks, Cody.... beat hell out of me...I, I...broke their noses before they...wrestled me down and tied me. Remember going over edge.... long fall. Knew it was end. I'm...awful tired. Dear God,...how I ache . . all over. Stick 'round, buddy. I found traitor on Cap'tol Hill. Sleep now...Bye." Leith Ci Ohmstead's eyelids fluttered; he coughed, eyes rolling upward. He passed out, returning to a deep sleep.

Cody's thoughts surpassed Mach Two speed. He had no choice: Slow down and wait for his sidekick to team with him again. Leith was the only professional he trusted. Dittus would give a minimal report to "the superintendents." They, in turn, would quickly know he was holding out on them. That made Cody grin. "Serves 'em right. They've done the same to me for years."

Some people might think him peculiar, but, when alone, Cody had a habit of talking to himself. And for good reason: Assignments lasted for weeks, often in extreme danger, during which it was essential to avoid human contact. Consequently, he appreciated the sound of his own voice. Consequently, it was no big deal for Cody to frown, stop, and ponder.

"Don't Oz Agents wonder what organization do the 'supers' work for? Perhaps I'm about to find out? I've lived a pattern of peril, traveled the world, followed orders to kill, . . yet, I still don't know who employs me."

Dittus' thoughts caromed inside his head like spent bullets: Who did this? What was so dangerous that it was necessary to exterminate Leith Ci Ohmstead? What had Leith learned to warrant assassination? On whose toes is he stomping? Do the answers lie among Leith's mumblings during his delirium?

Now Cody's voice bounced off the walls, "Just think, . . a police lieutenant stifled? Unwise to do that to a women, especially in rumor-rife Washington. Ohmstead mumbled, 'powerful traitor on Capitol Hill'—or did he say, 'traitors'? Ah, ridiculous. Not in our Congress or Administration.

"Nonetheless, what a story Leith might tell. Else, why would the muggers risk attacking him in downtown Washington? In a very crowded hotel? Particularly, on a busy Friday night? Why were the hit men willing to chance discovery while assaulting and tossing a man from the fifth floor balcony?

"Leith, my friend. You are up to your ears in something treacherous. Wait a minute, Cody. Does that hazard include his PARTNER?"

Jameson Dittus whirled, carefully looking behind, his fingertips caressing the blue gunmetal of his S & W automatic.

"Watch your backside, Cody. Now, more than ever, watch your backside."

4

Power Struggles

Charter Joseph Saladin was of Egyptian and Syrian extraction. A shrewd judge of people and vote-getting opportunities, he bragged to close cronies that his actual middle name was Yusuf; that his publicized name-ploy, Joseph, was deliberately Anglicized to neutralize prejudices against Arab-Americans in the New England states. Yet, his family surname, Saladin, was a real vote-stealer among descendants from the darker skinned Arabs who emigrated to the U.S.A.

Other ethnic groups never hesitated to vote for Charter, a handsome, appetizing male who made the women squeal at meetings and rallies. Charter Saladin would laughingly say,

"These new generations of Americans don't know a nickel's worth of history. They'd never believe I was a descendant of the great warrior, Sultan Salah-al-Din Yusuf ibn-Ayyud. My forbearer reigned from 1174 to 1193. In the 12th century, he and his army defeated England's King Richard and the Crusaders during the defense of Acre, a port city in northeast Israel.

"That's why I can lick any man foolish enough to seek office against me. I have the blood of Saladin in me, including his wisdom and craftiness."

Charter's close confidants were convinced he told the truth because no one could beat him. He had been reelected term after term for the past 14 years. He had wanted the senate. Charter felt the title carried more prestige. But, the senators from of New York and New Jersey were almost immortalized in stone due to their chronic tenure in Congress. Saladin's alternative was to run for the House of Representatives. Temporarily, that decision created problems.

For ethnic reasons Charter Saladin was bitterly opposed by a powerful Hebrew, the senator from New York, Abraham Lieberson Anselm, who was reputed to be a distant progeny of Baron Mayer Anselm who founded the world-wide banking enterprise, House of Rothschild of Frankfort on Main, Germany. Abraham was influential among the monied powers of America and Europe and an outspoken zealot for the Jews of America and the citizens of Israel.

Abraham Anselm's zeal often perturbed news columnists and commentators who accused him of being a Zionist. He literally frothed at the mouth over charges he nurtured a warlike "Israel Over All." Shouting obscene denials, he would initiate a tirade of counter-accusations: Racial prejudice; filthy Nazi Jew-baiters; vindictive Christian pretenders; and Ku Klux Klanners.

For some unknown reason, Senator Abraham Anselm had little use for the upstart, Charter Saladin. Yet, the powerful senator had never met the aspiring congressman. But, Anselm effectively slammed the door on Saladin in New York State. There was a consequence—but, to Abraham Anselm.

Because, shrewdly, during a quiet weekend, Charter Joseph Saladin moved to the State of New Jersey.

Clifton, N.J., was a short skip over the bridge into the Bronx and south into the heart of New York City. Charter Saladin had spent two years, well beyond congressional eligibility requirements, sustaining a home in Clifton and a condominium in New York. When the move was complete, records were changed in the county courthouses with the help of influential friends in both cities.

For the bargain sum of $ 1,000, Mrs. Elena Saladin, of New York, sold her condo to a campaign supporter who had generously paid the mortgage, upkeep, and expenses for the Saladins the entire two years. Political critics were candidly suspicious, but they could produce no evidence that would prove Saladin had met state requirements illegally. Even those in the camp of Senator Lieb Anselm knew Charter's action had been a strategic move. Not a few were wary, because they knew Anselm had made a bitter enemy. Charter Saladin, of New Jersey, had been seen at his residence by neighbors. In fact, Charter was the acknowledged "Good Neighbor Sam" who met and helped many district residents. He was warm, friendly, had a fantastic memory for names, and oozed maleness to adoring women. No opponent could argue Charter had not established residency. Saladin soon drew attention at party gatherings, society dinners, and statewide ceremonies. In a short time, he was a popular state celebrity. While currying favor from middle-class citizens, Charter docilely threw his hat in the ring for the upcoming congressional primary.

The unpredictable Saladin's swaying rhetoric during the campaign was inflammatory dynamite. And he didn't run on the Republican **or** Democratic ticket. Being an Independent had insured defeat for candidates in the past. However, Charter's coalition was a new state party, the United Reform Party...calling to every citizen of New Jersey who was searching for reform, hoping to find an honest nominee. Astute politicians from Democratic and Republican strongholds laughed—until the initial primary kickoff.

Then the neophyte, Charter Saladin, giving his first speech as a reformer, shook many Hebrews attending his first political rally. The Hebrews attended more out of curiosity than concern. Unexpectedly, Charter shook the Jews because, for the first time in memory, growing minority groups—Blacks, Hispanics, Slavs, and Asians—did not slouch around the political meeting, impotent with their hands in their pockets. Within minutes into Saladin's dialogue, the scorned, second-rate citizens began applauding, cheered wildly, and wondered aloud if this candidate could be one of them. After all…he was different . . and, they also noticed his skin was dark. Over the radio, and in a few brief public television film clips, the voice of the United Reform Party electrified the audience:

"Listen, you silhouette Jerseyites. Too long you've stood in the shadow of our eastern neighbor across the Hudson River. As New York goes, so goes New Jersey. That's what they told us, and we believed them—until now.

"In high society, where we ordinary folk are never allowed, New York's Senator Abraham Anselm says we can't exist without The Big Apple…including the personal beneficence of Anselm. Why, our own senator, Jacob Bergenfeldt, always seems to agree while basking in Anselm's shadow. Our dense, stubby, pudgy Bergenfeldt makes a fitting companion to the towering, flamboyant, 'Ichabod' Anselm. You could call them Mutt and Jeff or 'The Long and the Short' of it.

"Surely, it's no accident that our Senator Bergenfeldt never fights against banking bills charging the middle class high interest on your loans and your credit cards. After all, Senator Anselm permits—no, he champions large "octopus banks"—giants that absorb and merge with smaller banks to choke off competition. Benefits disappear for You, the depositors and borrowers. These giants boldly remove fair practices and protective restrictions which are good business. They now can make fantastic, and uncollectible, loans to foreign countries and foreign businesses, instead of helping our struggling, overtaxed state businesses.

"Yet, today, certain individuals are making fortunes by controlling and restraining trade. But, **we** are not. **You** are not. And **New Jersey** is not.

"Today, these privileged bankers and their perpetually-elected Washington cronies have obtained sanctions that grant and encourage ridiculous, liberal, financial policies. Just a few decades ago, these crushing policies against free enterprise would have sent corporate executives and their boards of directors direct to federal prison. Fraud, deceit, swindles, embezzlement, and political chicanery are now commonplace. Your taxes, your savings, and your investments have been squandered. Your hard-earned capital has already been stolen and forfeited in the name of foreign aid and One World Government.

"So today, I ask you, who gets those fantastic, deficit spending sums? Your billions of savings and investment dollars are not here in New Jersey. Where **is** our money?

"We MUST ask these questions, today—and learn why vital cash flows are drying up. Why are bankruptcies, and troubled businesses sky-rocketing off the casualty charts? WHY are you, and so many other middle-class workers, losing your jobs? We now face a growing monetary crisis just like that dreadful interval before the 1929 crash.

"The senate and administration have gone to bed with the big boys, and the wealthy interests...not only here, but abroad. But, we can close down their pipeline, their Horn of Plenty, by limiting spending bills and laws being crammed down our throats by an omnipotent U.S. Senate. There are too many hogs slopping from the troughs of our national wealth.

"Send me to Congress—the House of Representatives—and I'll turn off the 'money-valve' to those big boys who are living the high life while controlling the confiscatory taxes and lowering our standard of living.

"They've not only skimmed the cream off your efforts, but they're gobbling up your daily bread. They'll leave you exactly what they think you'll tolerate...an empty, crumb-laden pan.

"Send me to congress, good people—and I'll shove their bureaucratic schemes and one-world dreams right down their throats until they choke.

"You know the answer: Unite and Reform. And your first start is to send Charter Joseph Saladin to Congress."

Charter Saladin won the primary by a historic landslide. A runoff against a Republican or a Democrat was definitely unnecessary.

◆　　　◆　　　◆

The lights in the Senate Office Building, Washington, burned bright and late. Senators Anselm and Bergenfeldt raged. Their staffs, however, were very anxious about the future.

Anselm spoke, and Bergenfeldt parroted,

"I'll smash that S.O.B. so fast he'll take the first boat to camel-jockey land. He thinks he can turn all our good work around and…" His top advisor, Bergan Gruenspan, touched Abraham Anselm's arm,

"Senator, in the two weeks he's been here, Saladin's made unimaginable inroads among many senators. Some are your friends…and they are listening to what he says."

Abraham Lieberson Anselm snorted, "You think he can change the minds of my friends? I control them. As for this upstart freshman…"

"LIEB. Listen to me. I said some of these senators are listening. I did not say they were agreeing with him. However, that could come later. Right now your worry lies within the House."

"What do you mean, 'my worry'? Most of Congress, at least the influential representatives, follow my lead. Why, I'll break him…."

Gruenspan shouted, "DAMMIT, Senator Anselm, YOU DON'T HEAR ME.

"Next week, Charter Saladin makes his debut. It will be his first speech on the floor of the House. The flak is spreading, and the word is out that his address will be a spellbinder. This man will command unprecedented attendance by House members from the 50 states.

"You better be there…somewhere in the gallery. Our statisticians tell me Charter has already gotten the ears of nearly 300 Representatives. And, for the first time in his life, the Speaker is running scared."

"WHAT? HOLCOMBE BRODERICK? Don't make me laugh." snarled Anselm.

"Senator Anselm? You'd be wise to check your hole cards, because…

"Just this morning, the Speaker of The House pulled me aside. He told me to warn you,…'Watch your step.'"

Abraham Anselm's face showed surprise. Then sparks began to flash in his eyes as he glared intensely at his strong right arm, Bergan Gruenspan. A deep growl sprang from Anselm's throat.

"You are telling me that Holcombe Broderick told me to 'watch my step?'"

Bergan Gruenspan, an astute, wise, political fortuneteller, merely nodded vigorously several times. Further conversation was pointless.

Abraham "Lieb" Anselm responded. He, too, nodded slowly…and methodically. His extremely soft rebuttal disturbed Bergan Gruenspan.

"I see. So says Broderick. Very well. Just forget it for now, Bergan. I'm wagering Saladin will lay an egg. In fact, he may decide not to talk at all. Regardless, that's **my** worry."

For the first time in his life, Bergan Gruenspan looked askance at his chief, Senator Abraham Anselm. The senator acted far too calm, almost totally indifferent. Didn't he comprehend the threat facing him? A threat he, himself, had helped create? Didn't "Lieb" realize that his ineffectual New Jersey colleague, Senator Bergenfeldt, was riding for a fall?

Anselm's unsettling reaction made Gruenspan almost think out loud.

"Where, in Jehovah's name, did Anselm unearth this twisted logic that, of all people, Charter Saladin will scorn the custom allowing the newly-elected to address The House of Representatives?"

Inexplicably, Bergan's intuition made his insides grow cold, and he shivered. He surveyed the entire staff. No one seemed to think anything was affecting Anselm's responses, although his sudden composure, a detached self-control, seemed peculiar...even irrational...for him. There was the crux of the problem: Except for Bergan Gruenspan, no one in the entire staff thought.

◆   ◆   ◆

In the Samuel T. Rayburn Building, The Speaker of The House, Holcombe Broderick, was holding an intimate party inside one of the reception suites. The lavishly catered affair featured tables burdened with vast assortments of food and, always, the finest alcoholic "sundowners" that the scurrying, smartly dressed waiters could carry.

The gathering was a major highlight on "The Hill." A select group had been carefully chosen. They consisted of only 50 out of many hundreds of elected Representatives. But the 50, with their wives or husbands, were some of the most prominent and influential Congressmen in Washington.

The Speaker curried favor with both sides of the aisle because, by his very nature, he was, first, an American patriot, and, second, a Democrat. While treating both parties equally, he still needed a bipartisan coalition to hammer out the best possible proposals and legislation to benefit the United States and its people.

Speaker Broderick also needed powerful House leaders who could cripple radical, asinine attempts to subvert the Constitution.

No Congressman and spouse ever refused Broderick's coveted invitation. It was major proof on "The Hill" that a particular member of The House or Senate had arrived. He, or she, was a member of the elite.

Abraham "Lieb" Anselm would have been invited—should have been invited. But Anselm continually butted heads with Holcombe Broderick. During interviews, he also insultingly alluded to the Speaker as "my Boy."

In Broderick's mind, Anselm's mysterious arrogance reminded influential Congressmen, especially the Speaker of the House, that they had better join Anselm. Speaker Broderick distrusted Anselm, but did not fear him—so far. Broderick's close-mouthed confidantes would ask him,

"Why do you distrust Anselm?"—and Broderick could not answer. But, quietly, a sub-squad from the House Ethics Investigating Committee racked up hours of overtime. They would keep looking until they did find something.

In the meantime, Broderick needed another ally, a strong, fearless compatriot to back him when Anselm, and others who practice intimidation, challenged the Speaker's authority. He found just the man. One who, like himself, had been politically humiliated by Senator Anselm.

Charter Joseph Saladin and his lovely wife, Elena Imadie Saladin, were pleasantly surprised to receive a special invitation to the House Speaker's party. The invitation was special because of the attached handwritten note.

"For your eyes only: You are badly needed. If you only wish to feather your nest, I shall expect you to decline this invitation. However, if you are a patriot, please come. When you arrive, we must find time to talk."

The enclosure ended with the initials, "HB." Intentionally underlined, after the initials, was an endorsement that said, "Please destroy."

Charter burned the handwritten note. Elena R.S.V.P.'d.

Congressman Charter Saladin drove his Chrysler New Yorker down the ramp to the basement parking below the Rayburn Building. The auto was waxed, well maintained, and four years old. Its luxurious interior was befitting a popular Representative from New Jersey. But, Saladin knew his people…those who voted in amazing numbers for him. They were proud of Charter and his American car. The car was neither too new nor old. It befitted a congressman of the people. Had the "newly-elected" driven a Mercedes, BMW, Cadillac, or English Rolls Royce, he might have appeared to be rewarding himself. Although Middle Atlantic states want a knight in armor, they still resent an emperor.

The sleek automobile rolled into a parking space, poked its tires against the concrete wheel-stop, and nestled beside a heavy foundation pillar.

Always the gentleman, Charter rounded the car and opened the door for his beloved, ever-supportive wife, Elena Imadie Kassem Saladin. She slid gracefully from her seat and stood up beside her husband. Her captivating black eyes sparkled, and her adoring smile thanked him for his years of gallantry. He took her hand in his, gently squeezing it in a familiar message that intimately said, "I love you."

♦   ♦   ♦

Elena Imadie Kassem was the daughter of a wealthy importer of elegant household furniture and antiques. An immigrant from northern India (later to become known as Pakistan), Jeju Kassem fled the constant fighting along the India-Pakistan border. Jeju's wife, cruelly treated and malnourished by a decade of terrorist troop subjugations, died soon after her arrival in her newly adopted country. Yet, she left her heritage to the New World when Elena Imadie Kassem was born.

The father, Jeju Kassem, and daughter, Elena Imadie, resided in Portsmouth, New Hampshire. Elena was brilliant in school, spoke five languages fluently, graduated from high school at 16, and became an accounting whiz in her daddy's business. The import business thrived and Jeju Kassem became a millionaire. His astute investments in real estate, stocks, bonds, and shopping mall developments were blessed with the Midas touch.

And the guru of the Midas touch was Elena. She became wealthy in her own right. *Then came that unforgettable evening.*

The National Merchants Association was conferring its annual leadership awards. The gala function, held in The Towers Building, was at Ye King Charles Pub, a swank watering hole in Boston. Elena, weary, sitting alone at a corner table, was reassessing the week's profitable contracts she had negotiated. Looking up, she gazed across the floor...straight into the stare of a handsome man who appeared fascinated...or paralyzed. Slowly, deliberately, he walked across the ballroom, pulled Elena to her feet, and escorted her to the aged, hardwood dance floor. No word was spoken, but her princely escort glided around the floor as if he were skating on ice.

Elena's heart thumped, flopped, and bounced. She couldn't get her breath, but she, too, floated across the floor in concert with her partner. She was barely conscious of the applause as prosperous buyers and retailers moved aside to watch an exhibition of rhythm and grace. The couple danced for a half-hour before Charles Joseph Saladin introduced himself. He learned she was Elena Imadie Kassem.

He said, "I am from Connecticut. My grandfather was Syrian. You?"

"I'm also an American. My father is Pakistani, as was my mother."

"Ah, Elena. I must speak to your father very soon. It is an old custom and I must have his permission."

"His permission? For WHAT?"

"Our marriage. In the old country I might speak differently, but here, in this modern Western World, I must confess I've fallen hard for you. We must marry soon. Time is important. I have been looking for you too long."

Elena Kassem's jaw dropped. She stood aghast. She knew nothing of this lothario except that his passions were overwhelming. She stopped dancing, placed her fists on her hips, and, heart pounding, she spoke firmly,

"Don't be an ass. We are not in Syria. I don't know you…and you are **not** meeting my father. We are too busy. Have you been drinking?"

"My darling, Elena. Being the wife of Charter Joseph Saladin will be the high point of your life. And you will be the beacon of my soul. I am nothing, now. But, I lead people. With them, we will find our destinies."

Elena laughed derisively, "Saladin, you are a fool. Marriage? HA." Charter was silent, but his dark eyes penetrated to the very core of Kassem's daughter. Tenderly, he clutched Elena Imadie closely and whirled her around the dance floor. Her heart kept skipping and she kept swallowing.

The wedding cost a fortune. And father Kassem seemed the drunkest at the reception. A teetotaler, he sang and danced, inebriated with joy. And the city of Portsmouth had to admit it had never seen or experienced such an all-day, all-night jubilee since before the crash of 1929.

◆   ◆   ◆

And Charter Saladin gently helped his bride from the auto's seat. And as she peered into his face, he affectionately squeezed her hand once more…sending his secret message of love.

The explosion of the rifle shot echoed thunderously throughout the cavernous walls of the underground parking lot.

Elena Imadie Saladin staggered back against the steel frame of the Chrysler. Elena's expression of surprise was one that Charter would never forget. Her happy eyes changed to sadness when she said,

"Oh, my dearest Charter. What have they done to us?"

Congressman Charter Saladin was stunned—first, by the thunderous blast—second, by his lovely wife's sadness and puzzling question. "What do you mean, Elena? What has who done?"

But, by then, Elena Imadie began coughing; blood gushed from her mouth, down her chin, and dripped onto her velvet bodice. Her eyes peacefully closed, and she fell into the arms of her adoring husband. Slowly, as quiet returned to the underground cavern, the twosome slumped to the concrete.

Out of his mind in disbelief—and at the suddenness, Charter Saladin never discerned the slam of a car door, the squeal of rubber as tires spun, nor the roar of an engine. An unseen vehicle sped through the basement, and careened up the ramp into the obscurity of the Washington night. In moments the noisy blare of the engine evaporated within the security of darkness.

Holding Elena tightly in his bloodied arms, Charter rocked back and forth, moaning over and over, "My darling. My darling. Don't leave me. Oh, dear God, Why? WHY?"

Elena Kassem Salidan would never answer her devoted husband. Her face was tranquil. Elena's journey to another world was under way.

5

A Question of Honor

"Don't move, Mister. You do and I'll blow your damned head off."

Charter Saladin looked up from the composed features of his wife…straight into the barrel of a huge automatic—only feet from his temple. Behind the weapon stood a uniformed guard. There was no mistaking the dress of a Congressional Patrolman.

"Get away from that lady, Mister, or you're a dead man."

As he motioned to Charter with the gun barrel, the officer was radioing for assistance, "Lower parking, Zone D. Woman down, hurt bad,…I am holding the culprit. We need an ambulance—make it fast."

The officer's eyes squinted in fury as he nearly jammed the gun against Saladin's temple. With tears streaming down his face, Charter told him,

"Go ahead. Shoot. Life doesn't have much meaning, now. If you think I'm going to let Elena leave my arms, then do what you have to do."

The officer, a family man himself, slowly lowered the pistol. A softer expression enveloped his features.

"Elena? Hmmmmmmm, your wife?" Charter barely nodded.

"What happened, Mister?"

"I don't know—I just don't know." The officer frowned at Charter.

Charter yelled, "I don't KNOW what happened. Honest to God, I DON'T."

From a distance the wail of a siren grew closer, its sob resounding down the parking ramp. A flurry of feet pounded the cold concrete. The radio call had brought help. A man in a tuxedo spoke to the policeman,

"I'm Terry Thomlinson, Congressional Aide to Speaker of the House Broderick. Your Chief of Security yanked me from Speaker Broderick's reception. You say you apprehended a molester, a rapist? Good work, Officer. That'll be one less rotten bast—…."

"Oh, sweet Jesus. It's Congressman Charter Saladin. Charter. CHARTER? WHAT THE HELL HAPPENED? OH, MY GOD. IS THAT ELENA....?"

Charter only looked at Terry Thomlinson. Charter's tears divulged the answer. Terry was kneeling and holding Charter when the ambulance arrived.

A paramedic pushed Saladin, "Please move aside, Sir, while I examine the lady. Johnny, get the revive kit and resuscitator ready. This woman is unconscious. Now, move aside, Sir."

Charter Saladin moved sideways, but he would not release Elena.

"Mister, did you hear me? You must...."

The paramedic felt a firm hand on his arm and looked up to see Terry Thomlinson shaking his head reproachfully.

The medical technician understood and responded with a quiet, "Right."

The examination went swiftly, two attendants moving their fingers swiftly over Elena's chest and head.

A dozen people, including officers, congressional aides, and Representatives, observed the ministrations of the emergency paramedics. Elena's labored breathing echoed through the silent garage. Abruptly, the breathing stopped. Most noticeable, then, were the two technicians...glancing at each other. Without a word, the assistant medic began repacking his kit.

The first paramedic slowly rose, and addressed Thomlinson and the crowd,

"It's apparent the victim has been shot through the lungs, and, likely,...the heart. I'm sorry, there's nothing we can do. The lady's dead."

The elderly gray-haired man kept shaking Charter Saladin and tugging at his bloodied arms.

"You've got to let go, Charter. It's time—LET GO."

Congressman Saladin turned and gaped at the distinguished-looking gentleman kneeling beside him. Charter's face was immobile, his glazed eyes staring. He was staring into space—staring right through the fashionably dressed man beside him. Over and over the elderly man urged,

"Charter, the ambulance is here. The attendants and forensic physician are here. They're ready to take Elena away. Charter, you've got to let her go." But, Saladin remained in his dreamlike trance.

"Doctor, this man is a close friend of mine," whispered Holcombe Broderick. "Would you confirm he's in shock? I hope you'll give him a shot to make his sleep. I'll see he get's to my home. And, you detectives won't get anything from him now,...right? O.K., be at my home at 9:00 a.m. tomorrow and he'll answer all questions. Well, Worth, how about it?

Dr. Worth Miller Grossman, a wise and compassionate diagnostic surgeon, had taken in the entire picture along with the detectives. His actions were swift and professional. With a kind smile, Dr. Grossman said,

"I concur, Holcombe. The shot I'm giving him will make him sleep through the night." The hypodermic injection was a generous one.

Worth asked, "How soon do you want the autopsy, Holcombe? It's been a long day."

Holcombe Broderick didn't mince any words, "Worth, I want the autopsy report at my home by the time the detectives arrive tomorrow morning. Can you do me this favor, my friend?"

Dr. Grossman sighed, and closed his medical bag.

"All right, Holcombe, I'll be working all night, but you'll have it."

Speaker Broderick said, "Thank you, Doctor. Since I owe you one, how about coming over the week after next? I'm having one of my gourmet barbecued ribs and steak fries. Bring your lovely wife, Charlotte. The 'Attitude Adjustment Hour' begins at 1700."

The fatigued physician supervised the loading of Elena's body onto the portable gurney and ambulance. He would accompany her to the coroner's laboratory, but, before the ambulance door was closed, he yelled to Holcombe,

"You think you can bribe me to work all night just to attend one of your blasted barbecue and steak fries? Damn you, Holcombe, you certainly know me and my weakness. Now I know how you became House Speaker."

Worth Grossman smiled and waved goodbye. Yet, he knew tonight's work would be methodical and slow—his pathology exam must miss nothing—because the forensic facts must anticipate answers to every question that might be asked. Dr. Grossman shook his head in disgust, "Thank Heaven it's not too often a Congressman, especially his wife, is murdered. Hey. Waaaiitttt a minute. Was it caused by an attempted robbery?...Or was it an attempted **assassination**...of Congressman Saladin?

"Well, Worth, you'd better awaken your medical partner. A second opinion must corroborate <u>every</u> finding. We'll have to re-check <u>every</u> test."

◆   ◆   ◆

Charter Joseph Saladin returned to consciousness with two jolting affronts to his sanity: First, deep melodious gongs were steadily reverberating in his brain. His mind flickered into the 'distant past'—a travelogue into Colonial America with the hushed din of antique whirring gears—"What was that? Machinery?"

Second, there was the smell of coffee, . . fresh coffee. A white-capped woman with coarse hands, reddened from harsh homemade laundry soap, was turning the crank of a coffee grinder. Dark coffee beans, dipped from hundred-pound sacks, were being milled into fine granules. The "colonial woman" suspended a spouted blue-porcelain pot over a cheery fire. The vessel, hung over the hearth on a swinging iron hook, boiled and simmered the granules until a pungent aroma wafted from the porcelain pot.

"Hmmmm, coffee.... coffee? From where?"

Charter Saladin's eyes gradually opened and he stared at a sculptured ceiling replete with rough-hewn mahogany-stained beams. His blurry gaze dropped to sunlit windows, the sun masked by partially closed drapes. The windows were large and many; narrow, but tall; so tall that they extended inches above the floor and nearly reached the ceiling. Charter's eyes dropped to the wood-pegged flooring made of wide boards of creaking, old-fashioned yellow pine. He gasped,

"My God. Where am I? Are the British coming?" His hallucinating mind still heard the gongs reverberating, still smelled the delicious scent of coffee. He was inside an "old-timey lodging" of a colonial village—a way of life that Saladin had read about and admired. He turned his head, because the unmistakable aroma of coffee was titillating his nostrils. And, when he turned, he looked into the concerned face of Holcombe Broderick. Broderick was holding a steaming cup of coffee under Charter's nose. Saladin's stomach growled. He was ravenous.

Once more, Holcombe Broderick didn't mince words. His worried features were showing...even to a neophyte Congressman. "Welcome back, Charter. I am Speaker of your House, Holcombe Broderick. Your thrashings are a return to reality. I only hope you'll get angry when I tell you what your subconscious already knows.

"Your wife is gone, Charter. And, you are not mad, but only hearing the peaceful nostalgia of a bygone era.

"The bonging you heard came from a 200-year-old clock. The whirring sounds are the gears of the chimes. The Grandfather just finished striking 9:00 o'clock, and here is your morning coffee. God knows you were shouting enough about waking up. So wake up and take a look back at colonial times. You're in Georgetown, a part of Washington, which was built before the British burned the White House in 1812. This historic Early American house helps keep me in tune with the America we once knew—where patriotism, love of country, and integrity made the United States great."

Speaker Broderick continued, "The Washington police, the detectives and the F.B.I. are downstairs waiting for you. I know you are up to their questioning. It will be rough, but you **will** survive. I had told you, in my personal note, that we must talk. Before we both go downstairs to meet the police...and the dad-blasted nosy news media—we must talk, now. I must know, young fellow—

"Stupid as it may sound,...are you, Congressman Charter Saladin, willing to face `Death before Dishonor'? I must KNOW."

Congressman Saladin only closed his eyes, bowed his head, and responded, "I have just suffered death. So, I pledge you my Honor.

Broderick answered, deeply moved. "Then, my friend, when you recover a semblance of your former self, we will talk of many things.

Charter Saladin met the press, the F.B.I., and Washington Police. He conducted himself commendably. The legal fraternity, with vital facts already in their hands, asked surprisingly few questions.

The media learned even less. After all, they, themselves, knew more about the slaying than Charter Saladin did.

What the news media did not know, a silent Holcombe Broderick observed, was that Charter Saladin was doing an ever-growing "slow burn." Broderick smiled inwardly.

The young congressman was nurturing a burning desire for revenge. The warfare would encompass two methods: Either brutal or insidious. Neither one would be tempered with mercy.

◆   ◆   ◆

Speaker Holcombe Broderick kept the pace moving in the House of Representatives. He did not press Charter Saladin—yet. He wanted the man to show more evidence of recovery. Congressman Saladin zombied his way through the daily proceedings, walked to the Congressional Restaurant in a near-trance, and ate sparingly. Too sparingly. Charter was losing weight and his appearance was lined and gaunt. He remained ill from the trauma of losing his wife, but his integrity was never in question.

It seemed, more than ever, that Congressman Saladin was a man of the people. He acted in their best interest, and turned a deaf ear to imploring congressional associates on both sides of the aisle. Although he voted for some proposals, he fought legislation that seemed designed to line the pockets of particular groups. His vote and intrepid leadership helped defeat a juicy boondoggle for

New York State. His newcomer's effort was pronounced "only a pebble in a pond," by one prominent Senator whose House delegates followed his every whim. But, the rippling effect spread over that pond, to the chagrin of the Senator...and the measure was narrowly defeated.

Senator Abraham "Lieb" Anselm was livid with rage. That damned upstart from New Jersey had actually fought him and his bill...and won.

Saladin had effectively stopped the Corps of Engineers from building a questionable dam. This one, within the beautiful Adirondacks, would have created a new lake on the West Canada Creek near the foot of the West Canada Mountain. When the lake filled, the waterfront properties and tourist lodgings would have generated a fortune...a fortune for the big financier friends of "Lieb." Now Anselm would not get his customary kickback from the developers.

Anselm was gnashing his teeth and shouting, "There'll be another time, Saladin, and you'll pay again"

Counsel and top aide, Bergan Gruenspan, had been rather quiet, almost noncommunicative, these past weeks. He gaped at Abraham Anselm in wonder. Bergan's blood had turned cold weeks ago when he heard Anselm's calm remark,

"Saladin may decide not to talk at all. Regardless, that's my worry."

Saladin's awaited blockbuster speech was never delivered. His wife's murder had stopped the first speech of newly elected Charter Saladin. Now, Senior Senator Anselm had uttered another forecast.

And, Gruenspan found his insides churning, until he actually sickened. "What did he mean, 'You'll pay, again'?"

Bergan Gruenspan's suspicions were horrifying. He found himself at a crossroads. And he did not know where the trail would lead.

Congressional committee meetings were numerous as the new fiscal year began. Charter Saladin was cordial, but reserved. However, his internal fires were only banked, not out. He sat and listened in silence, his personal pain daily subsiding into a tolerable dull ache.

No Democrat or Republican was unaware of the unsolved, tragic, accidental shooting of Elena Saladin. Charter was wise, his words prophetic and sound, his common sense undeniable. So, amid his colleagues' respectful sympathy, he spoke and they listened more closely than ever before.

A simple wave of Saladin's hand, a gesture of dissent, repeatedly stopped the arguments of even the majority whips from both parties. His actions caused some partisan bickering and jealous objections. Yet, when Charter concisely expressed his reasons point by point, and backed them with a phenomenal battery of memorized facts, his opponents usually fell silent.

Members of the Senate and House were beginning to realize Charter Saladin was unique to the governing body in Washington.

No senator recognized this fact more than the senior senator from New Jersey, Jacob Bergenfeldt. He was habitually struck dumb or suffered a case of the stammers whenever he challenged the opinions of Saladin. The under-table leg kicks from his mentor, Senator Abraham Anselm, provided scant encouragement. Bergenfeldt was reduced to illogical babbling.

New York's "Lieb" Anselm neared apoplexy because of his frustration. His power plays were continually thwarted by Charter Saladin. What would fly through the Senate would strike brick walls in The House.

Abraham Anselm growled to his guru, Bergan Gruenspan,

"How can a guy so sick function so well in these meetings? He doesn't look well, does he? He keeps throttling me with his lies."

Gruenspan looked disgusted. "Lieb, you still won't listen to me. Saladin functions well because, although he's still suffering, he hasn't lost the will to fight for what he believes. Yes, he looks well…especially since last week. He's improving daily. And, he doesn't lie. His facts are irrefutable—he's right on the money. I've told you time and again you don't do your homework. You are beating you."

Abraham Lieberson Anselm's countenance grew menacing. He could not stand being beaten at his own game. His voice grew soft and deadly. He said, "So, Saladin is recovering quickly. I'm betting he'll have a relapse."

And, Bergen Gruenspan took several sharp breaths. His once-analytic mind was now blocked by fears he could not face.

◆   ◆   ◆

Charter Saladin whistled as he walked down the hallowed halls of The House. His troubled emotions were getting back on track due to his beloved, Elena Imadie. He could figuratively hear her chastising him because he was mourning her death.

"Now, stop it, Charter. You've cried long enough. I'm here. I'll always be here with you in spirit. So, cut the overwrought jazz and let's get to work. There are things we need to do."

Saladin laughed…a muffled laugh.

"All right, darling. But, oh, how I miss you."

Groups of congressmen traipsed down the huge corridor to their offices or scheduled meetings. They waved, spoke, and welcomed the surprisingly influential newcomer. And, for the first time in over a month, Charter Saladin smiled, spoke, and waved back. His gradual improvement did not go unnoticed. The bounce in his step had returned.

Suddenly, two beefy men, sharply dressed, stepped beside Charter, grabbed his arms, and steered him toward the nearest restroom.

"Relax, Mr. Saladin," said one. "You must see this. We believe it's a message for you. Please take a look and tell us."

The husky men gently released Charter in the middle of the restroom nearest to Saladin's congressional desk, and the one he normally used. Someone else knew his routine, too.

There, on the mirror over one of the wash basins, printed in red lipstick, were the words:

"YOU DAMNED FOOL. NO ACCIDENT. WE HIT EXACTLY WHERE WE AIMED."

"Congressman Saladin," said the other man, "we are Secret Service and we closed off this facility after an aide to Speaker Broderick, a Mr. Terry Thomlinson, found this message written on this mirror early this morning. Do you have any idea what the words mean?"

A pale Charter Saladin answered simply.

"Yes. My Elena was killed deliberately by some assassin. There was no warning, no notes, no messages—only this. Now you probably know more than I do."

Charter Saladin closed his eyes and collapsed on the tiled floor. He lay unconscious. The restroom was as still as a tomb.

From an unlighted corner, Holcombe Broderick walked to the center of the restroom. His commands were swift and promptly obeyed.

"Take color photos of this mirror. Touch nothing until the authorities arrive. Take Saladin to my home by ambulance. Notify the police and F.B.I. Close off this bath until the Secret Service, F.B.I., and Washington Police say it's Okay to reopen.

"I'll call Dr. Worth Grossman. Charter won't be around these halls for a while. He's strong, but someone has intentionally beaten him where it destroys him the most.

"Now we know. Elena's murder was planned. But, why her, not Saladin? For what reason? Incredible. Does anyone realize what a senseless puzzle this is? You detectives, . . anybody, please tell me: This is a new congressman—In God's name, WHAT'S the motive?"

6

Oz

Jameson Cody Dittus strolled leisurely down the tarmac of the Frederick Municipal Airport. The macadam taxiways were astonishingly busy for a smaller airport when compared with the traffic at Dulles International and Washington International Airports. Planes were coming and going continuously, like bevies of quail, throughout the morning and afternoon.

Cody scribbled in his notebook about the quality of the 40-passenger aircraft which were similar to planes flown by the airlines. But the average Frederick Municipal aircraft carried six to ten passengers and crew. The planes he studied were sleek and speedy jets, the slower turbine-engined craft, and the economy multi-engined prop planes. Cody Dittus noticed all the airplanes were new or in first-class condition. There were no dogs among them.

He spent the day portraying an aircraft lover who can't watch enough of those wonderful planes. He'd join the mechanics at lunchtime and work break. Pulling up a chair, he'd open his portable canvas ice chest and pull out a bottle of imported beer. Slurping noisily, and smacking his lips while praising the taste of real German beer, Cody had little trouble getting the attention of the A & E (aircraft & engines) technicians.

The floodgates of conversation opened easily whenever he offered any worker a Bavarian Beer. Cody was casual and unconcerned as he announced,

"I'm 'Jack Evans'. I've been looking for an old friend who used to work on a small Cessna plane of mine. Name's Cash Delway. Where do I find him?"

The two employees raised their eyebrows at each other. There was dead silence until Dittus gazed at them with a puzzled look.

"Did I say something wrong? Delway do something nasty to you boys?"

"No, Sir. I can see you haven't heard."

"Heard <u>what</u>?"

"He's dead ."

Cody acted shocked. After a proper amount of solemnity, he asked,

"Heart? Cancer? He was young."

The other mechanic smirked and facetiously said, "They found his body inside District of Columbia General Hospital, Mr. Evans."

Cody gasped, "I knew hospitals had their problems, but this is ridiculous. What was the problem? Doctors and nurses too far away?"

"The police didn't say. Believe it or not, someone found his body in the corner of a room. We suspect a sudden heart attack while he was visiting someone. I know Marchen Judisch was mighty upset when he heard the news."

"Marchen Judisch? Who's he?"

"He owns that King Air 350 twin turbo-prop plane right over there. He was a buddy of Cash Delway. Cash repaired everything on his plane. Isn't it a beauty? Man, the 'Washington Wheels' that Marchen flew all over the country."

Cody smiled and said, "Marchen must be an important man. What does he do? Who are the VIP's you've seen him with?"

"We really don't know, Sir. Maybe he's a lobbyist, industrialist, or an overseas diplomat. He's thick with the Ambassador from Israel, Bergenfeldt of New Jersey, Anselm of New York, . . sometimes his chief counsel, Gruenspan. There's Mirish from the President's Cabinet,...plus a group of trench coated uglies with bulges under their jackets. Man, you look at them and you leave them strictly alone. Mr. Judisch spends a lot of time picking them up from all over Canada."

"How do you know he flies to Canada?"

"He tells us 'fill those tanks full. I'm going to Montreal'. Or, 'I'm going to Quebec'.

"He might mention he was on his way up to Halifax, or St. John's, . . even Goose Bay. He's not kidding us 'cause we inspect his pilot's briefcase, and it's always crammed with USA high altitude in-route charts and a Jefferson's USA Airport Approach manual. A Canadian Mapleleaf compartment is stuffed with Northwest Sectional Airway Charts and Approach Guidebooks for Canada, Newfoundland, and Labrador"

Cody Dittus was missing nothing. Keeping a low-profile, while listening, Cody quietly opened two more Bavarian beers and handed them to the technicians. They accepted the brews without slowing the conversation.

Cody stood, stretched, and asked, "How about showing me that beautiful King Air turbo-prop? Just how many does that multi-windowed fuselage hold?"

As the three walked out to the plane, the chief mechanic said,

"It has a club car arrangement. Seats face each other with a card table in between. It holds 8 people very comfortably. Each engine is over a thousand horsepower, and the '350' cruises better than 350 miles per hour at 18,000 to 22,000 feet."

Ambling around the beautifully streamlined craft, Cody did an abrupt "double-take." Beneath the aircraft's nose hung an L-shaped pipe...with a canvas and Naugahyde wrapping around it.

Dittus said, "What is this? Why is it covered?"

The assistant technician answered,

"Mr. Evans, that's what we call a Pitot tube. It measures air pressure, air speed, altitude, and supplies other vital cockpit instruments."

"Wow . You boys don't miss anything. New paint job and new instrument covering. How long does this Pitot Tube cover last? Years?

"Not when someone steals it. The cover protects the air tube from blowing dust on the ground. The pilot insisted on an immediate replacement. Keeps the moisture out of his blind-flying instruments."

Cody said, "I can see why Marchen Judisch is so particular about his plane. It even looks like a bird. Those long flights into Canada must wear him out."

"No, Mr. Evans, we said the pilot. Judisch is the owner and always flies the co-pilot's seat. When he's not hauling the Washington big shots, the pilot jaunts around the country to the numismatist shows."

"The what?"

"The coin shows. He's big on coins—you know, numismatics—the study of coins and medals—silver and gold coins. Rare and valuable coins. Ancient copper, bronze, silver and gold medals. He's got one of the best collections in the country. He often carries satchels of gold and silver coins with him. He's a real wheeler-dealer."

Bingo. Jameson Cody Dittus blinked. He had struck paydirt: The dead man trying to kill Leith Ohmstead was Cash Delway. Delway was close to Marchen Judisch, the aircraft owner. But his pilot cavorted around the country buying and selling precious gold and silver coins. And...he flew a plane from which a Pitot tube cover has been stolen. Judisch flies people in and out of Canada and points North. DOUBLE BINGO.

Cody Dittus could not believe his good luck. He said, "Fellows, I'll bet the police have been grilling you over the death of Cash Delway. Right?"

"And how, Mr. Evans."

Cody, still carrying the canvas ice chest by a shoulder strap, smoothly took the empty German beer bottles from the A & E employees, and just as smoothly opened up two more of the strong imported brew. The technicians started to object as the freshly opened beer was placed in their hands.

However, the day was sunny, the air was bracing, and the Bavarian ale delicious. As the maintenance men swigged the liquid in appreciation, Cody continued his questioning.

"Tell me, who is this skilled pilot who also transports 'trench-coated uglies with bulges under their jackets'? Do they fly with the senators and Washington officials, too?"

"Never . No way . It's either the tough guys or influential Washington VIP's...'Mark' Judisch and Vier see eye-to-eye on that."

"Vier?"

"Only thing we know about him is that his name is Vier Dyan, a Delegate-at-Large from the Israeli Embassy here. I have heard that Marchen Judisch, who lives here most of the time, is a Diplomat-at-Large from Jerusalem, Israel's capital. When the police found the trail of Cash Delway ended here, they had to drop the matter because they were dealing with the Israeli Embassy and its diplomatic immunity.

"By the way, during the investigation concerning Delway, a policewoman, a Lieutenant Priscilla Kozac, was grumbling that a lot of pressure was coming direct from Congress and the White House to stop the investigation. That's all we know, except that those passengers using the King Air sure tip well." Cody Dittus was breathing heavily. He was trying to mask his feelings which had suddenly jumped to the surface. He asked,

"Would a full name such as Danvier Dyan better identify the pilot?"

"Say," said the chief mechanic looking at his partner, "Remember when Cash Delway called him 'Dan'? Dyan told him he preferred 'Vier'."

The other mechanic agreed, "Come to think of it, it is Danvier. How did you know his name, Sir?" Cody was slow to answer.

He finally said, "Thanks fellows, I'll see you around. Here, you two finish these."

Dittus handed them the last two bottles. Before they could thank him Cody was walking to his car with a shocked expression on his face.

"It surely pays to keep a trunk full of premium iced beer. It gets better results than a rubber hose and a hot spotlight."

The stunned agent reached his car parked in the shade. Cody slowly sat down and leaned back against the headrest. His mind spun with remembrance:

"Dear God . So we meet again, Dyan . You sadistic bast—."

◆   ◆   ◆

Agent Jameson Dittus was running for his life—fleeing down a back alley, away from the side street where heavily armed, fanatical madmen were screaming and yelling—chasing him through the battered streets of Beirut. He could hear the angry orders shouted by the leader of the well trained mercenaries. And he would never forget the soldiers howling,

"Down this way, Colonel Dyan? Danvier, which way now?"

◆   ◆   ◆

Cody Dittus and Leith Ohmstead were part of a select group that spoke at least one foreign language, sometimes two. The Counter Intelligence Agency (CIA) of today is an all-purpose spy organization with many specialists functioning in countries all over the world.

But, Cody's and Leith's team was dead...supposedly phased out after World War II. But his select group had a name: "Oz," a play of words on OSS.

Over 50 years ago, America's only overseas surveillance and sabotage force was the specialized Office of Strategic Services (OSS). Disbanded after the war, the powers behind the defunct OSS kept an extremely secret nucleus operating, although their headquarters continually moved from building to building in Washington, D.C. The only criteria for "Oz" was that the Headquarters be located, temporarily, in a deserted part of a building with dark corridors, few access doors, few offices, and a security entrance and exit second to none.

An agent carried no identification revealing his government agency. For the special group of Oz, if anyone carried such a card, it would state his name and address beneath a logo of a twister, a tornado, . . plus a shock of wheat and the word, Kansas. It meant an American to anyone who could read English...and to a certain few it meant Oz. All activities were covert undercover operations. The generous salaries (actually hazard pay) were cleverly paid through a recognized government agency, the Social Security Administration.

Social Security is an accepted institution for paying disability or retirement income to the American public. There was no way to prove income came from any military branch or quasi-military U.S. Government agency. Even CIA members did not know Oz existed. But, foreign agents overseas knew there was an elite group—its name unknown. Most international leaders know the major infiltrators are either Russia's KGB, England's MI-6 (called SIS—Secret Intelligence Service), or the United States' CIA. At least they are the easiest to blame.

◆   ◆   ◆

Cody Dittus ran through the alley until it intersected another side street. He turned right, dashing past doorways, studying a possible escape route through one of the entrances to the mortared buildings. Cody darted across the narrow alleyway toward an open door. Half way across, he ran into two khaki clad figures…swinging the barrels of their machine guns upon him. Cody's 10-millimeter automatic, with his favorite silencer attached, bucked hard in his hand.

He fired three times, "Whip, Whip…Whip." The first two shots hit the larger man. One through the bridge of his nose, the other through the heart. The second man hesitated. The surprise over Cody's attack slowed his response—Cody put a slug through the target's vocal cords, shattering his neck vertebrae. The smaller mercenary collapsed without a sound…a broken sack of wheat. The first man struggled for air, dropped to his knees, then pitched forward on his face.

But, not before he grabbed for Dittus' jacket. The mercenary's hand fell lifeless to the dirt, and Cody finished his run across the alley, vaulted a set of stairs, and dodged through an open door. He slammed it shut, his chest heaving with the exertion. Cody ran through the Lebanese house, finding it empty. The occupants had flown after hearing nearby gunshots. Cody took the steps two at a time as he bolted upstairs to the bedrooms. He found a closet where the family's clothes hung. Behind the apparel was a small door into the wall. Cody almost ripped the storage room door off its hinges. Cody plunged through the hole and lay among dusty boxes. He pulled a paper clip from his pocket, fashioned a small hook, and pulled the door shut. He held the paper clip wire firmly, the hook doing its intended job…keeping the thin plywood door closed.

How they knew where to look in this particular house mystified Dittus. Yet, come they did, tramping up the stairs, footsteps pounding on the wood flooring…directly into the bedroom. Suddenly, Cody heard the hangers being pushed aside on the crossbar. The next moment he heard a faint "beep, beep, beep…" when a heavy leather boot SMASHED the storage door to kindling. A brilliant flashlight cast its powerful beam precisely on Cody's body and he was exposed like a fish in a lighted aquarium. Dittus shut his eyes and waited for the burst of bullets that would chop him to mincemeat.

Instead, strong hands grabbed his legs and dragged him, face down, across the rough splintered floor, down the bone-rattling steps, across the first-floor living room, down the steps into the grimy street dust. He was almost senseless by that time, his head a mass of cuts and bruises. Dittus was yanked to his feet where, for the next several minutes, he suffered the cruel blows of a wicked palm slapping him forward and backward across the face. Blood flew through the air like a mist…blood spewed from his throat, his mouth, his lips, and his nostrils.

The Colonel stood before him, breathing heavily from his grueling exercise. One fist was planted on his hip; the other hand clutched the wallet brutally torn from Cody's hip pocket.

"I am Colonel Danvier Dyan, your captor. You may live or die in the next hours…slowly and painfully…depending on your answers to me. This card says your name is Jameson Cody Dittus. Obviously, you are a European spy here in Beirut. What was your assignment?"

"I am Cody Dittus, from Hutchinson, Kansas. I am an American. I'm not a spy. I came here to buy Lebanese products for my Middle East Import Company."

"BAH . You ran . Only a guilty man runs ."

"Colonel, there's a big difference in being dumb and being stupid. You let me and a batch of khaki-clad soldiers chase you with machine guns, and we'll see just how still you'll stand ."

Colonel Danvier Dyan's answer was a vicious smashing right to Cody's jaw. The blow almost took Cody's head off, but it did not put him down.

Through bloody, swollen lips Cody said, "You've got guts, Colonel, especially with my hands tied. Tell me, just how in hell did you know exactly where to find me?"

This time Danvier laughed,…and held up a small button which he removed from the shoulder of Cody's jacket. "Even while you were killing him, my lieutenant placed this little 'bug' on your back. You were scurrying, but we did no hurrying—Hey . That's a good rhyme—we just followed the 'beeps' to your hiding place. You Americans are children in a Middle East man's world. We Arabs know just how to deal with American weaklings and your impotent country."

In spite of the pain, Cody laughed, spitting blood through lacerated lips. "Dyan, you are no Arab. You are a Jew. Why you'd lie to me, a captive, is cowardly. But, your eyes gave you away. You are a brown-eyed Hebrew. Probably a Zionist, since you and your hit team are warlike. What's the real reason you are attacking an innocent American friend?"

"Damn you—DAMN YOU . Hold him…hold him tight and hold him up ."

The flurry of fists, the unmerciful punches, the staggering blows, came hard and abundantly. Colonel Dyan did not answer. He gave vent to a rage that was inhuman. He battered Cody Dittus into unconsciousness. And Cody welcomed the black veil of oblivion that was drawn across his senses. His world of blinding pain and blood-letting revolved into peaceful nothingness.

Cody Dittus slowly awakened. His swollen eyes peered out from eyelids that were mere slits. Fortunately, daylight diffused through small iron-barred windows at one end of the smelly room. The dim light was gentle on his eyes. Cody lay on a dirt floor. He didn't rate the comfort of a mattress, or even a blanket. His good jacket was gone. His shirt and pants were torn and soaked with blood. Wherever he lay, or turned, the powdery floor mixed into his clothes…making a paste of dark red clay. His body cried out for water and, finally, so did Cody.

"Water . Water, please . Please, some water."

The room door opened and boots scraped across the soil. Without warning, cascades of water soaked Dittus. Two, three, four buckets of water drenched him from head to foot while his caretaker's voices roared with laughter. Cody got a few drops by licking his hands and arms. But, the moisture had blended into bloody clay on his body, and the mixture turned gritty between his teeth. The soldiers left, the door slamming shut loudly.

Then the initial torture began. Cody's adversaries <u>had</u> to know what would happen. The blistering floor and walls were bone dry like a desert.

And the bugs came from everywhere—searching for moisture—the water that had drenched Cody's clothes. The insects sucked the water from the fabric; sucked and ate through the fabric; then, sucked and ate Cody Dittus.

As Dittus screamed in agony from myriad red-hot stings, he became aware of laughter from the adjoining room. Every body movement tortured him as he braced himself on an elbow and looked at his cell door. Heads were rimmed around the door's small observation window, and howls of mirth punctuated Cody's screams.

His torso was purple and black—a mass of bruises. His thighs and legs were covered with red, distended, bites. By now his body was a collection of oozing punctures caused by the bites and bug saliva deposited in his subcutaneous tissue. The terrible beatings should have critically injured, perhaps killed, Dittus. But, Cody was saved by a snarl.

Biting his puffed lips in pain, Cody laboriously stood. He stripped naked to his shoes, then brushed off the carnivorous pests. He snarled.

He was at the end of his rope. Every movement of his bones, every muscle contraction was so painful that he growled. His mind, highly disciplined, had snapped. Perhaps he was actually deranged…unbalanced. At last, the "breakdown" conquered his disabling pain. He staggered to a corner, outside the vision of his guards. It was nighttime, and his captors relaxed with glasses of wine or Middle East whiskeys. But, the prisoner could not be seen.

With a crash the door flew open and several guards rushed in. They encountered Cody standing in a corner, eyes shut, mouth slanted at an angle, his arms dangling helplessly at his sides. Cody was barely conscious on his feet. Then a sergeant, speaking with an unusual accent, said,

"Enjoy yourself this night, Mr. Dittus. That is, you and the bugs. We have great plans for you tomorrow morning after you get a good night's sleep. Do you wish us to bring you some more…water?"

And the sergeant chuckled. What the squad leader did not know was that, if he had been alone, he would have been dead.

Cody Dittus refused to answer. His blood-sucked body ached for cooling water, but he knew he could not survive another bout with the insects.

He only babbled like a demented being. The other guard cautioned the sergeant, "Careful, Aaron, he must be alive tomorrow for the Colonel." The guards withdrew after locking the door. The drinking party began anew.

Cody let time work for him. Although he ached to lie down, the crawling insects made him snarl. The longer he stood, the more his blood coursed through his being, and his mind calmed.

Suddenly, without warning, the door burst open again, and another soldier outlined Cody in his flashlight. The guard literally weaved toward Cody's face, while examining him. His captor reeked of drink. And Cody displayed a state of stupor. The guard snickered and left. Now the entire group next door could carouse and sleep without worry. Which was exactly what Cody Dittus planned.

Dittus shuffled to the door, stifling any outcry of pain. He looked into the adjacent room. His drunken captors never heard nor saw him looking through the porthole of the door. But Cody instantly recognized instruments of torture that apparently had been used before:

The first obvious satanic instrument was a testicle crusher. Beside it, on the wooden rack, lay a penis vise. Its crushing sheath would mangle any man. Specifically designed irons, when heated red hot over burning coals, would sear, create hideous wounds, and then cauterize the wounds so that a pitiful victim would not bleed to death. A headband of iron, when screwed tight, could crack a man's skull as easily as a walnut. There were even adjustable rods meant to slowly push a man's eyeballs from their sockets…or back into his skull. These were tools that no man could tolerate. They would kill him or disable him permanently.

Jameson Cody Dittus strode to a wall, supported himself against it, and removed a shoe. With a proper series of twists, pushes, and pulls, he removed the heel. From its hollow interior, he pulled out a coiled wire with latex-coated nooses at each end. It was a survivor's kit cable saw—a strong steel cable imbedded with diamond dust. The tiny diamonds were razor sharp, indestructible, and could cut through steel. Cody stepped to the small barred window just above his head, pulled the cable around a corner bar, hooked his middle and index fingers through each rubber-protected noose, and sawed.

Using a strength born of pain and desperation, he enabled the steel-cabled diamond-bladed saw to slash through the iron like a hot knife slicing butter. The particles of iron shavings built a mound on the window sill around each bar. First, Cody sawed the top of the bar where it entered the brick. Then, he sawed the bottom of the bar, snapping it off and placing it quietly on the floor just before it would have fallen. There were four bars to remove...and one chance to escape. Cody weighed 180 pounds. He wished he were 160. He crouched, ready to spring into the now-open window, and squirmed his way to freedom. He heard the doorbolt slide back, and the hinges creaked.

A fatalist at heart, Cody believed life was "Kismet"—an appointed lot, fate. He would go down fighting and killing instead of caving in like a helpless mortal.

The ruthless sergeant entered Cody's domain, watching him stagger toward him with his hand held out...a hand holding two metal rods? As the sergeant moved closer with a puzzled frown on his face, Cody dropped the sawed iron bars on his boot. The double thump of the iron striking leather hurt.

Surprised, the sergeant, gun in hand, jumped back. And Cody Dittus swatted the gunhand aside. With three fingers, he landed a wicked blow to the captor's Adam's apple. The sergeant experienced paralyzing shock. His hand, still holding the pistol, dropped while he shouted for help. He strangled; he could not breathe; he could not swallow; and his shout was a feeble whisper. Dittus sprang behind the sergeant and didn't worry about the gun. The prisoner wrapped the cable saw around the sergeant's neck—and whipped the blade back and forth.

As the captor fell, Cody braced his knee on the back of the sergeant's head...and sawed. The deed was easy and fast. Cody did not stop until the head rolled on the floor and the body plopped to the dirt. There was moisture in the dust now. And the bugs would get their fill of drink...and food.

Without one qualm of remorse for his tormentor, Cody jumped to the window, wrenching his shoulders one direction then another, his indispensable cable saw still gripped in his right hand. He was halfway through the window when the stubs of the bars caught his hips. He twisted, pulled, and wrenched...ignoring the sounds of tearing flesh on the sharp stubs. He never even noticed the anguish. He had long ago reached the threshold of maximum pain his body could feel.

Then Cody groaned. He hung high outside the building. His prison was an upstairs room, and his headfirst drop would be to stone steps below. He could not go back—and to go forward was certain death. And someone would soon investigate the whereabouts of the squad leader sergeant.

Death below, and death behind. Cody noticed his arms were wet and warm. He was bleeding again, from reopened wounds. With a macabre touch of humor, Cody Dittus began chuckling. He could hear the droplets of red splashing off the stones below. It was ironic: Most of his body faced freedom outside, while his derriere flashed a message to his captors inside.

"Quit your idiotic giggling before you wake everybody, you imbecile . If you've examined the terrain to your satisfaction, then kindly drop your skinny-dipping frame down to me. I'll catch you...maybe ."

Below Dittus stood an...an Arab? He spoke English, but wore a burnoose, a hooded cloak. Cody moaned again,

"Hell, why not . You only live once. It's Kismet time." He dropped from the cell's window.

The man below braced, caught Cody's plunging body, and appropriately said, "Ooooffffff."

He caught Dittus by his shoulders and hips. Cody's head missed the stone-work. His feet did not. He felt his shoes strike the rocky doorsteps, but so lightly that no toes protested. The next instant he was walking across the dirty street, al a bare bottom and male accouterments, assisted by his Arab confederate. In the black of night the pair headed across a traffic square toward a parked automobile. Cody could not believe his luck. He sighed and breathed deeply...when from the dark appeared two uniformed men...well armed. Both carried pistols in their hands and automatic rifles strapped across their shoulders.

They spoke Arabic, "Just a minute. Where are you going in the middle of the night? You should.... WHA—? Allah in heaven. This one has no clothes on. Look at him, he's been in a fight ."

Both patrolmen looked military. But on whose side? They nodded courteously to one of their own, the burnoosed Arab. Fortunately, they were flabbergasted by Cody's appearance. He was a spectacle to behold with white skin, purple-bruised, bug-bitten physique, and only shoes. For an instant their pistols were pointed at Cody.

The Arab rescuer raised his white-sleeved hand at the patrolmen.

"Whip. Whip."

The unmistakable sound of a silencer, barely echoing through the square, was almost a sneeze.

Before the two forms lying on the ground had quit convulsing, the Arab stuffed Cody into the auto, threw a trench coat at him, and smoothly drove the car down a deserted street. The speed was slow; the engine was quiet.

"Thanks, buddy. You saved my life. That's twice I've escaped from the authorities in the past 15 minutes. Just who are you?"

"Cody, why in hell are you walking around the neighborhood naked? You look like you've been through a meat grinder. Lord, man . Was she pretty?"

Dittus was really confused. He yelled,

"I'm an American. Now, WHO THE HELL ARE YOU?"

The car sped down a modern highway, making turns, up and down hills, until it sped into a high-walled compound. The Arab drove into a courtyard and parked in front of a white painted residence. The white-cloaked man jumped from the auto and assisted a shaky Cody Dittus inside the home into a cozy study. The host then poured a brandy and handed it to his naked friend.

"I've had a bad time of it following your trail. Looks like I made it just before the 12th-hour. Drink up. You need it; then we'll talk.

"Buster, you're no Arab. Turn up the lamp and introduce yourself. You talk like an American...or are you British?"

The Arab threw the hood back on his shoulders. He was grinning at the naked, astounded member of Oz.

The benefactor was also a member of Oz. Cody had not seen him in years. Before him, reloading the clip on his automatic, then pouring himself a drink,...stood Leith Ci Ohmstead.

7

Mossad Encounter

Leith Ohmstead and Cody Dittus sat in upholstered chairs, sipping their brandies. Neither spoke. The silence of the night was like a cloak, shielding and sheltering them from the stress of the day. Leith grabbed a bronze velvet-headed mallet and struck an intricately etched gong sitting son the sidetable. A deep bass sound rolled softly throughout the quarters.

Cody thought, "What a beautiful tone. That small gong resounds with a deep rumble. How do they forge such metals? How do Arab craftsmen do it?"

In answer to the gong's summons, a dusky-skinned servant, dressed in a sky-blue two-piece uniform, materialized from nowhere. The whites of his piercing eyes contrasted with his olive skin. Leith said,

"Jabal, get a doctor here immediately. We have a badly beaten man who needs care." As an afterthought, Leith added,

"And, Jabal, be sure he is a doctor to be trusted."

"Yes, Sahib. It is done." Just as suddenly Jabal was gone.

Cody Dittus raised an eyebrow. "Sahib? He's Indian?"

"Jabal comes from the mountains of India and Pakistan. I know little more about him, except he is a magnificent fighter and loyal to the death. Many such family servants trained for generations under the British. The British are gone. So, selected Americans have become shoddy substitutes. Now, tell me, how in the world did you get yourself in such a mess here?"

Between gasps of pain, Cody told what he knew…and didn't know.

"Orders assigned me to a tour of Beirut. My time in Lebanon was not disclosed. I was to find out: 'What was the political and military structure here? Who really ruled a frayed and tattered Lebanese government? Was it Iran? Perhaps Iraq? Better yet, Syria? Were there Egyptian forces or representatives here?'

"Normally, Americans are received congenially and warmly. Beirut had been cordial to Americans until the terrorist activities began. My avocation as head of an import company was a very good ploy. Local businessmen enjoy selling their wares. Imports, as you know, are big business all over the world. Everyone makes good money…and some strange bedfellows have flourished—not in the name of Allah, of course, but dollars! After all, Leith, everyone seems to agree: Commerce is commerce…whether in peace or in war."

Leith interrupted, "That explains why you're here. Just untangle the confusing 'What happened mess?'"

"Leith, yesterday I was minding my own business, visiting merchants, buying products. Without warning, a squad of mercenaries ran through the street straight toward me, shooting bursts of automatic fire at me. Man, you should have heard the bullets pelting that poor merchant's shop. And I ran. It was run or become a human sieve.

I ended up hiding in an upstairs bedroom storage space…where some psychopath yanked me from my cubbyhole into his fists. This sadistic crazy was intent on breaking every bone in my body, and planned to torture me into talking. About what, I have no idea. By the way, this psycho calls himself Colonel Danvier Dyan. I sawed my way through the bars before they could begin their torture, and…"

Cody tried to continue, but he could not stifle a groan. He tried to avoid the slightest movement. By now, he appeared a mass of caked blood. The brandy revived his spirits and circulation, but his grievous blood loss had left him weak. Cody feebly looked up. Leith Ohmstead was gone.

Alarmed, Dittus struggled to rise when, abruptly, Leith reappeared and laid a robe beside Cody, who said,

"Thanks. Can you help me into this? I'm a little embarrassed to be a charter member of the 'Beirut Nudist Colony'."

"No way, Cody. You're dressed exactly as the doctor will want you. No clothing. I imagine he'll be doing some painful cleaning and stitching."

Outside, a car door slammed. Jabal effortlessly glided in, inspected the premises, then beckoned to the physician to enter. The doctor was accompanied by a nurse. The nurse, also olive-skinned, wore western dress.

Within minutes, via the doctor's instructions, several blankets were unfolded on the dining table, and Cody was laid on the blankets. The sick expression on the physician's face showed the seriousness of Cody's injuries. The doctor began his ministrations. The nurse was examining the wounds on Cody's naked thighs, and Cody's face grew beet red. Leith Ohmstead stood nearby, chortling at Cody's embarrassment while Dittus glared at him.

The woman "inspected" her patient and then spoke a dialect to Jabal which Dittus did not understand. Jabal shook his head, "No," but was grinning and looking at Leith...who was smirking, also.

"What'd she say? What was that?" yelled Cody.

Jabal answered. "She asked me if Americans are Jews. She believes you are Hebrew."

Cody snorted, "Many Americans are Jewish...why does she believe I'm Jewish, too?"

"Your, er, ah,...privates."

"Private WHAT?"

"Sahib, she has noticed that you are circumcised!"

Cody blushed six colors while he mumbled disgustedly,

"Noticed? Oh, Joy! What a great way to end a perfect evening!"

The doctor and nurse jabbered some more. Cody couldn't stand it.

"NOW what?"

Leith Ohmstead answered, "She says you are small-peckered!"

Cody Dittus raged...and almost came off the table. Leith Ohmstead began roaring his head off while Jabal averted his eyes and covered his giggling with the palm of his hand. By now, Cody's big toes were blushing.

Leith pushed Cody back on the table and said,

"Don't get excited, Cody. She and the doctor were actually discussing which antibiotic to use. You've got some infection."

The doctor nodded, and his assistant measured liquid into a syringe. She administered the shot gently and professionally. The nurse smiled and patted Cody's cheek, but he only glared back at her with suspicion.

"Just what did she give me? What kind of anti...anti . ." Cody's head dropped back on the table. He was out cold!

The real work began. The doctor cleansed Cody's body with a small scrub brush and antiseptic soap; then came alcohol and so much methiolate that Cody's body was painted orange; next, penicillin shots, sutures and needles, a hundred and fifty stitches, salves and Band Aids, and a major body-wrap of gauze and elastic bandages. After nearly two hours, Agent Dittus was still out cold as Jabal and Leith carried him to bed.

"I will return at noon tomorrow," the doctor said. "Make sure he takes one each of these medicines every three hours. He needs time, now. We've halted the wild infection. He's young and will heal quickly, but his bruises will bother him for weeks. Who did this terrible battering?"

Leith Ohmstead could only shake his head, "That's the trouble, doctor, we just don't know. I found him in the street and brought him here."

The perplexed Arab physician mused, "Ah, yes. How like Beirut today. Everywhere in Lebanon lies danger. Too many factions, too much shooting, and too many innocents killed. When will it end...if ever? Until tomorrow."

Leith Ohmstead gripped the doctor's shoulder. "Is your nurse....?"

"Good Samaritan," the physician answered, "this case will not be discussed. Only symptoms and treatment. She does not see what I do not see; she hears no more than I do; she speaks less than a 'Holy Man'...aaahh, I believe a similar word you use is . . monk?"

Leith smiled, and pressed a hefty sum of Lebanese bills into the doctor's hand. The exchange rate would have exceeded an American hundred dollar bill. The doctor blinked,

"This is far too much. I would, as customary, bill you at the end of the month."

"No, Doctor. No names, no address, no writing anywhere except on the medicines. Lebanese money—cash—is difficult to trace. I wish it so."

The practitioner bowed, "Tomorrow." He disappeared into the night.

◆   ◆   ◆

Tel Aviv, a city in Western Israel, lies on the Mediterranean Sea, and provides warm beaches for swimmers and sun worshippers. Here, Cody Dittus recuperated after a week in Beirut.

The inner-city sections of Beirut seemed to have one or two suspicious characters on every street corner. During the day things appeared normal in the bazaars and private homes, including the square where Cody had been so brutally treated. Occasionally, there were shootings and assaults on individuals, but nothing compared to the nighttime mayhem. Yet, armed soldiers, identification questionable and loyalties suspect, roamed the streets. Leith Ohmstead reasoned it was unwise for Agent Dittus to be seen outside the house.

The puzzle was why had Cody Dittus been attacked and horribly beaten? Why was torture planned to make him talk? Talk about what?

By the time a week had passed, Cody was mending amazingly fast. Stiff and sore, he was able to move without great pain. The fresh air and lack of stress also contributed to his body's recovery quicker than expected.

One morning, in the early hours before dawn, a swift four-man jet landed on a makeshift runway located miles from the capital city. Dittus was carefully loaded into the craft, then joined by Ohmstead and Jabal. Both Oz agents had that "gut feeling," an intuition developed by experience and close calls. If someone had been informed that both were in Lebanon, then the life of servant Jabal was probably in jeopardy. Lebanon bordered Israel. Israel stood alone, strong, dominant; therefore, a bitter enemy of Arab States.

So, requests filtered through international channels. Coded messages traveled by wireless, by camels, and by human couriers. An unmarked Israeli plane landed between hand-held flashlights that outlined the improvised runway. The pilot locked the plane's brakes, pushed the throttle to 70 per cent, and reached the point where the brakes would not hold. The pilot released hydraulic pressure and the craft gathered speed. After a hundred feet he rammed the throttle to the stop-gate, cut in afterburner, and guided the howling jet into the deep purple sky. He was flying southwest. Navigating by computer, the pilot punched in his destination and the airplane streaked above the sands and mountains, flying only a hundred feet above the contours and ancient terrain. Distances from country to country, and city to city are short; nothing approaches the far expanses of the United States. The 140-mile trip takes a quarter-hour or less, depending on speed.

The Israeli aircraft was on final approach to Tel Aviv only 15 minutes after takeoff. But the minutes determined the difference between danger and peace—at least enough difference to die among friends.

◆   ◆   ◆

Weeks passed swiftly, and Cody's daily walks on the beach, under a warm sun amid bursts of cool ocean spray, brought him back to his former self. There were no more indications of blood in his body wastes; his muscles loosened and grew strong; his lungs and heart welcomed the exercise and fresh air. The only remnant of his torturous encounter was a dent in his manly proboscis. Thanks to a broken nose, he could pass more readily as a Jew.

The Israeli Mossad was located in a nondescript building among other government offices. Brigadier General Moschi Rubinstern was commander for that military zone. Somewhat reserved, he politely received Leith Ohmstead and Cody Dittus…although the general seemed baffled.

"Er, Misters Ohmstead and Dittus—you are Americans?"

Both visitors nodded.

"We are known to you Americans as Israel's FBI. Have you not made a mistake as to the government service you need in Tel Aviv?"

Ohmstead quickly answered, "The Mossad is not FBI. Its activities parallel our CIA and England's MI-6."

General Rubinstern raised both eyebrows. He thought to himself,

"Always Americans—typically rude, blunt, and straight to the point. Not like the French, delicate while fencing with a rapier. These Americans use a battering-ram." With his feelings showing, he brusquely asked,

"And just how can the Mossad help its 'brother', the FBI—if you have the credentials from your bureau?"

Ohmstead handed Moschi his calling card, the picture of a twister, a stem of wheat and the name, "Kansas," across it.

General Rubinstern was now scowling. "What the hell is this?"

Cody Dittus said, "You are looking at Oz. You do know Oz!"

Moschi Rubinstern started, then gasped, then looked at his visitors.

"Good Lord! I'm too young to have worked with the OSS fifty years ago, but I know their remarkable history. They're defunct—extinct—you can't be the Oz organization rumored about for years? That's only legend…an intriguing story!"

"Re-al-ly? You're looking at two in the flesh, Brigadier."

Rubinstern fell back in his chair, stunned. His mouth hung open as he studied the unique calling cards. He slowly turned, facing the men, and said, "All right, just what is it you wish, Gentlemen?"

"Cody is going to tell you a story, General, and then we're going to ask you a key question—about one of your men."

"One of my men? Are you talking about the Mossad?"

Moschi was given no answer, but he did sit back as suspicion clouded his face. He listened intently as Dittus told him about the beginning gunfire in the market and his desperate escape from torture—a sentence of death by torture for information he did not have, because his captors never told him what they wanted. When Cody finished, Rubinstern was gripping the edge of his desk, his eyes boring into those of Ohmstead. The Brigadier was almost cringing, dreading the question he knew Ohmstead would ask.

"WHO, General Rubinstern, is Colonel Danvier Dyan?"

Brigadier General Moschi Rubinstern was startled again. His head jerked backward as he exclaimed, "Danvier Dyan? Colonel WHO?"

It was Leith's and Cody's turn to be startled. They gazed at each other. The general was not faking. Obviously, Dyan was unknown to him.

Moschi pressed a button and barked orders into an intercom. A major appeared and silently handed the general a thick black bordered file marked, "TOP SECRET." Rubinstern thumbed through the pages, his index finger scanning lists of alphabetically arranged names. Disgusted, he slammed the file shut,

"NOTHING!" He pressed an entire row of buttons. He pressed quickly six or eight times. There came the THUD of boots and running feet.

Six physical specimens of high rank marched into the office and, saluting, stood at attention. The lean and mean men were heavily armed.

"Messrs. Ohmstead and Dittus, please meet my Chief of Staff, Colonel Marseille LeBourget. Lee, meet our allies from the U.S.A.."

Cody chortled, "Marseille LeBourget—a Frenchman?"

Moschi chuckled, "There are Jews from France, too, you know."

Ohmstead smiled, "General, Israel will never be whipped. Father Abraham was too prolific!"

Staff Head Colonel LeBourget was grinning, "Right on, Yankees. Welcome to Tel Aviv. You are tourists to our country?"

General Rubinstern interjected, "Gentlemen, you are looking at two of Uncle Sam's finest agents."

The Mossad staff was not impressed. They just looked Leith and Cody up and down. A young captain barely concealed a smirk. His hand surreptitiously crept to the holster on his side, and gripped the butt of his automatic pistol. As he stealthily pulled the weapon free of its holster, he heard two ominous, unmistakable sounds: "Click—Click!"

The captain froze. He stared into two pairs of eyes that were no longer smiling. He looked down...and his heart skipped a beat. His dry mouth made him swallow, and his swallow was audible in the room.

He grasped into the barrels of two 10-millimeter Smith & Wessons...hammers cocked. One moment the Americans were empty-handed; the next, they held two formidable automatics with muzzles that could have served as tunnels for trucks. The captain's hand sluggishly returned to his side. Leith Ohmstead figured a lesson was in order.

"Shall I kill him, or you want to do it, Cody?"

Cody responded with, "Whatever the General says. Been a long time since I killed a Hebrew—'twas yesterday afternoon, I believe."

General Rubinstern stifled a laugh while shaking his head. He said,

"If our guests will holster their guns, I'm sure the captain will appreciate it. Incidentally, Staff, these agents are members of 'OZ'."

Eyes widened in disbelief. One of the staff muttered, "Impossible! That group has gone by way of the dinosaur."

Moschi said, "Was the response by two seated men that of archaic dinosaurs? Captain Wollenski had his hand on his gunbutt before I even saw them move. Now, all of you sit down and listen to a very, very interesting story. Please proceed, Mr. Dittus. Leave nothing out, including your remarkable escape, and you, Mr. Ohmstead, tell them how you helped stop the two mercenaries while you were holding Dittus, and of the surgery on the dining table, and your flight out at night."

Just that statement by the general brought immediate attention. The staff was fascinated as both Dittus and Ohmstead told their respective tales. When the explanations were finished, the entire Mossad staff looked with extreme respect at the Americans. Captain Wollenski spoke up,

"I was a fool. I thought I was well trained, but I've never seen such instinctive reactions as you two possess. I apologize."

Colonel Marseille LeBourget said, "I'd hate to have both of you against us in the Middle East. I believe you two could start World War Three!"

General Rubinstern asked the key question,

"All right, Staff, I don't know this Colonel Danvier Dyan. Who knows anything about him? Speak up. These men are being pursued by him."

There was dead silence. The staff's faces were blank.

Captain Wollenski sat, pondering. Reflecting upon his military life since age 18, the 23-year-old officer mused thoughtfully instead of voicing a convincing opinion.

"I barely remember a time four years ago when I led my squad against some insurgents who were fleeing from Old Palestine into Jordan. Even then they wanted a united Palestine at our back door right on the heights overlooking Jerusalem. We couldn't allow that—we'd be at their mercy. So, the fighting was fierce with no quarter asked or given. Our losses were heavy, but I'm positive we gave them a lot more than we received. The bodies we passed were everywhere, but their leader, a whale of a commander and fanatical fighter, cleverly led them over the Jordanian border before we could get him. We made him run, but we didn't defeat him.

"He was **not** an Israeli, definitely not on our side. Yet, I am just as positive he was not Arab. Certainly not from this region. When we stopped at the border sign, this commander stood on the next rocky crest holding a machine gun high in his hand, bandoliers of cartridges crisscrossing his chest, while he taunted us.

"'You will meet Danny Dan again. You will die, filthy Jews. Danny Dan has pledged...you will roast in hell!'

"My Israeli first sergeant heard the same words Danny shouted down at us. We were out of bazooka rockets, or we would have blown Danny Dan to Allah's heaven. But now, he could have been shouting Danvier Dyan and not Danny Dan. The distance was great, but this coincidence is too much. The Americans' stories tie things together too well. His skin was dark, tanned, from the sun. He was not quite an olive-skinned Arab. Yet, he may have been an insurgent Jew. Perhaps a European. Reports said he flew west looking for financial support.

General Rubinstern asked, "Where would he fly to in the Middle East?"

"That's just it, General. He didn't—according to our sources."

Ohmstead leaned forward, "Then, to where?"

"The United States!"

"WHAT? HOW?"

"He was seen in Spain. Next, he was identified in Lisbon, Portugal. That is, his picture was recognized. It was a positive ID."

"How do you know his face?" asked Cody Dittus.

"You see, during the fighting we took pictures. We still do, using telephoto lenses. We know Dyan's face. But his name, Danny Dan, meant nothing...until now."

Colonel LeBourget said, "Then why are you sure he's in the U.S.A.?"

"Colonel, our Lisbon Mossad confirmed he bought plane tickets for himself and several allies for Washington, D.C.."

Cody Dittus healed even faster the following week. His anger was growing daily over the Beirut incident, and Leith Ohmstead was almost convinced their cover had been blown. Had Cody not been captured, it would have been Leith, next. And right in his "secured compound."

Both had been given separate assignments, but both had come from Oz Headquarters in Washington. Now HQ wanted to know: Oz compromised? Oz infiltrated? Since secrecy was so rigidly enforced, Ohmstead concluded that information must have leaked from the highest echelons.

Leith and Cody flew back home unannounced. Sending any form of message was now suspect. They must confer in person. Their companion was a shrewd, cynical man, dressed in western garb, but wearing a purple turban—a sign of high caste. Jabal, the British trained soldier, was guarding their backs.

8

Something Wrong

Britain's Lord Acton, whose English name was remarkably elaborate—John Emerich Edward Dalberg-Acton, was a prominent English historian (1834-1902) who enriched the literary world with famous maxims. One of his best truths is often quoted today:

"Power corrupts. Absolute power corrupts absolutely."

And that adage kept repeating itself, like the crack from a broken record, over and over again to Bergan Gruenspan, the brilliant counselor to New York's Senator Abraham Anselm. Gruenspan had almost driven himself into an acute depression. However, there was no melancholy in Senator Anselm, who walked around elated, sometimes rubbing his hands with glee. His outlook effervesced, and he bubbled over with euphoria.

Like a young man in Springtime, deeply in love, Anselm appeared abnormally buoyant and vigorous. Gruenspan had not seen Abraham Anselm act this way for over a decade. And **that** was exactly what disturbed Bergan Gruenspan.

"My reintroduced bill for the new vacation development in the Adirondacks will pass both houses now," chortled Senator Anselm. "And the Corps of Engineers will dam the West Canada Creek. We should have some good times up there in a few years, Bergan. At the same time, we can ram Senator Bergenfeldt's plans through Congress, too."

This sudden success where, before Anselm had been sandbagged, shocked Gruenspan. As for Bergenfeldt, his pork barrel proposals had been outlandish. His bills were too obvious, self-serving, and unquestionably larcenous. Yet, Abraham Anselm anticipated no rigorous opposition in both houses for his New Jersey crony. Then Anselm loftily said,

"Bergan, I'll be leaving for the Middle East soon. Be gone a week."

"Lieb, the Senate is in session. You can't leave a busy senate schedule for an overseas junket. Besides, what business do you have over there? Your use of commercial aircraft is an expense the voters don't appreciate. The newspapers can make a big 'to do' about such a trip."

Abraham Lieberson Anselm just laughed. "Not to worry, Bergan. Marchen Judisch and his pilot are flying me there. It'll cost the taxpayers nothing."

"But, Senator, why go in the first place? What about your bill for the Adirondack dam?"

"It should pass the Senate next week. The House may take longer, but there's little opposition there. I'll be back before the House passes it."

"Anselm! Exactly what will you be doing over there? Does the President approve? Is your staff traveling with you?"

"Now, Gruenspan. Don't get your bowels in an uproar. It's strictly a vacation, . . nothing more. I want to see some places I've not visited before. You worry too much, Bergan. Take some time off and relax while I'm gone. The rest will do you good."

With a patronizing pat on the Gruenspan's shoulder, Abraham Anselm turned away and began rummaging through his desk. Bergan Gruenspan had been curtly dismissed.

From the moment he left the senator's office, Bergan Gruenspan literally paced his steps down the long corridor. He was reaching a distasteful judgment. Hearing a door open, Bergan looked up and saw Senator Don Boren closing his office door, preparing to lock the security deadbolt.

Prominently displayed on the heavy oak was a semi-circle of letters that spelled, "Oklahoma." Just beneath was painted the beautiful flag of Oklahoma, a feathered Osage war shield with a branch of laurel leaves crossed over a long-stemmed calumet peace pipe. The Indian design was outstanding on a field of sky blue. The Senator's name and key staff were listed farther below.

The sunbelt senator was highly regarded by both parties. He also showed his savvy when he said, "Problems, Bergan? Anything I can do to help?"

Gruenspan started to say "no," when a sob burst from his throat,

"Yes, you can! I need to talk to someone. I'm greatly disturbed, and I need counsel with...with..." Gruenspan lapsed into silence.

Senator Don Boren said, "Someone recognized as very tight-lipped and, more important, absolutely trustworthy?" Bergan nodded his head vigorously.

"In this Senate Building you might talk with me...if you don't think me too egotistical saying it. But, if you wish to take it <u>outside</u> this building, then there's only one man—a unique, one-of-a-kind man. He's in The House. I'm referring to Speaker Holcombe Broderick."

Bergan said one word, "Outside!" Senator Don Boren cocked his head and indicated his office door.

The Senator opened his unoccupied suite and motioned for Gruenspan to sit down. Don Boren picked up the phone and dialed.

"Senator Don Boren here. Is Holcombe available?" After a pause there was a click on the line.

"Senator, how are you?"

"Fine, Mr. Speaker, but I've got a worried man here...you know him. It's Bergan Gruenspan—he needs to talk to you—and talk now."

"You know what it's about, Senator?"

"I know Gruenspan, Holcombe. He rarely gets upset. Right now he's a seething volcano. It must be something 'hot', and he wants to take it away from this building. I recommend you see him right now."

"Send him over. My door will be unlocked. My staff is just leaving."

Speaker Holcombe Broderick opened his office entrance and was shocked to see a disheveled beaten man. The Speaker locked the door, escorted Gruenspan into his private sanctum, and placed a goblet of burgundy in his hand.

Bergan asked, "Have you anything stronger?"

Holcombe gave him a double shot of brandy. "Chase it with the wine."

Bergan Gruenspan did. He sat quietly a few minutes, easing. Broderick was an old hand and knew the signs. He remained mute, allowing Gruenspan to start the game. Ten minutes passed. In the late hours, except for occasional footsteps echoing from the corridor, the House chambers resembled a mausoleum. Broderick's inner offices were so hushed that the air moved audibly as the filtered-air blowers operated. A small Grandmother clock ticked loudly, and the creak of the executive chairs sounded like distant gunshots. In that ten minutes, Bergan Gruenspan bolted down his brandy and sipped his burgundy to the bottom of the goblet. Then he spoke, as if from the grave.

"I've decided to go back into private practice!"

"WHY?" was Broderick's only answer. Holcombe waited, watching Bergan place his face in his hands. The wait was like a slow-motion movie.

"Something is very wrong, Mr. Speaker. I've guided Abraham Anselm through 20 years of politics, infighting, power-grabbing, but always with integrity. Or so I thought! But, he has changed. Lord, how he has changed! Anselm speaks in double-entendres, hidden meanings, and he laughs joyfully when things happen to his enemies...or should I say his 'imagined' enemies. He's beginning to hate anyone who gets in the way of his schemes."

"Schemes?"

"Yes, Holcombe, schemes. They are no longer plans. For instance, he's succeeding in putting a boondoggle dam in the Adirondacks. He's been flying to Canada, perhaps overseas, and always with Marchen Judisch, an Israeli diplomat, and Marchen's pilot, a sinister looking man called Dyan. Anselm's gone a week here, a week there. No explanation. No reasons. I was scrutinizing his desk one time and he screamed at me...ME, the man who, for decades, has guided him away from pitfalls and his own folly.

"His mortal enemy seems to be this new representative from New Jersey, Charter Saladin. When Saladin was to make his introductory speech, Anselm quipped to the staff, `Saladin may decide not to say anything!'

"Can you imagine THAT? I laughed and told Anselm not to count on Saladin not making a speech. I understood it would be a lollapalooza. And `Lieb' plainly said, `You let me worry about that'.

"Well, Sir. Charter did not make his speech because of his wife's tragic death. I was flabbergasted at Anselm's insight. Yet, after Charter partially recovered, he was able to block the Adirondack deal cold. Anselm was furious. I advised him not to make another enemy. And Anselm told me he was sure Charter hadn't fully recovered. I informed him Charter looked surprisingly well. And Anselm got real quiet...so quiet it scared me...and then he said, `I'm betting Saladin will have a serious relapse'. The next thing I knew I heard Saladin had collapsed in the House restroom. That really scared me. No ordinary mortal can prophesy like that!

"Now, my longtime friend and oracle from New York will propose the same Corps of Engineers dam again. However, this time he is sure he'll get it...from the Senate and House. In the meantime, after the senate vote, but before The House can act, Anselm is leaving for a week or more to visit the Middle East. He won't say to where, nor what he'll be doing. He may well throw a wrench in the President's overseas negotiations.

"I'm telling you, Speaker Broderick, something is very wrong. No, Sir, I'm bailing out. I won't be a party to corruption—or treason."

Broderick asked, "Why, in God's name, would you ever say treason?"

Gruenspan, nervous, jumped up and shouted, "REFILL, . . PLEASE!"

Broderick repeated the double brandy with a goblet of Burgundy chaser.

Gruenspan, hating to voice his suspicions, answered in a whisper,

"Because Senator Anselm is privy to vital internal plans and top secret developments; because Anselm has reached an imperious plateau. He feels infallible; he's acquired strange friends; he's begun globe-trotting without approval or instructions from the White House; he ignores me and his entire staff. Ignores ME! I, who has been his confidant over 20 years.

"I tell you, Broderick, something is <u>very</u>, <u>very</u> wrong!"

Bergan Gruenspan lapsed into silence, alternately sipping his brandy and then his Burgundy. It was evident confession had been good for his soul.

And Holcombe Broderick sat back in his swivel chair...stunned. He had known Abraham Anselm since his first day in the Senate. But, it was devastating to hear an acknowledged top aide, respected throughout Washington, reveal such suspicions—suspicions backed by extensive circumstantial facts. Broderick's eyes were wide open, unblinking, dazed. He refused to consider the rabid thoughts crossing his mind. The possibilities were too horrible to contemplate. Bergan Gruenspan had said, "Treason!"

Gruenspan stood, his heavy sighs permeating the room. He was a tired and weary man. He looked at Speaker Broderick and smiled,

"I honestly pray I've done the right thing. You can end my career, you know. But, Senator Don Boren said you were different. I can only hope so."

"Mr. Gruenspan, I am as different as you are. You do not realize it, but you may have done a great service for your country. There now exists a great debt to a courageous man. Your career is safe with me. Somehow I believe your career will truly grow from this moment on."

Speaker Broderick picked up the phone. "Lawrence, have a limousine stand by, and have the driver come to my office immediately."

While the pair waited, Holcombe refilled a third round of drinks for Bergan Gruenspan. Bergan objected, "I'll get tipsy. I can feel it already."

"No problem, Bergan. You'll be escorted to your home in style. You should sleep better, too. Have a good night's rest and report to me tomorrow morning by 10:00 o'clock. We'll work out your future plans."

The chauffeur arrived and helped Gruenspan to the limousine. Bergan was feeling little pain. But, then, he had been hurting for many months. As they left, the House Speaker sadly shook his head. He hadn't the heart to tell Bergan that Charter Saladin was convalescing at Holcombe's home. Nor would he admit that a prime suspect was emerging as the culprit behind Charter Saladin's appalling turn of fortune.

Speaker Broderick locked the door and returned to his office. Pulling out a bottom desk drawer, he braced it on the edge of his desk while he squatted beneath the woodwork. With a penlight he carefully read a faint phone number.

Its sequence renewed his keen memory since he would never, never write this number on paper. He replaced the drawer and penlight.

Picking up the telephone, he cautiously dialed that faded number.

There was a 'Click' on the line, followed by silence.

"This is Speaker of The House, Holcombe Broderick. Let me speak **to Oz.**"

◆   ◆   ◆

The crippled man got out of a cab two blocks away from his destination. Non-chalantly, he wobbled across the street, reached the opposite side, and leaned against a beautifully trimmed tree. A pretense of studying the view, across the avenue from the house he would visit, granted him time to study the entire block ahead.

Dressed in a gray loose-fitting western shirt with a turquoise bolo, charcoal slacks, and cowboy boots, the man looked like a Texas rancher. His coat, a pale ocher buckskin jacket with leather fringes, was complemented by an expensive silver-gray cowboy Stetson. He walked stiffly on his right leg, assisted by a dark walnut cane with a bulb-shaped handle.

The cane gave good support for the lame rancher, but it was more than that: It was a weapon of lethal capability. A flexible Solingen-steel saber lay buried within the cane. Also, if the cane head should be twisted, a small trigger snapped into position by the user's finger. The bottom portion of the cane was a 7-inch barrel firing 15 extra-long super .22 caliber cartridges. If hit anywhere, a live target would die. Each hollow-nose bullet was filled with cyanide crystals. Within seconds, what a mushrooming bullet did not destroy, the deadly potion would.

The westerner's superior had phoned him at his home where he was healing after a long siege in the hospital. It would be a minimum of two more weeks, the doctors said, before he would be able to stroll without a cane. Now, an urgent request had come from the Speaker of The House. Until this moment, the months of inactivity had brought him nothing but boredom and discouragement.

Limping, happy to be back into his element of clandestine travels and danger, a wary Leith Ohmstead walked down a street in Georgetown, a suburb of Washington, D.C. After walking a half-block, he stopped and rested the femur bone and sutured muscles of his hip. His stitches and the surgical incisions through his thigh, along with the bone that had not fully knitted, hurt like Hades. But, Leith was on the job and looking forward to meeting Holcombe Broderick.

Ohmstead hobbled another block before he neared the address with numbers he could read from across the street. Outside of mild traffic, the only individual he observed was standing several houses down from Leith's destination. The man stood by a lamp pole, reading a newspaper. Reading a newspaper on the street in an exclusive section of Georgetown?

That old feeling tingled on Leith's backside. He decided to test the waters. Leith entered an ivy fenced courtyard. He went in one gate, but did not exit the other. He stood quietly behind a thick growth of green leaves, watching the dubious man hidden behind the newsprint. Five minutes passed…ten minutes…that reader's arms must feel like lead weights by now. Yet, the suspect never once turned a page of the paper. It might be a good idea to know the "reader" before Ohmstead walked the steps to Speaker Broderick's house.

Leith left the courtyard by another gate, noting that he, too, was being observed from behind closed curtains. The lady of the house was worried about the man in her ivy-covered garden. Just before he opened the wrought-iron gate, Leith turned and tipped his Stetson toward the fidgeting curtains. He could just hear the woman of the manor muttering,

"Damned Johnny Reb Texans. Never had, still don't have, any manners."

Leith Ohmstead hesitated by the closed gate, as if he were confused, and then limped across the street. He started walking up the street, snapped his fingers as if he had just remembered something, and then reversed direction. His walk carried him toward the lamp pole and the man with his fascinating newspaper. Only, up close, Leith could see the paper had a slit cut from it. And, an eye watched, following Leith's every move.

Ohmstead's actions were concise and planned instinctively. He passed the lamp pole reader and his peekaboo newspaper. Still limping while relieving the pain by bracing himself with his cane, Leith walked several paces past the shady suspect before he turned. He stopped, as if resting his game leg, which he really had to do because of his suffering, and found himself being studied. The furtive individual still hid behind his newspaper. However, he, too, had turned and now faced Leith…still watching him through the slit in the front page. Leith walked into troubled waters.

"I may only be an ignorant Texas rancher, but your arms have to be tired, or that one page must contain a whale of a story."

The pole leaner didn't move. One eye continued to stare through the peep hole of the newspaper. Worse, he declined to speak.

Leith had enough. Groaning convincingly, he limped up to the man and, with an adroit upward sweep of his cane, trashed the paper out of the man's hands.

Ohmstead's sudden move caught the quarry unaware. He stood there, each hand grasping a torn piece of newspaper. With a curse, the man grabbed at a now exposed shoulder holster.

Again, Leith swept the heavy cane upward. As the man pulled a lethal looking automatic from the holster, the cane collided with his jaw. The noise of the resultant "whack" betrayed the force of the blow. The adversary's head popped backward, and he staggered rearward into the light pole. After a moment he recovered and began to lift his gun—when he suddenly felt a sharp instrument cutting a hole between his neck and chin. Leith's opponent glanced down and saw a long thin polished blade. He didn't need to reason that the foil was razor-honed. Although he felt little pain, he did feel the trickle of warm blood down his neck. He looked up…into the eyes of Leith Ohmstead…and his blood ran cold. The alien was a professional, but he was staring into the eyes of a "ranch garbed Texan" with a face that was impervious. Yet, the stranger could sense Leith's absolute ruthlessness.

The stranger heard, "Lower your Uzi, gently release the cocked hammer, and hand it to me,…butt first."

The antagonist thought fast, but he had no alternative options. The sword was in his neck and the Texan had only to fall forward to plunge the rapier through and out the back. He lowered the Uzi, slowly uncocking the weapon. A strong hand jerked the gun from his possession.

The entire scene was incongruous—two men in quiet, opulent Georgetown, standing on a street corner, a mahogany cane lying in the grass at their feet, and one man holding a gleaming silver blade at the other's throat. It was typical Class-B movie stuff. The scene was unreal—incompatible—but, deadly!

Ohmstead said, "All right, my friend. Who are you? Who do you work for?"

The stranger replied, "I'm a private investigator. I'm on a simple surveillance case."

Leith snorted, "You can do better than that. I'm holding your weapon, an Uzi 9-millimeter. That's Israeli…that's Mossad. Either way, that means 'assassin'. You are either a Zionist, an Arab, or a Revolutionary. So, which?"

"I'm a P.I. May I withdraw my I.D. from my wallet?" Without hesitation the pole-leaning investigator reached toward his back pocket.

Leith Ohmstead relaxed his rapier, and dropped it downward.

When he did, the P.I. yanked a small "midnight special," a .32 caliber pistol from a back holster.

Any other man, even well trained, would have been dead within seconds. Yet, Leith Ohmstead was far from an ordinary man…which a certain Brigadier General in the Mossad could affirm. As the concealed gun zipped forward ready to fire, Leith drove the razored blade through the man's navel. The sword tip exited swiftly, its keen edge slicing through a disc of the lumbar vertebrae, cutting the spinal nerve column. As his adversary collapsed, his lower body paralyzed and useless, Leith twisted the honed blade.

Keenly sharpened on both edges, the slashing steel severed the abdominal vein, and sliced through the stomach and intestines. The body's collapse became total, its effect extending from the victim's navel to his head. His thoughts quickly faded.

"Funny, how did those clouds cover the sun so fast? What good is this gun...when all I need is a good sleep. I've never been so tired..." Before he hit their ground he was dead.

Leith Ohmstead thrust the Uzi automatic pistol behind his belt, withdrew the sword and wiped it clean on the victim's shirt. The blood would mingle with that streaming from his belly. Leith replaced his rapier within his cane. He looked up the street just in time to spot a cruising police car approaching. He quickly removed the dead man's wallet, then removed a memo pad from his inside coat pocket. That was enough. Leith knew the man would carry nothing more.

Like a lame bystander, Leith staggered to the curb and, with his cane, signaled the Washington patrolmen. Within moments he explained he was a Texas cattle rancher visiting his friend, Speaker Holcombe Broderick. He happened on this body lying on the grass and was limping to a phone when the patrol car arrived. Leith's ID, as always, was perfect, having been professionally forged by Oz. Speaker Broderick's confirmation provided support that the police should look elsewhere for the assailant. Ohmstead knew nothing, and the body held no clues. So, temporarily, the corpse went to Washington General Hospital as an unidentified "John Doe."

Holcombe Broderick made another secluded phone call to Oz. Perceptively, arrangements were made so that television broadcasters and Washington Post reporters gave news coverage to the John Doe cadaver. Purposely, another Oz agent waited at Washington General. Their belief was that someone would come forward to claim the body. The jackpot question was: "Who would it be?"

From the interval when both men engaged in their fatal conflict, to the moment Holcombe Broderick verified his friendship with Leith Ohmstead, Speaker Broderick had never even met agent Ohmstead. Now, after the police and ambulance had left, Leith stood painfully on the bottom step of Broderick's Georgetown mansion.

"Mr. Speaker, the world has too many prying eyes. I recommend you get me inside as promptly as possible. I am the man you were expecting."

Broderick assisted Ohmstead up the four steps into the marbled foyer of his home. Leith found climbing the steps particularly painful.

Broderick said, "My God, Man! You look like you're in agony! I understand from Oz that you're just out of the hospital. Why did you come? Better yet, why did they send you?"

"Mr. Speaker, the greater the challenge, the more anguish you can tolerate. Just let me sit down, and I'll feel my body healing."

"Mr. Ohmstead...."

"Please, call me Leith."

"All right, Leith. How were you able to shoot that man without arousing the whole neighborhood?"

Leith smiled and slowly pulled the thin sword from the cane.

"If you'll provide me some rubbing alcohol and a cloth, I'll be able to wash off the bloodstains. Agent "X," or whoever he was, attempted to use a 9-millimeter automatic, and then a .32 special...on me! He left me little choice. I used the first thing that was handy."

Holcombe Broderick choked and coughed. From his door to the street corner was only several hundred feet. There, he suddenly realized, a man had died...silently. The episode seemed unreal. But, his respect for Leith and the Oz, was multiplying beyond count. Broderick almost whispered,

"Do you know what the corpse was doing?—I mean, before you..."

"Holcombe, I studied him a quarter-hour from both sides of the street. He was a trained professional. The only reason I got the upper hand was my Texan impersonation. I looked like a cattle rancher should look, at least in his estimation, until I had my rapier in his neck before he could touch a trigger. This I do know. He was watching your house for one of two reasons:

"The worst possibility was finding an opportunity to terminate you, right on your doorstep. The other was to see who entered and exited from your home. A list of your visitors would answer someone's questions involving you. Frankly, as an afterthought, I believe you are being shadowed at home and on Capitol Hill. Why? Especially, why would a person, or persons, spy on the House Speaker?"

Holcombe Broderick and Leith Ohmstead wandered over the aged, but polished, hardwood floor to a study at the back of the house. The study exuded charm and peaceful quiet where the sun shone through tall windows and smoked glass skylights. If the room grew too hot or excessively bright, the skylights darkened, restricting Old Sol's penetrating rays. Thick draperies could be pulled to shut out all views and assure privacy.

The study's rear windows overlooked a flagstone patio nestled within a beautiful garden. In Leith's mind, there was little doubt that Broderick drew great comfort and serenity while walking among the flourishing greenery, or while resting in the hush of seclusion in the study where he found strength and clarity of purpose.

It was here both men relaxed in silence, each man contemplating past and present events that led to this meeting.

A glass of wine bubbled at his elbow, and Leith relaxed as he rarely had these past months. His pain diminished when he placed his feet on an upholstered footrest. He closed his eyes and drifted, while the world spun by, and tuned out his thoughts. Soon, his snores made Holcombe Broderick smile. The Speaker tiptoed from the study and called his office to tell his secretary to make Bergan Gruenspan comfortable. He would be late for his appointment. Regardless, Bergan was to remain until the Speaker arrived.

Broderick returned, stamping his feet loudly and whistling a merry tune. With a start, Leith Ohmstead jerked awake, the cobwebs clearing from his mind. He was embarrassed to hear himself sounding the last snores of a deep sleep.

"Oh, no! My apologies! How long have I been asleep?"

"About 10 minutes or so. With that pain, I figured you needed a snooze. I'm betting you've been keyed up for quite a while…particularly when you know you just killed a man a half-hour ago. You look better now, . . refreshed. Now, tell me how I may help you—and how will you help me?"

Ohmstead answered, "Like any story, you usually start at the beginning, and the best place to begin is to describe the events that finally led you, of all people on Capitol Hill, to call Oz. I don't believe you are the type to overreact to circumstances, so something has occurred that made you feel you must have Oz instead of the FBI or Washington police. Furthermore, it has to be serious—involving national security—or you would not have called us."

Broderick stared at the floor and sighed, "It's nothing I can prove, but incidents are of such a nature that I crossed off the CIA. Counter Intelligence has been under fire too long. If I asked the FBI to investigate, consequences could be terribly damaging. We have too many leaks. Somehow, such a monumental investigation would probably seep out and turn Washington on its ear…let alone ruin reputations. Frankly, Agent Ohmstead, I'm talking about treason. You might wish to takes notes."

Leith Ohmstead slowly sat up, his eyebrows raised.

"Don't worry, Mr. Speaker. I'll remember everything, including names, with no trouble. We're trained that way, you know. Please continue."

For nearly an hour Speaker Broderick discussed the seeming moral morass within Washington circles. He openly discussed many Congressmen and Senators who had integrity; then he named the publicity hounds who would reveal any confidential or secret information just to get their names in the news; he mentioned the newly elected, such as Charter Saladin, and an Eastern Bloc of Senators who fought Saladin at every turn.

The discussion covered the bewildering case of the unsolved murder of Elena Saladin and the restroom mirror message which renewed the traumatic shock to Congressman Saladin, who was recuperating upstairs at this moment.

Holcombe's concluding remarks reviewed the strange behavior and the Middle East trips of Senator Abraham Anselm. Holcombe finished his tale explaining the despondency of Bergan Gruenspan and why he intends to resign and is waiting at Broderick's office for advice and an opportunity to find a new position.

Broderick asked, "What am I to do, Leith? What should I do?"

Ohmstead, astonished, understood for the first time how these facts might be the **key** to his and Cody Dittus' attempted murders. Evidently, the answers lay right here in Washington. Cody had told Leith of his conversation with the A & E Mechanics at Frederick Municipal Airport in Maryland.

A shaken Leith Ohmstead was thinking, "The Middle East fugitive, Danvier Dyan, is a delegate operating here from the Israeli Embassy? Incredible! Worse, Dyan is now associating—or perhaps is involved—with some powerful and prominent senators from New England.

Leith and Cody believed covert activities had been compromised. Leith thanked God for men like Holcombe Broderick and Bergan Gruenspan. They did not understand what was transpiring. But, Leith was convinced, now more than ever, that the extreme secrecy of the little known OSS, Oz, had been breached. A most dangerous problem was taking form. The problem, so far, had only shown the tip of the iceberg.

And Leith kept remembering Gruenspan's reiterated quote to Broderick, "Holcombe, something's wrong. I'm telling you something is wrong."

9

Pursuing Evidence

Jameson Cody Dittus crumpled his handkerchief into a simulated bar towel and wiped the sweat running down the back of his head. The janitorial closet was stifling. The air was dank and, he thought, probably rank from the mannish smell of his perspiration. He was soaking the good clothes he had worn since noon yesterday when the body of "John Doe X" had been delivered to the hospital morgue. A phone call had gone to Oz and the call was forwarded to Cody's home. The caller was Leith Ohmstead who suggested Cody go on surveillance, take pictures, and trail the person or persons appearing at the hospital to claim the body.

Cody groaned, cursing the portable telephone. It was required. He was paid extremely well for his dangerous vocation and much of the land in view was his, although being on call seven days a week kept him traveling over the world, everywhere...excepting his magnificent hideaway.

He sat on his backyard patio, a marvelous kaleidoscope of multi-colored aggregate bedded inside an epoxy coating. The rainbow finish was laid over a concrete foundation. The grounds were comprised of a sculptured lawn of dense green grass fed by a deep-well irrigation system. Well sprayed and trimmed American elm trees mingled among October Glory maples, sky-reaching pines, and beautiful blue spruce. The elms grew tall and arched themselves as they tunneled a path to God's Heaven.

By judicious spraying and pruning, Cody had, so far, avoided the fungus blight carried by the Dutch elm beetle. He paid a local farmer well for taking care of the landscape. The log cabin ranch home stood on a wooded Virginia hillside far from the civilization of Washington. This paradise was unblemished by neighbors and noisy 4-wheel drives or dune buggies. While land developers drooled, the indomitable Cody Dittus acquired the land under questionable circumstances. A Washington law firm with many wealthy investors and a Virginia land developer were running pell-mell over anyone in their way. The two groups would make a fortune building homes for politicians, civil servants, and military personnel.

Then, along came Cody Dittus, the homesteader.

Several blithe-spirited fellow agents were enlisted. It wasn't that they were dishonest,…but, because of their hazardous profession, their personalities reflected the attitude, "I don't give a damn—what can they do, shoot us?" attitude. Besides, the plan, when set in motion, would give the Washington power structure a royal shafting.

With impressive governmental credentials, courtesy of Oz headquarters, the collaborators called upon the law firm's chief attorney, followed by a clandestine appointment with the senior land developer. Cigarettes dangled from their lips; hats were pulled down to hide their faces as the agents depicted trench-coated "hit men" skulking into the affluent offices.

Often looking over their shoulders while "accidentally" flashing heavy handguns in their shoulder holsters, the agents commanded rapt attention.

"You have forced our hand, Sir. We must tell you to cease all negotiations and back away from your real estate plans. If you do not, you will probably kill yourself and every buyer who purchases your property. Not only would you have to explain so many deaths, but the government cannot afford to create mass panic in the nation's capital."

The response was as expected. "Now, see here. We'll decide what we'll do. We're not afraid of you hired thugs. Our influence extends directly into the White House. Name me **one** good reason we should not make a fortune!"

"All right, here's your answer: A few years ago, a terrible plane crash scattered a bomb bay load of plutonium cartridges over a hundred-acre crash site. The nuclear fuel residue will last over a hundred years."

"WHAT? You mean atomic bombs?"

"Exactly! You say one word of this and the military will categorically deny it. It took us three days to locate every container most of them were smashed. We remove them and the aircraft remnants from the crash area. Even with protective clothing, we lost three men from radiation sickness."

"My God! We hear everything, but I never heard any rumors about that!"

"It was a top secret military operation all the way. No one was allowed anywhere near the area. Using armed troops, our security stretched for miles. It was a miracle that we avoided a panic. Even today, parts of that locale are patrolled because the ground is red hot for over a mile."

"What should we do? We've got a bundle invested."

"Get back what money you can; absorb your losses; and, pray you weren't near the contaminated soil. Since then, we've lost another man."

"Good Lord, WHO?"

"Some ignorant woodsman. He squatted on some of the land before we saw him building his log cabin. We're taking care of him, . . even sending the doctors to him, but he won't be around much longer."

"You mean...?"

"Yes sir, he's a goner. Our Geiger counters go off the scale when they get near him."

"Oh, the poor Devil! Gentlemen, thank you for coming. You'll excuse us, but we've got some telephoning to do."

The phone lines buzzed between the law office and land company. Within hours construction personnel, including every piece of equipment, had plunged away, driving frantically into the wind. No one wanted even a puff of contaminated dust blowing in his direction from the crash site. Later, the staff of a District of Columbia medical clinic was dumbfounded when every employee from a large legal firm and construction company insisted on immediate medical examinations.

Homesteader Dittus still ruled his domain—usually in absentia.

Cody could stand the closet heat no longer. He could hear occasional footsteps from a hallway adjoining the wall. Still wiping sweat, he kicked backward with the heel of his shoe, and punched a hole into the fiberglass insulation. A red Swedish Army pocket knife slashed the fiberglass away, and once more Cody's heel crashed against the outside wall. The plasterboard shattered and Dittus yanked the broken piece inside. No need to scatter plaster across the hallway. Cody's effort bore fruit.

When he cracked open the janitorial room door, a cooling rush of air blew from the cold morgue into Cody's hiding hole. The cross ventilation achieved its purpose. Cody cooled down—once again he could pay attention to the cadaver's resting place. Now, if only someone would step forward to identify this John Doe body.

◆   ◆   ◆

The incredibly expensive Mercedes 500 SEL cruised slowly around the driveway entrance behind the District of Columbia General Hospital. Including taxes, title, and tags, the wedgewood blue sedan's price readily exceeded 100,000 dollars. It was a showpiece and usually required a chauffeur for an ego trip to exhibit immeasurable wealth. The Mercedes SEL and Rolls Royce were the dominant automobiles used by Governments or Embassies the world over. But this auto displayed no government license plate, nor the flag of a particular country. The lavish car was driven by a man in his middle 30's. He was handsome, somber in appearance, with piercing eyes. Closer observation would have revealed thin cruel lips. A conspicuous bulge showed through the drape of the driver's shirt...a lacy sport shirt hanging over his trousers. After thoroughly investigating the entire area and parking lot, plus every person coming and going through the back-entrance hospital doors, he parked in the driveway with the attitude that the space was reserved for him. He exited the Mercedes, eyes searching left and right, and entered General Hospital.

Marchen Judisch, Israel's Diplomat-at-Large, knew exactly where he was going. He walked directly to the morgue, checking his backtrail the moment he passed through the morgue doors. He saw no one except orderlies and nurses and occasional resident doctors with their endless stethoscopes. A uniformed attendant, sitting at a desk and reading a magazine, looked up and saw a casually dressed man standing before him. The visitor's eyes were cold; the expression on his face was all business; and, the bulge under his expensive shirt told the attendant he'd better be all business, too.

"You have an unidentified body in the refrigeration room?"

"Yes, sir. Are you a relative claiming the body?"

Marchen Judisch did not answer the attendant. But his eyes pierced the guard and made him uncomfortable. The guard rushed to open the refrigerated vault. By now the attendant was only interested in getting rid of his visitor first, then the body.

Cody Dittus heard the aluminum door open and slam shut. He readied his camera and stared at an athletic young man, striding to the cold room's guard.

Cody blinked! It was not the expected Danvier Dyan. Cody had never seen this man before.

While hoping the attendant was making enough noise running to the refrigerated vault, Cody snapped frame after frame with his 35-millimeter camera. Although the film and shutter moved quickly and electronically, the whining servo-motor of the camera seemed to create a wailing din inside the janitorial closet. Cody kept advancing film, and kept taking pictures—noise or no noise. Dittus watched the caller approach the pullout drawer holding the body. The voices were muffled due to the distance, but he heard most of the conversation.

"Is this a relative, Sir? The ambulance brought him in yesterday. He was found alone, and he had been knifed with something through the neck."

"You say he was alone?"

"Yes, sir. Our ambulance was called by the police. A patrol car was passing when the officers spotted the body. They saw a crippled man standing at the curb hollering at them."

"Crippled man? Know what he looked like?"

"I didn't see him, sir, but our ambulance men said he was a Texas cattleman, who wore cowboy clothes, a big hat, and cowboy boots. House Speaker Holcombe Broderick lives down the block and he vouched for the Texan as a personal friend. I do know the guy probably fell off a horse, 'cause he sure couldn't ride one now. He really leaned on his cane. In fact, our boys said he could hardly climb the steps. Congressman Broderick had to almost carry him into the house."

Marchen Judisch said nothing. After all, he was paid to think…not talk. He only muttered a grouchy, "Hummpphhh!"

"Mister, you know this man? You claiming the body?"

"Yes, he was an employee at the museum. I'll send a hearse to pick up the body."

"What was your man doing in Georgetown? That's a peaceful place."

"Just walking the city. He was a great one for studying history and architecture. Probably some mugger knifed him from behind. The limo drivers will complete what papers you require. Thanks for your help."

Judisch slipped out the door, jumped into his expensive Mercedes, and was gone in an instant. The two-way entrance doors were still swinging when Cody Dittus quickly pursued, taking pictures of the Mercedes driver, his auto, and the license plates. The man was doing too well for a museum employee. The "500 SEL" might be owned by executives of a large firm, not by an employee. Also, there was no identifying name or emblem usually found on a company car. This man, who never gave the attendant his name, behaved like the privileged few in the top 5% income bracket. And he was getting away.

Cody Dittus jumped into his older model Pontiac. He pressed the pedal.

The wheels narrowly held to the pavement. Had Cody pushed the accelerator a fraction more, he would have spun the rubber off the tires. Maintaining control at the maximum limit, Cody sped down the avenue in pursuit. There was no way the Mercedes could have escaped Cody's auto.

Special men did special jobs for Oz; these special men never knew their employer. The agreed price was paid into their own bank accounts. Upon completion of the job, each checking account would show a hefty deposit, a deposit that came from nowhere.

So, Cody slowly gunned the motor, increasing his speed remarkably as the engine purred with power. The technicians who juiced the Pontiac were NASCAR mechanics and innovators who tuned and rebuilt engines only for world racing champions. The autos became souped-up explosive bombs when the NASCAR technicians plied their trade. As to the engines: The specialists began where Detroit quit. Engines of 220 horsepower were redesigned and re-machined, reaching a peak of 660 horsepower. And, that was a controlled peak. The same engine could be reworked to attain horsepower of 850 to 950. However, given too much throttle, the engine could blow up. The available 600-plus horsepower was far more than ample for Oz agents.

Dittus drew within a hundred yards of his quarry. Suddenly, two cars filled with yelling high schoolers cut in front of him and blocked his view. When Cody started to pass, one of the autos swerved in front of him, again blocking him from passing. The teenagers' hand signals and shouted lewd insults were far from complimentary. Cody, losing his quarry in traffic, had time for only one response.

"Well, youngsters, you wanted to play—so now it's my turn."

Cody whipped his car left, and as the taunting teenagers again jerked their auto left to block him, they were, momentarily, driving partially sideways. Cody pressed the pedal, accelerated, rammed the rear of the tormentors, and then gave them a surge of 400 horsepower. The front auto jackknifed, flew sideways down the avenue, tires screeching, when Cody slammed on his four-wheel racing brakes. The surprised youngsters found themselves alone with their car spinning end to end. Out of control, the auto met the curb with a BANG. The rear axle bent, then shattered, and the curb's immovable construction flipped the car onto its side. The troublemakers slid down the roadside, with metal grinding, and came to a halt when the roof crunched under the impact of a wire-braced telephone pole.

"As ye sow, so shall ye reap," Cody remarked as he passed by.

Cody sped toward the next car ahead, noticing the bug-eyed expressions on the faces of the teenage occupants. The driver desperately tried to leave Cody behind, because he floor-boarded the pedal. But, Cody was the cat toying with a mouse. As the high schoolers increased speed, so did Cody—only his "NASCAR Bomb" gave a burst of speed that caused the trouble-making driver to think his brakes had locked. Dittus was roaring up for another bumper-bending lesson.

Without hesitation, the teenage driver tried to escape by swerving from the roadway. He smashed the car's front end against the curbing and felt the two front wheels rip away from the frame under his car. Cody's last recollection of the adventure depicted an auto, full of screaming teenagers, plowing on its front chassis and rear wheels, disappearing from sight down a dirt embankment. A huge cloud of flying dust marked the spot.

Cody mentally summed up the escapade: "Man! I'd sure like to have owned the toilet paper concession on this one."

In less than 30 seconds, Cody, roaring down the straightaway, had the Wedgwood blue Mercedes in sight. Its owner had missed all the excitement. And Cody was shaking his head in disbelief at the young troublemakers.

"Did they actually believe no one would dare retaliate? That everyone would run? That no sane person would challenge their menacing antics?"

He was still shaking his head in disbelief as he followed his target off the busy avenue. Suddenly, his bewilderment over such an irrational, idiotic performance by high school teenagers, changed to astonishment when the blue Mercedes slowed, then turned into a wide driveway where armed guards patrolled the ornate iron entrance gate.

What flabbergasted Cody Dittus was the familiar sight of two sizeable brick and stone columns, one on each side of the drive, leading into a large fenced compound. There, superbly etched on marble in each column was a government crest, a Star of David, and the prominent words, **Israel Embassy.**

Driving moderately to the blare of horns from impatient drivers, a concerned Agent Dittus traveled to a drive-in window at the building housing Oz Headquarters. The small facility was a film development laboratory operated by Oz. Cody's roll of film was speedily processed while he waited at another window marked, "Pick Up." The film lab was one government facility that made a profit for taxpayers. Although designed to process secret pictures and movies for undercover agents, the lab had to handle a substantial flow of camera bugs visiting or living in Washington. Cody had his picture package in minutes. Civilian customers received one-hour service. Oz's camera technicians were so quick and professional in their film processing that they out-performed Wal-Mart and K-Mart.

What annoyed the Oz executives was the continual surprising profit over and above expenses. Oz leaders were refunding remarkable sums of money unheard of for a budgeted agency, . . particularly when the refunds were untraceable, charged to a non-existent organization which continually sent baskets of legal tender back to the treasury.

Such a singular response from somewhere caused confusion—especially within a mega-bureaucracy. Such incidents brought excessive stress and migraine headaches to the Secretary of the Treasury. Each year the government expects tremendous deposits of cash to flood the U.S. Treasury—the annual tribute of riches from the American people—where vast credits are harvested from over 200 million IRS tax returns.

But, somebody, something, some ghost…returning tens of thousands of dollars…why, it was…was…Un-American.

Demands for a thorough investigation increased the migraine attacks suffered by the treasury Secretary. The cries also scared the Hades out of Oz administrators who underwent a new siege of ulcers.

"Someone is trying to shame us with honesty and integrity," shouted one congressman. "This must not continue!" That congressman was reelected.

Cody Dittus reported to his superiors. Neither they nor Leith Ohmstead could identify the blue Mercedes and the driver who had access to the Israeli Embassy. The Director said, "It's got to be someone rather new. Perhaps our New York contacts know him from the United Nations. Drive down and check."

"Right," said Dittus. "May I take Ohmstead with me? We can cover more territory with less suspicion." When the boss nodded, Cody added, "We'll have the answer for you next week."

There was no objection. Both agents jumped into the Pontiac "NASCAR Rocket" and rolled out of town.

Cody nudged Leith, "We'll spend that enjoyable week at my place. You need some rest and more healing. But, right now, we're going to Maryland."

"Maryland? I thought our orders were for New York City."

"That was to find an answer. I'm betting the answer may be closer. We're going to visit an airport and watch the Spads and Sopwith Camels fly."

Leith grinned, "Okay, Red Baron, you're driving."

After exiting Washington, D.C., and its heavy traffic, the pair spent the next hour enjoying the countryside and absence of civilization. The sign at the gate announced the complex was the Frederick Municipal Airport of Frederick, Maryland. This time, Leith Ohmstead, still painfully hobbling, joined Cody Dittus in a short walk to one of the aircraft hangars.

Cody waved and gave a friendly, "Howdy," to two surprised mechanics working on a handsome twin-engine Beechcraft plane. Cody introduced Leith as "Ken Mowry," and then opened the auto's trunk. As before, he handed each A & E Technician two bottles of imported Bavarian beer. Both mechanics spoke with one voice, "Lunchtime!"

And the two sat down and began popping bottle caps.

Cody looked at Leith, "Go ahead, `Ken'. Tell them about the wreck."

Leith Ohmstead followed the play without missing a line. He handed both mechanics two pictures: One a frontal view of the hospital's mysterious caller; the other, a side view of his face. Cody could use a telescopic lens like an aerial photographer. The prints were in color, concise and in focus.

Leith continued, "Fellows, this guy hit me broadside coming from this airport several weeks ago. I was in no condition to catch him. He seemed in a real hurry. Fortunately, I was at a wedding reception in Washington this past weekend. There he was...I'd know his face anywhere. I had the wedding photographer snap several pictures, and these are the blowups of him. Would you know him?—That is, has he ever been at this airport before?"

Both repairmen, between swigs of the tasty German beer, looked and then grinned at each other.

"No doubt. That's Mark. I knew he'd clobber somebody someday. He drives way too fast. What say, partner?"

The other technician agreed, "No doubt at all. That's Judisch. Was he driving his blue Mercedes 500 SEL?"

Leith interrupted, "Just who is this guy?"

"Marchen 'Mark' Judisch. Diplomat-at-Large for Israel in D.C. Remember when I mentioned him, Mr. Evans? He's the guy who owns that King Air 350 passenger plane we looked at." Cody replied, "You told me he's the one who had employed a pilot named Danvier Dyan, a coin collector. Right?"

"Exactly, Mr. Evans. And you, Mr. Mowry, have the man who hit you. Happy lawsuit. That is, when he gets back."

Leith 'Mowry' Ohmstead, surprised, said, "When he gets back?"

"Yes Sir. Judisch left for Canada with his pilot, Vier Dyan. But, they'll probably change to a long-range jet for the next leg."

Ohmstead was puzzled, "Why a jet for the next leg?"

"Look at it this way, Sir. As usual, following the flight plan, we stuff the appropriate maps into the pilot's briefcase. But, this time, they're taking a real long ocean-hopping trip. That's why they'll probably use a jet from Canada. The maps were of the Atlantic, the Mediterranean, and the Middle East."

"Just the two of them going to the East, eh?"

"Oh, no, Sir. They're carrying two passengers. Senator Abraham Anselm, with a ravishing redhead. Brother, what a build! Anselm should have a ball."

"Is his wife that attractive?" asked Ohmstead.

"Mr. 'Mowry', we know the Senator's wife...and she's no redhead. Honestly, you should have seen this one in her thin blouse and skirt. Wow! Obviously, Anselm's traveling to a hot climate, with a hot redhead, for a hot time."

Leith Ohmstead and Cody Dittus glanced at one another. Both knew Senator Anselm didn't need to fly to the Middle East to do his philandering.

10

Homecoming

The automobile ride back to Washington, D.C. was quiet. The engine purred softly, but conversation was sparse. Leith Ohmstead curled his fist, his fingers touching, then tapped his lips. His thoughts were random—now and then documented by vocal ramblings in meaningless outcries. Leith's growls and angry snarls would have been incomprehensible to a listener—baffling to anybody but Cody Dittus. Leith would periodically gasp with anguish, although he never complained. Unconsciously, he revealed his constant torment by vigorously rubbing his thigh. Confinement within a car's seat belt gave him little chance to exercise or change position.

Cody Dittus, still listening carefully, drove off the highway onto an outlying expressway, which looped around Washington, and took another four-lane toward Virginia. Once on the road leading to his wooded cabin retreat—his "hidey hole" as he called it—Cody pulled over into the first roadside park. There were few people parked there, so Cody, with his thermos of coffee, and Leith with his supportive cane, walked to a picnic table.

Cody sat high on the table, his feet braced on the bench seat. He "cleared the area" of possible assailants. From force of habit, neither man allowed easy access to his backside. Leith walked, did leg stretching exercises, and finally surrendered to his pain by tossing a long overdue analgesic tablet into his mouth. All the while not a word was spoken.

Then, Leith suddenly spoke to no one in particular. His and Cody's minds were in tune in reasoning and judgment, so Leith blurted out,

"I know the b—d did it. Maybe it took several of his men. But a Representative...a Senator...wouldn't do it—couldn't do it. Not against me." Turning toward Cody, he said,

"Only you might give me trouble, Dittus. So, any attempt by a Congressman would be the height of stupidity.

"No, by God, it had to be him. But WHY? For oil? For access to plans of a minuscule nuclear device? Maybe munitions and weapons?

"Hell. I had no proof, . . no evidence, . . just a hunch. And the suspicions came from the Director of Oz. I knew nothing. And the b—d threw me off a five-story balcony. For that he will pay."

Cody asked, "All right, which one of the two did it? You've only seen one of them—and from a photograph I took."

Disgusted, Leith took a medicine bottle from his coat pocket. He shook out another pain pill. Cody took the tablet and returned it to the bottle.

"Leith, that may stop the pain. It will also stop your thinking. You don't need a drug that kills all feeling. What you need, buddy, is a 'body toddy'. So, wait till you see my paradise. I'll pour you a stiff one while you explain the WHY to me, and how my photograph ties everything together...including your five-story plunge."

The trip to Cody Dittus' "hidey hole" was surprisingly rapid. After inspecting the highway a mile in front and a mile behind, in case the long arm of the law might be cruising nearby, Cody pressed the foot pedal. The Pontiac Special gave a deep throaty growl and rocketed down the highway with such acceleration that both men sank into the back of their seats. The exhilaration Leith Ohmstead felt made him forget his suffering from the throbbing misery of his shattered thigh. Mentally he compared this impression of speed to his first trip on a commercial jet aircraft when he felt the tremendous power as the plane took off. There, too, he was firmly pressed back into his seat.

The twosome exited down a dirt road. Unexpectedly, the road disappeared into a thick forest wilderness. Next came a steep climb up a dim mountain trail...actually, more like a squirrel path. With a sudden turn, the car paralleled a stony precipice for miles. The drop-off from the cliff vanished into trees far below. The traveler would fall but once, and die in a grave of emerald green grandeur.

Abruptly, the auto dipped into a hidden brush-laden passage that led to a valley plateau. There, where the ground rose and fell for a quarter section, lay 160 acres of low-cut grass...almost a lawn. A paradise. Green grass had been brush-hogged low to the rolling hills. Assorted trees grew and bloomed, amid sunlit leaves in varied shades of green.

And there, with varnished logs harmonizing with the foliage, stood a rustic cabin, snuggled in a scenic clearing. Cody's "Hidey-Hole Lodge" extended Leith the warmest welcome he could ever remember.

Cody drove the car behind the cabin to a concealed shelter. Leith said nothing. He stepped from the auto, and limped along pine-needled footpaths to the rainbow-floored patio. The setting sun filtered through the rustling leaves, and the winds whispered greetings to a wounded and exhausted man. The cabin beckoned to Leith Ohmstead. And the uncontaminated primeval forest greeted a new mortal blessed with a rare appreciation and love of such beauty. Here was another one like "Cody, the homesteader."

Dittus watched Leith Ohmstead sit down and lean back in the comfortable wood hewn chair, and slowly relax beside the polished natural wood table. Leith had found sanctuary in the Lord's vineyard—a healing place where he could return to the soil "from whence he was created."

Cody Dittus, pouring the promised libation for his hurting friend, observed the emotions flooding through Leith as he rested in nature's nirvana. As Cody Dittus silently set the drinks on the attractive table, a tear rolled down his face. He had been wise in his judgment concerning Ohmstead.

At last, Leith Ohmstead had finally found a home.

◆　　　◆　　　◆

Charter Saladin sat in an easy chair, dressed in a green satin robe that covered his knees. A pair of comfortable fur-lined slippers warmed his feet. He was staring...staring into the hypnotizing flames of a cheery fire. Charter's mood was serene—tranquil in his every expression—composed as he had never felt since the death of his wife. The welcoming fire was an evening fire. A ship's clock, from somewhere in Speaker Broderick's house, chimed four bells. Eight o'clock. The night was warm. The small breeze blew from the Potomac River. Saladin sensed the needle on his energy scale was steadily climbing toward the peg. He jumped up, strode through the den, and out the door to the native stone walk in the garden.

Pungent odors from cedars, beds of clover, and intoxicating cherry blossoms floated throughout the dimly lit haven. Saladin sighed. He was at peace, but his mind had been purged. What remained was calm and cool. Charter's eyebrows raised when he heard soft footsteps behind him. Then, a hand gently gripped his shoulder while the other hand slowly handed him a small goblet of brandy. Holcombe Broderick stood beside Charter with an affectionate grin on his face. Charter felt like talking.

"I've been doing some hard thinking,...and I'm sure my conclusions are striking close to home."

Holcombe Broderick sat down on the ornamental iron bench and said, "I'm listening."

Saladin took a deep breath, paused, and began a step-by-step monologue. Broderick never ceased to be amazed at the young congressman's ability to follow a regimen of facts arranged in logical order.

"The perpetrator behind my wife's murder accomplished his goal. That goal was to crush me so thoroughly that I was unable to perform my governmental duties. But, Elena's spirit stayed with me and I returned to the Halls of Congress to represent my people. The instigator of such hate knew he had to cause a greater shock to my already-weakened system: A confession that my precious Elena was always the intended target—that her killing was no accident. So he...yes, He—the odds greatly favor a man because, in comparison, there are so few women in Congress—he knew he must provoke an even worse shock within me than ever before. Whoever this ghoul is, he knew the best way to destroy me. He succeeded.

"Yet, in his cleverness, he exposed his neck to the noose. I mean by that, the horribly graphic note on the restroom mirror struck me so emotionally,...that I passed out. That trauma made me lose my mind. And, that was his exact intent. And, for a while, he succeeded. Fortunately, he underestimated Charter Saladin.

"In his gamble—that's exactly what it was—he won...and he lost. He incapacitated me for Congress, but he forgot that the mirror episode narrowed the hunt to Congress. Holcombe, it's a powerful man behind this. A very powerful man. Only, a Representative would have to be a damned fool to pull such a sick stunt in his own office building. He might be sitting just a few seats away from me in The House. Therefore, the criminal surely could not be idiotic enough to cast suspicion on himself from only a few aisles away.

"No, he's located in the upper house, The Senate. The guilty party has to be a Senator, his top advisor, or a top aide. Such acts could not be trusted to a staff member. That would be even more stupid.

"No. He's from the upper house. Powerful, but ruthless. We've narrowed the field to those who did it...or know all about it. So, tell me Holcombe, how am I doing so far?"

Broderick was smiling inside. This kid was sharp. He answered,

"Why would anyone in the Senate Building go after you? Explain that."

"Mr. Speaker, I've become somewhat influential. I'm only in my thirties, but most of the newer 20-year-olds and 30-year-olds have rather allied themselves with me...or behind me."

Holcombe Broderick snorted. That was one of the understatements of the year from Capitol Hill. "Charter, just who, or what group, have you alienated in Washington? Better yet, whose feet in New Jersey or nearby, have you stomped on?"

"It's not in New Jersey. I know Senator Jacob Bergenfeldt would never orchestrate a "hit" and a follow-up "mirror trick." He lacks guts. In fact, he hid in the synagogue's cellar while the Lord was passing out the brains." Broderick was thankful for the night. He was choking on his laughter.

"Tell me, Charter, why do you think anyone would hate you enough to kill…especially a man's family?"

"Holcombe, I've given much thought to that question. But, I doubt it would be racist."

"Why do you say that? Racist, of all things?"

My family came from the Arab nation. One of many tribes. My ancestors were famous, and, also, great warriors. Saladin was from Persia. In battle, he often defeated the Jews as well as Richard the Lionhearted—during the Crusades. But, to suspect racism because someone lived in the 12th century, say, in the 1150's?"

"Has any other person given you a hard time since Congress?"

"Only one. And that was even before Congress. Senator Anselm of New York certainly was difficult."

"How long have you known him?"

Charter blinked in surprise, "I don't, Holcombe. Fact is, I've never been allowed the opportunity to meet him. Doesn't make sense to dislike a man before you've even shaken hands."

Broderick suddenly asked, "Have you ever talked with Bergan Gruenspan? I understand he's available."

"Senator Anselm's super advisor? He wouldn't give me the time of day."

"You might be surprised, Charter. I'll arrange it. You might find him very informative."

Saladin sniffed, "It'll be a waste of time for us both."

Broderick added, "I'll also be contacting a very special man. I believe you should get to know him. He might have some ideas of his own."

"And who is that, Mr. Speaker?"

"A very aggressive fellow by the name of Leith Ohmstead."

◆   ◆   ◆

House Speaker Holcombe Broderick picked up the telephone in his study. Only one small fluorescent bulb glowed from a desk lamp, and Holcombe sat in literal darkness. The paneled study reflected a warm aura, and Holcombe sighed, recalling the limitless hours he had studied legislative bills pending before the House. Never-ending research enabled him to coerce Congressional action toward certain domestic and foreign policies.

Broderick was troubled by a nagging ache—a foreboding—that emanated from the back of his head. The cramp was familiar. This was one of those times when his "intuitive hunches" surfaced. The discomfort coursing behind his head and neck gave him warning: Each time he had ignored that sense of foreboding, he had made a mistake that accomplished little,…and more often damaged his country. That sense of apprehension told him he had overlooked something; there were bases he had not covered; in effect, someone was trampling Miss Liberty and the Constitution right in his own backyard. The problem was that Broderick could not fathom the cause. Yet he knew he had to do something. That dilemma meant using the telephone.

He pulled the receiver button up until he heard a click. The special switch on the Study telephone effectively disconnected all other telephones within his home and even hampered any attempt at wiretapping. He dialed.

"Speaker Broderick here. Let me speak to Oz."

◆   ◆   ◆

The hour was 0430. The pink tinge of a galactic fire bordered the distant horizon. On the airdrome it was impossible to discern the rendezvous spot of earth and sky. Thin pencils of orange light traced arcs through the ebony dark…like sparklers on a Fourth of July. There was activity on the airdrome—weak beacons of gold penetrated the misty morning blackness—and the deep purple of an airship's belly flashed momentarily. Another beam shone into a cavernous door on the side of the ship. Suddenly, two men, guided by a third, walked toward the open door. The two being led almost stumbled. They were cautiously feeling their way. They were blind.

From nowhere appeared another individual. Athletic in build, he skipped up a foot brace inside the ship. He helped each man inside, and seated them in the narrow cabin. In minutes both staggering men were strapped into primitive bucket seats. There was no comfortable upholstery. The craft was spartan. It was built for special use…strong and durable. A study, also, of the two safety-belted men would have shown them wrapped with a wide band of black cloth. They saw nothing—they were blindfolded.

Dawn cracked the sky. A faint, ever growing, light penetrated the ebony and indistinct tracings disclosed hangars, parked airplanes, and a vacant tarmac. Beside the asphalt taxiway a concrete apron stretched to tire-marked runways. The airdrome would be very busy when it awakened.

The yawning doorway gave way to a long black metal frame. A tail rotor propeller and a giant windmill topped the aircraft. The word "Huey," was stenciled on the empennage. It was an attack helicopter, a Huey Cobra gunship. This time it was unarmed, but ready for flight. The individual who had led the two blindfolded men to the door strode to the pilot's chair, turned on dim cockpit lights, and actuated the turbine motor. An increasing whine shattered the stillness of early morning, and the copter blades turned slowly…then faster and faster. The attendant, who had strapped the passengers in, slammed the door shut. Within moments the helicopter had risen, dipped forward with speed, and quickly evaporated into the light of a new day.

The Huey gunship never climbed more than 500 feet above ground. It followed a major highway off to its right…just enough to keep the expressway in sight, but well out of view of early morning motorists.

Flying at a surprising speed, the bird turned away from the interstate and followed a dirt road through a profusion of forests. Just as the ground below met the light of a rising sun, the helicopter flew past, then hovered, at the back door of an attractive cabin nestled within green trees and rolling hills. The Huey landed briefly; three passengers disembarked; and, the pilot pulled the gunship once more into the sky. He disappeared from sight and sound within one minute.

Only then did their attendant, Cody Dittus, take off the blindfolds. An astounded Bergan Gruenspan and Charter Saladin blinked at the unexpected sight of this pristine paradise. Then shock and astonishment showed on their faces as Saladin and Gruenspan looked at each other. Both knew one another, but the atmosphere at certain Capitol Hill parties was not conducive to friendship—their politics were too diverse.

Gruenspan asked the question for both abductees, "Where in hell are we?"

Cody Dittus knew exactly what to say, . . and how to mislead…

"You are in Maryland. Over that far rise is Chesapeake Bay."

It was a reasonable answer to a fair question. The site might have matched some area of Maryland, but Saladin and Gruenspan had not seen the cliffs and small mountains foreign to that state. The "guests" were satisfied with the answer. If ever the two were questioned, they would point searchers in misleading directions that would guarantee Cody Dittus the preservation of his home, and safety from detection.

Years of "batching it" as attractive, eligible bachelors, whose romances had been short-circuited by extensive worldwide travels demanded by Oz, had produced dual vocations for Leith and Cody. A decade of eating at global restaurants patronized by the elite, the so-so, and the abominable stratum of society, had forced each agent to become a chef-d'oeuvre. Both had become Masters of the Cuisine. While Cody was hijacking Saladin and Gruenspan, who were expecting to meet Speaker Holcombe Broderick at the airdrome, Leith tossed his cane aside and limped happily through "his" kitchen in the log cabin. Ohmstead prepared an early breakfast that would have delighted the Queen at Buckingham Palace.

Charter Saladin and Bergan Gruenspan had barely been seated on the patio when the sun broke through the night's overcast to illuminate a silver service groaning under a load of: eggs overlain with sweet/sour sauce resting in the center of glazed cinnamon-sugar toast; a hint of mustard mixed with a mushroom sauce basted over slices of clove-spiced ham; a salad bowl of French-Algerian ambrosia, a smorgasbord composed of fresh diced fruit garnished with shredded coconut beneath a cap of brandied apricot chips; finally, a real waker-upper eye-opener, . . from Tanganyika, a just-below-boiling vessel of high mountain grown Kilimanjaro coffee, sweetened with a tinge of black molasses and topped with a float of thick beaten cream.

Both politicians began enjoying their abduction. At the sight of such a scrumptious feast, their saliva flowed and their stomachs growled. There was a peaceful silence, broken only by the sounds of swallowing, munching, "Oh's" and "Ah's," and appreciative lip-smacking as the diners sipped their coffee. Cody, however, rolled his eyes and commented,

"The eggs were slightly overdone; the sauces need more salt, and . ."

"Shut up, Cody. Just eat and grow fatter." growled Leith.

His remark drew a dirty look from Cody Dittus. Yet, Cody kept eating. And the food generated congeniality. After empty stomachs were filled, and a second full coffeepot was placed on the table, the group began to tell their stories: Leith Ohmstead was, under orders from Oz, tracing the secret lives of certain globe-trotting Congressmen—with emphasis on Eastern State senators. For no apparent reason he was attacked, bound, and thrown from a high balcony of Washington's Stouffer-Mayflower Hotel.

Cody Dittus recounted his escape from torture in Beirut.

Charter Saladin retold the strange, but deliberate, assassination of his wife, and the effort to incapacitate him as a new leader on Capitol Hill.

There might be a tie-in for all three. No one was sure what the Mossad had to do with it, if anything. There was no attempt at maintaining secrecy. Obviously, someone was shadowing the trio's every move; surveillance was in progress on The Hill and at residences. Speaker Broderick had to chair The House, and was doing his own probe from his office.

It was Bergan Gruenspan's observations that began to turn the key.

11

Moil for Oil

Sultan Sadah Diyarbar stepped from his extravagant nomad's tent and surveyed the sands and rocky crags from horizon to horizon, and smiled with satisfaction. His hair, eyebrows, eyes, and mustache were jet black. His physique was impressive…wide shoulders, a slim waist, rippling muscles concealed in an Iraqi army uniform. In combat boots he stood 6' 3", and weighed a solid 220 pounds. His medium-sized, sharp nose and sparkling white teeth disguised a ruthless will to win. Sadah might smile, but his eyes pierced his inferiors like daggers. He could kill a guest, or a prisoner, without a qualm. He had done so, many times, even to terror-stricken women consigned to his chambers. Diyarbar appeared handsome, but his lovemaking was as brutal as his treatment of foes.

This morning he was in a fine mettle, bursting with male energy and the thrill of conquest. As he breathed the fresh air of dawn, a pair of attendants quickly carried away a whimpering, bloody 12-year-old girl from his den of erotic passion.

All of this before him was his…the women, fulfillment of his insatiable lust, the submission and allegiance of his people, the vast domain he ruled. Sadah's empire included ancient Mesopotamia, an archaic country of Asia between the lower Tigris and lower Euphrates rivers. A smaller northern region had been added along with a new name, Iraq. Man's eternal wish to be free, soon inspired an element of democracy, and the 172,000-square-mile territory became a Republic in Southwest Asia. Its modern name became Iraq. Then once again, as in ancient times, the Republic's population, now numbering ten million, saw a cruel ruler emerge. He called himself President Diyarbar. Old people called him the old name, "Sultan."

As he gained power, Sadah Diyarbar wisely moved around. Although his troop of bodyguards had sworn his protection to the death, Sadah knew assassination or another military coup—not necessarily in that order—could surface anytime. Reared in small towns, Diyarbar soon discovered the practicality of a nomadic life; he traveled in clandestine comfort using an ingenious nomad's tent of canvas and skins; a modern canvas tent built for great strength. It was acceptable to desert bedouins because its design featured traditional animal skins throughout.

Nevertheless, Sadah permitted himself a lavish lifestyle. His perpetual-motion entourage boasted stainless steel tanks of flowing hot and cold water, silent electric generators for assorted equipment, lights, air conditioning, and an army field kitchen capable of producing menus for the Waldorf Astoria. He lacked nothing, but he craved more. His latest relocation should bring him world power and influence.

Now, his convoy lay nestled among palm and date trees, surrounding a small oasis. He was camped on the southeast tip of Iraq, by a lake south of Al-Basrah, known as Basra. Lodged near a restricted waterway to the Persian Gulf, the location was only miles west of Iran and almost touched the border of Kuwait. A simple runway rolled north and south several hundred meters from the campsite. An obedient aide bowed low, groveled, and informed his sultan, President Diyarbar, of a radio message just received.

"My Sultan, an airplane will soon be landing on the runway."

"Have my driver and staff stand by the Landrover auto. I will want an honor guard for a welcoming salute. Arrange it immediately."

The aide retired, bowing ceremoniously. Even the Queen of England was shown no better homage. However, she earned respect without threat of death.

A two-engine jet flew low and slowly, barely pulling itself over the burning sands, with its wheels and flaps fully extended. The plane gradually sank, disappearing behind a distant hill of sand and rock.

Sadah Diyarbar jumped into the British desert truck and rushed to the airstrip. The jet's engines were just winding down when the honor guard aligned itself on both sides of the fuselage door. As the hydraulic actuator hissed, and the passenger door opened upward while the stairway descended, a cluster of bugles sounded with an accompanying drum roll.

A distinguished western-garbed dignitary, slightly balding with salt and pepper hair, carefully walked down the aluminum stairs straight toward the outstretched hand of President Sadah Diyarbar. There was a feigned affection in the handclasps and broad smiles from the two important men. Both men stared unflinchingly into each other's eyes. However, the impression, gathered by Diyarbar's closest lieutenant, was that the eyes of the men were only reflecting each other's most coveted aspiration, a bountiful harvest from a crop of megadollars.

The visitor inquired, "Are we near the property you've informed me about? You said some arrangements had been made?"

Without a word, Sadah's Landrover, followed by three truckloads of armed soldiers, drove westward over the crests of several hills. At the top of one, President Diyarbar waved a sweeping hand over a level plain. Within view stood six oil wells, their beams rocking up and down. They were separated a half-mile from each other, and actively pumped night and day. A pipeline ran the length of the well sites, and the pipe continued eastward until it became a tiny thread receding into the horizon.

"The pipeline goes to a collection point on the lake where a Japanese tanker is waiting to transport it through the Strait of Hormuz into the Arabian Sea."

"Are these good producing wells?"

"Of course. They are producing only meters from the boundary-line stones marked `Kuwait'." After his statement, Sadah began laughing.

"What is it you find so funny, Mr. President?"

"Please understand, Sir. My engineers contrived a plan for drilling on a **slant,**...so that the drill stems are actually pulling from reservoirs of oil beneath Kuwaiti territory. Production here should last a lifetime."

The Western dignitary said, "Phewww. I can hear the hum of the oil gushing through that pipeline. These wells must be producing oil worth millions every month."

Sadah Diyarbar shook his head, "No, my honored friend. Production is one or two million dollars <u>daily</u>. And these, plus many more wells beyond the following hills, are yours. They are my gift to you.

"I do this in appreciation of your visit and our arrangements, . . er, shall I say...our mutual concessions, . . a, ah, that we make for one another. Your gift is this segment of land and all its production—in perpetuity. Please accept this as a token of my esteem for your association. It is my welcome to a great Western leader."

The visitor gasped, "In perpetuity? All, everything...mine?"

"Yes. To do with as you please, Senator Anselm. Do with the income as you please. Tell me, where do you wish your monthly checks mailed?"

Without hesitation, Abraham Anselm scribbled on a small slip of paper. He unobtrusively handed it to Sultan Diyarbar who stared at Abraham Anselm's bank account number...in Zurich, Switzerland.

Sadah Diyarbar smiled inwardly. This highly publicized senator was hungry. By gorging Anselm's personal piggy bank, Sadah could be assured that Abraham

Anselm would be instrumental in obtaining a source of weapons and munitions. He would ably assist Diyarbar in his pursuit of vast sums of international credit.

Tragically, making such an accommodation with an anti-American tyrant of Sadah Diyarbar's ilk never entered Anselm's mind. As his confidant, Bergan Gruenspan, had already bemoaned, something was wrong with Abraham Anselm. The acceptance of a foreigner's gift—an obvious munificent bribe—had placed him beyond the crossroad of integrity or dishonor. Although some observers suspected Anselm's corruption, the extent of his deterioration would have shocked even the most unscrupulous members of The House and Senate. His character could no longer elude depravity.

Senator Anselm had sold himself into immorality. Its iniquity was too rewarding to resist. Immorality's price was no longer a few hundred dollars here, a grandiose favor collected there, but millions of dollars, harvested monthly, like wheat into storage bins.

And the transformation did not occur among the opportunists in his own country, but along a water-laden, oil pumping, plot of ground below Basra in Iraq. The real calamity was that Anselm felt no remorse. His jubilation was in knowing his political power had finally reached fruition. He could stop counting expenses, cease denying his every whim. There would be no cap on his living standard, and he could look down on most public servants struggling behind economic barriers.

For the first time in his life, Abraham Anselm was a wealthy man.

The subsequent meeting inside the cool tent was productive. Whenever one of Sadah's staff entered or exited the tall shelter through the thick canvas folds, a literal blast furnace blew its hot breath among the assemblage. The noonday sun pounded and baked the earth. Without thick-soled shoes, a man's feet would burn. Yet, even the gas-engined equipment was under cover. Protective shields, like open-sided wigwams, covered everything. Relief, from the terrible heat and constant sweat almost insured accord among the bargaining parties. Instead of stoically enduring the enervating heat, the "movie theatre air conditioning" proved exhilarating, and prompted far more agreements than disputes.

Diyarbar, whose chair was the center in a four-man staff, looked across the circle at Anselm.

"How soon can arrangements be made for a, ah, er…"

"A representative?" suggested Abraham Anselm.

"Yes," answered Sadah. "A, . . as you say, . . 'representative' of a munitions company to come here and take an order? Mind you, the 'request' will be extensive. The supplies will be paid for in cash,...or with a Letter of Credit from our bank in Switzerland."

Sadah Dayarbar stared at Abraham Anselm. So far, there had been no mention of a commission or fee for the senator's help. Sadah simply said,

"How do you wish to be paid? And I mean the representative, too."

There was no pause in the conversation. The senator easily repled, "My compensation is 15 percent. Good faith to the supplier is half of the cost up front, then the remainder when the first delivery reaches you."

"Senator, I might mention previous finder's fees have been 10 percent. I estimate my first order will surpass 100 million dollars. Your compensation would exceed 15 million. Your portion could be considered exorbitant.

Anselm answered, "Mr. President, your equipment will be first-rate, modern, and not outmoded World War II weapons. I can flood your warehouses with rusty 50-year-old arms at bargain prices. I'm talking about the finest we manufacture and the best Europe can produce.

"Besides,...I've got Eastern Seaboard ports we can ship to and through for any place you designate. There are maritime union chiefs who can thwart government inspectors,...and who will transport the goods quickly.

"Also, Mr. President, I'll be doing it right under the noses of the administration. I have that situation under control—one way or another."

Sultan Sadah Diyarbar was impressed. His thoughts missed little of what was implied. He nodded at Senator Anselm while he mentally accepted the Senator's terms. Sadah's thoughts said it all:

"Whoever controls the unions dominates shipping. Anselm even infers he can bypass the President of the United States. Sadah, you've struck gold."

◆   ◆   ◆

Mohabe Hejira was a close friend of Jabal, the British-trained soldier. Jabal had adopted Leith Ohmstead in Beirut, and helped saved the life of a terribly beaten Cody Dittus. When both men escaped Beirut's roaming bands of scavenging mercenaries by fleeing to Tel Aviv, "Jabal, the Jackal" accompanied them. He was too good to be left behind, and the enemy was too close.

Upon his arrival in America with Leith and Cody, Jabal confounded the clerical bureaucracy of Oz. Applications and records for an agent with only one name? Impossible.

Regardless, Cody and Leith continually explained his cleverness and deadly conduct when caught in tight places. They respectfully called him The Jackal.

Ultimately the ex-British soldier became known as Jabal, the Jackal. Naturally, a brilliant personnel manager figured out the new agent's real name: Jabal The-jackal (pronounced Thej-a-kal). And that was the way Jabal, the Jackal, was carried on all Oz records—Jabal Thej-a-kal.

Jabal ended his "American vacation" by joining Oz and attending its one-year training course: First, in the Florida Everglades; then, traveling west into a sparse desert basin in southeast California, called Death Valley. Training requires a year or more to qualify for graduation.

The agent must be multi-lingual in foreign languages; therefore, Jabal would fit the Middle East since he had grown up in that far frontier. However, Jabal already spoke six languages fluently, plus many tribal dialects. Unfortunately, Jabal's hand-to-hand combat training was a disaster—a disaster for the instructors. One Oz instructor suffered a broken leg; another, a broken arm; and, countless dislocated shoulders and collarbones. Obviously, Jabal had killed before.

Only when a "consulting" British Commando visited the secret base in Death Valley did the executive staff of Oz recognize Jabal's true worth. Radio and Morse Code almost put Jabal to sleep because he was so proficient. The Commando, a British Colonel, advised the staff to assign Jabal to train them. Jabal's scores on required combat training, linguistic abilities, and geography of the Middle East were almost perfect. His teachers stood in awe.

It had to happen. A stunned staff from both Oz training schools watched as one of their "green recruits" received his graduation diploma in only two months. No one, including Leith Ohmstead and Cody Dittus, had ever advanced that fast.

Now, operating from Jerusalem, Beirut, Teheran, even Baghdad, Jabal was a sinister specter moving from country to country exposing ruthless and murderous leaders of the Arab world. Jabal was a blessing to the West.

Now, Mohabe Hejira, a resourceful friend of Jabal, was working as one of the chefs in Sadah Diyarbar's field kitchen. He also took pictures with a miniature camera with a super lens. Mohabe needed only two buttons: one to turn the film to the next frame, and the other to snap a self-regulating shutter. And, it was here, below Basra, that agents of Oz learned of unusual and highly suspect relationships.

As the jet aircraft passenger plane readied for takeoff, Mohabe Hejira got good pictures of Abraham Anselm shaking hands in warm goodbyes with Sadah Diyarbar. Approaching the plane from a restricted area of the tent motorcade was a ravishing hunk of redheaded pulchritude. She said goodbye with a kiss on the cheek.

Diyarbar's eyes undressed her from head to toe. Had she been an Iraqi woman, she would have been Sadah's until he finished with her. The redhead was plainly glad she was leaving. There was something about the Sultan.

Then the aircraft commander saluted and also bade farewell to Sultan Diyarbar. The Sultan had called him—what was it? Marken or Marcus?

The aircraft's pilot was the surprise. He got on his knees to Sadah Diyarbar and kissed his hand several times…in servitude. Yet he and Marken looked like Jews from Jerusalem. Both men had those piercing dark eyes. But this particular one they called…Vier Dan…or Dan Vier? Just for luck, and one more snapshot, Mohabe took a shot of the hand kissing episode. Why in Allah's name would two Jews revere a tyrant like Diyarbar? Diyarbar, until this accession, personally shot them or had them executed. President Diyarbar hated…and feared, Israel.

Maybe Oz could make sense from the film. The private jet took off and disappeared toward the west. For the next two days Mohabe Hejira cooked meals unknown to that region. Hejira only saved his life by outwitting his cruel troop commanders: With his bedroll, clothes, and tent area subject to continual searches, Mohabe kept and slept with the minuscule camera stored between his buttocks.

Three days later the entourage returned to Baghdad in a joyous mood. The Sultan was happy with the pacts and the prospect of the machines of war. Already arms merchants were in Baghdad awaiting his arrival. Anselm moved fast—and, apparently, without hindrance. Sadah's joy infected his loyal troops, too. There were no attempts at search and seizure. It was the only relaxed part of the trip.

Mohabe Hejira took time off for family and shopping in the Casbah, the native quarter of Baghdad's Arab population. Within hours the tiny spool of film, wrapped in a methodical report of everything that had occurred during the Basra meeting, was on a camel train of Arab traders. Two days later, at a green oasis holding a temporary tent town, the merchants displayed wares of jewelry, cattle, rugs, and clothing. From every valley and sandy knoll came bedouin and city customers. Haggling, arguments, and laughter filled the air. Sales were brisk. A young man, a son of one of the merchants, had pottery for sale. A handsome, high caste Arab, with dark penetrating eyes and a purple turban, strolled by. He examined the pottery piece by piece while the young man faintly shook his head. Abruptly, the youngster smiled and nodded. The required haggling went on for minutes until the young merchant let the customer steal it.

Jabal Thej-a-kal placed the vase beneath his robe and left. A British jeep, common in the cities, departed for parts unknown. Within hours an Israeli jet was winging its way to an American base. From that base an American F-16 roared down the runway. At 60,000 feet altitude, its long trip to the U.S.A. was amazingly brief. Mohabe Hejira, and Jabal, the Jackal, had completed one of the most dangerous missions possible—and survived.

It was late afternoon when the group of men gathered around the table behind the handsome log cabin. It was the home of Cody Dittus and Leith Ohmstead. There, in the warm autumn breeze—actually a magnificent Indian Summer—lay the Basra pictures expertly enlarged by the Oz Film Laboratory. The men were relishing The Hidey-Hole Lodge. Over coffee and hot tea, they were studying the amazingly clear photos and their companion report.

12

Misgivings

The expressions on the faces of Attorney Bergan Gruenspan and Congressman Charter Saladin were completely opposite. Both men, after the first shock, glanced down once more at the table top, and intently scrutinized the compromising photographs.

Initially, Bergan Gruenspan's face was horror stricken, then ashen gray. Leith Ohmstead and Cody Dittus, trained to observe closely, missed nothing. Bergan Gruenspan was actually physically sick. The effect of the photos became more apparent when he walked to the edge of the patio and retched. Bergan had spent a quarter-century training, advising, and guiding Senator Abraham Anselm into that rarified atmosphere few senators attained: a reputation of being a great leader.

Bergan's thoughts were like blows. He reeled under the emotional impact tearing him apart. His thoughts raced,

"Has, is…he, one of our nation's most influential leaders, committing treason?"

Bergan staggered under the load of his thoughts. Leith Ohmstead jumped to his side and steered him into a lounge chair. He whispered to Cody Dittus,

"Better get him a snifter of brandy or he's going to lose everything he's eaten the past week."

Cody moved quickly. Soon, a deep crystal goblet was placed in Bergan Gruenspan's hands. Gruenspan nodded his thanks as he sipped, still retching between swallows. Cody Dittus hissed at Ohmstead,

"Do I get a waste basket…or the mop?" Just then Bergan belched.

"If you're smart, Cody, you'll get both." answered Ohmstead.

Charter Saladin's expression was one of insight. Had his look been portrayed in an animated cartoon, the picture would have shown a large lightbulb above his head, burning out with a tremendous "FLASH."

Wonder flashed in Charter's wide-open eyes when his mind registered an explosive comprehension of his brief tenure in The House of Representatives. Because, with that flash of revelation came the first rational clue that might explain the death of his wife. If he understood correctly,—and, this time, his instinctive hunch was overpowering—then he had learned the answer to the question he had asked over and over: "WHY?"

Charter Saladin, a newcomer to congress, had led a potent coalition of Representatives and Senators who were determined to prohibit all trade by the U.S., or any other nation, with Iraq. The coalition had been far more effective than newspapers or journalists could report. However, President Sadah Diyarbar of Iraq could testify how shortages of supplies and growing hunger had caused his people to suffer...almost toppling him from control. The prospect prompted Sultan Diyarbar to act.

During that interval Charter's beloved, Imadie Kassem Saladin, was murdered. The trauma of seeing the killing, and holding his wife in his arms as she died, caused his collapse and lengthy absence from Congress. Only the FBI's belief that Imadie had not been the intended victim sustained Charter during a remarkable recovery. But, the "lipstick on the mirror" episode caused a relapse far more critical healthwise to his career. His recovery, and sanity, became a prolonged disability. Only the support and merciful care by House Speaker Holcombe Broderick kept Charter Saladin from losing his mind. The intense pain and suffering resulted in months of absenteeism from congressional duties which had curbed open commerce with Iraq. Without Charter's leadership in the coalition, the blockade of Iraq floundered. Openly, in contempt of the United States, heavily loaded trucks crossed the border from Jordan. King Hussein of Jordan had done another flip-flop while urging the U.S.A. to increase his loans.

The understanding was twofold: First, not only did Congressman Saladin have an Iraqi adversary, including Iraqi agents in America, but, second, incredible as it seemed, there might be a force from Capitol Hill behind the struggle to remove Charter from congress.

The discussions, and plans to be augmented, lasted until dusk. Leith and Cody could only emphasize they would be traveling between Washington and the Mid-East. Any warnings or instructions from them would come through Oz; and Oz would only talk to top, highly trustworthy, leaders. This edict meant that any "suggestions" from Speaker Holcombe Broderick were to be obeyed. Charter Saladin would continue investigating certain Eastern United States senators and representatives. Charter, now more than ever toying with opponents in an adversarial role, would observe and report any actions or reactions that seemed peculiar. The focus of the New England investigations would center around Senator Abraham Anselm. Yet, a suspect, without proof of guilt, is no suspect; circumstantial evidence, without supporting facts, is indictment without substance.

Charter, Bergan, Leith, and Cody stayed overnight in peaceful surroundings to give themselves time to think...and ask questions.

◆   ◆   ◆

The Chevy Caprice leisurely drove past the ornate brick columns signalling the Israeli Embassy. The engine of Leith Ohmstead's auto also growled. It had been attuned by NASCAR technicians and was the only car able to keep pace with Cody Dittus' Pontiac. This particular day was similar to an earlier day marking the excursion to the "Virginia Hidey-Hole." It was another Indian Summer day, and Leith and Cody were vibrant with energy.

The previous week at the secluded cabin worked miracles for Leith. The muscles of his wounded leg had healed, their restored strength confirmed by the absence of Ohmstead's habitual limp. Leith had decided to park his cane in the Caprice's spacious trunk. He never reclaimed that "third leg" from storage.

Oz agents had gone on full alert after Marchen Judisch had visited Washington General Hospital. Cody Dittus had followed Judisch and his handsome blue Mercedes SEL to the Embassy compound. Not long after, an unmarked black hearse called at the hospital's mortuary and picked up the body of John Doe X who had been shadowing Speaker Broderick's home.

Marchen Judisch was, no doubt, checking on—trying to trace down—the Texas cattleman who had "found" the body of the snoop and turned it over to Washington police. That cattleman, limping on an obvious broken leg, had been Leith Ohmstead.

Although the identification of the Southwestern cattleman by Speaker Broderick may have misled Judisch to believe that a Texas rancher had only happened along to find the body, Marchen was no fool. He was not an Israeli Diplomat-at-Large by accident. Marchen Judisch was smart, cunning, and suspicious by nature. He strongly suspected that the Texan had been the catalyst in the murder of one of Marchen's men, a dangerous surveillance mercenary. But, two things muddled the usually accurate logic of Judisch: Washington police, Speaker Broderick, and Marchen's own espionage force had verified that the "Texan" was almost physically incapacitated. Shrewd judgment reasoned that no such handicapped individual, such as the cattleman, could have killed Marchen's highly-trained spy; second, when Leith Ohmstead returned to the furnished apartment he used when in Washington, his convincing disguise with a slicked-back-wig, fake wrangler mustache, and typical cowboy garb stayed with him. Even at night, his windows, when viewed with a powerful infra-red nighttime telescope, showed Leith either in his favorite chair reading, watching television, or preparing for bed. Roaring with laughter inside, while maintaining a straight face, with difficulty, Leith served a nighttime dessert to his window-peepers by wearing long winter underwear to bed. Shockingly, the long underwear was a vivid red.

Judisch became convinced the Texan was just that—a cattleman—when a verbal report, from several snooping nighthawkers, revealed,

"Honest to God, Marchen, he really goes to bed with the darned thing on; probably dreams about pushing herds of longhorns across the Brazos River. So help me, that passionate-red costume actually has a trap door over his bottom...why, I'll even give you odds he goes to that 'Great Outdoor Potty' right from his saddle."

An Oz agent followed the hearse from its automobile paddock at the Israeli Embassy. The funeral car drove directly to Frederick Airdrome in Maryland. The same King Air 350 turbo-prop passenger plane was loaded with the casket and soon howled down the runway and lifted into the sky. The two technicians on the airbase were handed an ice cold pack of Bavarian beer, "With respect from your airplane buff friend, Mr. Evans."

The A & E specialists laughed and thanked the agent who never even introduced himself. But, he had one question,

"I didn't know you hauled coffins from a private field? I thought only commercial cargo planes or the airlines did that. I wonder where it's going?"

"Just who wants to know?" answered one of the mechanics.

"Fellows, I was coming out here with Mr. Evans when he got called out of town. He said to ask you if you knew 'cause he saw the hearse come from Embassy Row. He thought it might be someone important from overseas. If the man was famous, then somebody may be trying to keep it quiet—and Evans is a magazine publisher, you know. He thought there might be a story here?"

Both A & E mechanics glanced at one another. The tall one spoke,

"It's our guess he's an employee at the Israeli Embassy. Nobody known, but Mr. Judisch is flying him home. We stuffed the pilot's briefcase with maps of Newfoundland, Israel, and Lebanon. That's all we know."

"Shucks, Evans will be disappointed." The agent returned to his car.

"We're close to traveling abroad again, Cody," said Leith Ohmstead.

"What does that mean?" asked Cody Dittus.

"The maps were of Newfoundland, Israel, and Lebanon. If that is the actual itinerary, then progressing from the West to the Mid-East, the route of that casket is Newfoundland, then to Israel, and, final destination, Lebanon."

Cody spoke, "We know the Mossad, . . and General Moschi Rubenstern. The way this 'Diplomat' Judisch is acting, we must assume one of two theories."

"And they are?" countered Leith.

"Either Judisch will be reporting to Tel Aviv, or some equivalent military hierarchy in Jerusalem, in which case he will be met by The Mossad. Do you agree?"

Ohmstead cocked his head, "Unlikely, but go on. The other theory?"

"How's this one? Otherwise, Judisch lands in Lebanon. That location is 'persona non grata' as far as Israel and The Mossad are concerned. We have few remaining "friendlies" covering Lebanon. We've lost too many agents—that is, they've disappeared—never to be heard from again. Right?

"You're talking," said Leith.

"Suppose Judisch lands at Beirut?"

"General Moschi Rubinstern wouldn't like that worth a damn."

"Exactly. What does that tell you...if Judisch does land there?"

"Your theory, Cody. You tell me what that would mean."

"That would tell me he's pulling a double-cross; he works at the Israel Embassy, but he's landing in a militarized city that kills and tortures Jews without any compunction. Ergo, Judisch is on Israel's payroll, but is actually working for someone else. He's a double-agent."

"Come on now, Cody. Just to deliver a body?"

"Damn, Leith. Whoever that mercenary was—a spy—paid assassin—enemy agent—he was working against the U.S. He tried to kill you in Georgetown when you approached him...without any explanation whatsoever. And he certainly wasn't going to play 'tiddlywinks' with Speaker Holcombe Broderick, either. Furthermore, what reasons would Judisch have to take the body and land somewhere like Tel Aviv to confer with his boss, the general? You think the body is one of the general's men? Come on, now, Leith. What does it take to persuade you?"

"Cody, you've forgotten to ask one thing."

Cody raised his eyebrows, "And that is...?"

"We don't know where the plane is at this moment. But, I'm surprised, especially with what you've been through, that you haven't speculated about...just who is the pilot on Judisch's plane?"

"Now, wait a minute, Leith. Neither of the A & Es mentioned anyone except Marchen Judisch. They would certainly have told our man that the pilot was Danvier Dyan. Right?"

"Not necessarily. They saw Judisch pre-flight the plane. They received Judisch's orders on what maps to package. That's the only person they saw."

"Okay, Leith. So, Judisch is a lone eagle this time. Why not?"

"Not if you check the control tower."

"Man, the tower only operates from dawn to dusk. This is not Dulles International."

"Agreed. But think on this. There's no report—written record—with the FAA (Federal Aviation Authority) of Judisch's aircraft, NC 587640, taking off for a cross-country U.S./Canadian flight."

"So, somebody goofed?"

"No, Cody, nobody goofed."

"What the hell does that mean?"

"Flight Service records anyone plotting and reporting a cross-country flight. At Frederick Municipal they operate from dawn to dusk. Ergo—it follows—Judisch, and pilot, took off between dusk and dawn...when the field communication was inoperative. No one would have known, at that time, who was in the plane. In fact, I believe it was deliberately planned that way to keep their departure secret. They never filed a flight plan."

Cody blanched, "Lord. We gotta' contact Jabal and Mohabe Hejira."

◆   ◆   ◆

Jabal Thej-a-kel had departed London on Austria Airline and landed in Beirut. Oz had notified him on one hour's notice. So, Jabal had selected Austria Airline—a wise decision because Austria was one nation that had, so far, created no ill feelings among the Arab population of Lebanon. El Al Israel Airline didn't even venture near the border because of the previous ground fire. British Overseas Airline, BOA, had discontinued their flights due to strained relations, and any American airline was as welcome in Beirut as the bubonic plague.

Jabal, whose skin tone and features resembled a citizen of India or Pakistan, was dressed in a bedouin burnoose and robe. He was masquerading as the sheik of a desert tribe. Deliberately "professorial" in appearance, Jabal carried his books in a slightly-battered leather briefcase engraved with "American University" and "Professor Habeen Sakeen" in gold lettering.

Jabal, the Jackal, avoided waiting taxis, and studied intently the interiors of available cabs, the cabbies themselves, and any individuals loitering nearby. Many a kidnapping began here.

Standing away from the curb outside the airport, Jabal tarried. A nondescript medium-sized auto, dented and dirty, drove to the curb. The driver, dressed in Arab garb, waved at Jabal. Jabal moved quickly, climbed into the front passenger seat, and pointed toward the university. The auto took off in a cloud of exhaust smoke.

"Welcome to Beirut," said Mohabe Hejira, while his eyes searched the roadway for unusual traffic jams, or possible life-threatening ambushes from gangs of pedestrians lining the crowded, dirty streets. Mohabe Hejira skidded the car to a screeching halt. Jabal, opening the door, hid a large envelope behind Mohabe's back.

"First chance you get, memorize everything, then burn it. We'll meet later. We must find Judisch and the body. Allah be with you."

Jabal disappeared up the front steps into the university. He checked one or two classrooms, found one empty, entered and locked the deadbolt from inside. He wasted no time in disrobing and, like a chameleon changing color, his disguise changed to another type of tribal leader, a Holy Man. Wearing the simple white garb of an impoverished Holy Man, Jabal opened a classroom window and let himself drop to a shaded bench-lined patio with a marbled mosaic flooring of terrazzo. Walking swiftly, yet inconspicuously, he soon disappeared among the marketplaces of the city.

After a few Syrian silver shekels changed hands, Jabal rode to the outskirts of Beirut by the private airstrip where he had been rescued once before. His Iraqi friend, the spy, young Mohabe Hejira, loitered near the international airlines' airport. Both men were sure Marchen Judisch would not reveal himself by bringing a casket to the Lebanese Airport on a private jet. Immigration checks, or lack of them, would be hard to explain.

In his ruse as a Holy Man, Jabal begged for alms from passing travelers and trade caravans. The airstrip near the road was easy to see during daylight. At night, wrapped in a desert nomad's blankets of animal fur and skins, Jabal slept. In the blackness of night, he lay on a sandy hillock where he could doze lightly, yet detect every activity at the landing field. Jabal was rewarded when, just at dawn of the second day, a small jet, cruising slowly to minimize sound, began a straight-in approach to the runway. Jabal could see a radio pack on the back of one soldier, while another was speaking into a portable radio-telephone. Plainly, the plane and ground crew were in contact. The craft landed with hardly a bump, and a small lorry backed up to the cabin door the moment the jet quit rolling. Several uniformed guards muscled the coffin onto the flatbed while a conversation continued with the pilots and welcoming committee.

The sunlight broke over the horizon and illuminated the parties. Jabal's camera, a duplicate of the one used by Mohabe Hejira, hummed steadily as he took pictures through the telephoto lens. Looking through the lens while he took each picture, Jabal was stunned by the seeming appearance of President Sadah Diyarbar and, . . yes, definitely, Marchen Judisch. The only discrepancy in the Jackal's mind was the terrible scars on Sultan Diyarbar's face; worsening the confusion was the violent argument between Diyarbar and the second crewman. Pictures taken by Oz, and memorized by Jabal, almost convinced him that the assistant to Judisch was the dreaded Danvier Dyan who was raving. But, Diyarbar was adamant. With a sweep of his hand and arm, Diyarbar ended the argument. He whirled and marched to his waiting limousine. Danvier Dyan, thoroughly chastised, meekly followed him to the car. Dyan never spoke another word.

But, the actions were explicit. The jet taxied away as the sun rose to confirm an early dawn. In the plane was the one crewman who had handled the casket, and only one pilot, Judisch. This time Danvier Dyan was staying.

◆　　　◆　　　◆

Mohabe Hejira was agitated; riding a burro, and dressed as a low-caste beggar, he approached the knoll where "Holy Man" Jabal was resting at dusk near the quiet isolated airstrip. By the time the small cavalcade with the sealed coffin had departed, Jabal Thej-a-kal had shot an abundance of telescopic lens photos recording the activity at the secluded landing strip. The sparse runway lay hidden, visible only from overhead, or to those pilots who knew its exact location outside Beirut.

Therefore, "by accident," the grimy beggar hailed the resting Holy Man and just happened to dismount from the burro's crude saddle. The heavily loaded donkey, one of the freight-laden animals for a small band of touring merchants, continued his loping gait, glad to be rid of his human burden.

Mohabe spread his blanket, and knelt beside Jabal while he removed the travel gear of a footloose vagabond. Fatigued from a long day of snooping, Mohabe rolled on his back and tucked a camelskin robe around his neck, shielding himself from the cold night air of the desert.

"Jabal, I thought I saw President Diyarbar leave International Airport on a small commercial plane. He had a bearded companion with him; and that confederate had one of the meanest, evil faces I've ever seen."

Jabal was disturbed, "I can see why you're so agitated. How could the airport security allow Diyarbar to schedule a flight, let alone fly out of the airport? It makes no sense. Diyarbar is an enemy; almost any Arab nation's enemy. He wants to be another Darius the Great of Persia, or worse, Alexander the Great who ended up ruling all the known world."

"I would agree, but Beirut authorities paid him great respect because it was someone who looked like the Iranian Sultan—maybe a relative."

"Allah praise you, Hejira, you've found the whereabouts of Hadallah, Diyarbar's brother. Hadallah, hasn't been positively identified for years."

"Perhaps, `Master' Jabal. But, I know of only one man, a `Will-o'-the-Wisp,' who is quietly welcomed by the anti-Western nations of the Mid-East. And, one who would treat the assassin, Danvier Dyan, as one of his own. Dyan, in return, is loyal to the death." It was Jabal's turn to be worried.

"Dyan and this `counterfeit Diyarbar' were together at Beirut's airport? How do you know it isn't the brother?"

Mohabe Hejira said, "I saw him among the close confidants of Sultan Diyarbar when they welcomed Senator Abraham Anselm to Basra.

"This `counterfeit' likes to show the left side of his face to his audience. Yet, I often saw his right face, . . and he has a terrible jagged scar—no doubt a war wound—which is unmistakable. This revolutionary is not even trusted by Diyarbar. He is `Kahn the Scarred,' the cousin of Sadah Diyarbar."

"What is his name?" asked Jabal.

"Druid Kahn Membossie. And before you begin the inquisition, Master, let me tell you that all the Sultan's chefs, while preparing food and drinks, have a pipeline to the choicest rumors and unusually-reliable secrets. Kahn Membossie comes from the mother's side of Diyarbar's ancestry. Membossie's mother was a Celt.

"Yes, I said a Celt, which is one of the sect of Druid priestesses from Stonehenge, England. The Celts were probably the first to navigate ocean-going ships to Egypt.

"In their religious ceremonies, the Celts practiced blood-letting, or human sacrifice. I personally saw Druid Kahn Membossie, and only God knows his mixed racial background. But, I tell you I've never seen more cruel, vicious features on any man. He lusts for power, like Diyarbar, but his ambition is what makes him so dangerous. Killing anyone—men, women, children, even babies—is an acceptable end to his ambitions. So far, his ambitions have exceeded his grasp.

"However, he is getting some American backers. Guess who was with him at the airport? Another American. I heard him paged, then saw him board that aircraft. The plane flew due East—straight toward Baghdad, . . and President Diyarbar."

"Well…well? Mohabe, who was it you saw?"

"The American? They paged Senator Theo Dennahy."

"The senator from Massachusetts? Don't be an ass, Mohabe."

"I've got a telescopic snapshot, Master. You wouldn't believe it was Senator Anselm, either…until I showed you film from this same camera."

13

The Pernicious Parley

The Honorable Mangel Mayer Mirish was a member of the exclusive "President's Inner Council" and was officially listed as the first recipient of the newly created post, Secretary of International Protocol and Trade. In this sacred trust, he was privy to the President, able to initiate vital Balance of Trade negotiations with foreign powers, and firmly influence most of the administration's forthcoming plans and policies.

Mirish's duties took him all over the globe meeting with world leaders and high-placed officials. He reported only to The Secretary of State, and the President. Such sudden power is a heady wine to a struggling politician, and Mirish had spent years in The House of Representatives. After continually "stroking" whatever administration was in power, he finally ingratiated himself to the President.

Although the incumbent congressman, at the height of his personal relationship with the President, Mirish had been narrowly defeated by an aggressive, new-broom candidate. The supporter of Mirish's opponent in Connecticut was a crowd-pleasing young New Jersey go-getter named Charter Joseph Saladin. For him, Mirish nurtured a bitter hate. Those who knew Mirish questioned his size—he was 6' 2" tall, acknowledged large in personal aspirations, but, secretly, was genuinely small in character and principles. He vividly remembered how he had struggled, as a young man, through a lesser known eastern university with a low "C" grade point average.

After his congressional defeat, and descent to a mediocre job as a professional lobbyist in Washington, Mirish remained a modest man; modest because he had much to be modest about. Since he was not a controversial person, his middle-of-the-road fence straddling in Congress had made him an appealing choice to the President. Mirish was humble; he was non-controversial; he was cautious; in fact, so cautious he always looked even when he didn't leap. In the President's view, Mirish was an eager team man who generated no adverse publicity, and who was no threat to the staff. Mangel Mirish was a natural as the new ubiquitous Secretary.

Although insiders might consider him modest and mediocre, Mangel Mirish had learned how to hate. Only an astute few on Capitol Hill recognized his unfulfilled ambitions and burning hate.

The assessment of the newest member of the Administration's "inner circle" had attracted the attention of New York's Senator Abraham Anselm. A confidential report disclosed that Mangel Mirish had a pathetic bank account, even poorer living standard, and a suffering family whose children would never be able to attend Ivy League schools. Anselm had uncovered Mirish's weakest points: Bitterness in failure, a raging hate, a longing for revenge.

Senator Anselm's somber face broke into a satisfied grin. Possibly, a larger cast of "kindred characters" might be molded into a behind-the-scenes force where he, Anselm, would direct a new playhouse in Washington.

◆   ◆   ◆

Congress had adjourned for the Easter Holiday, and the Senate Office Building lay cloaked in the misty night of a foggy autumn. The normally raucous senate chamber was dark and silent except for a dim light outlining the drawn curtains of one office.

The profile of the archaic stone office building pierced the murky gloom, and, through the swirling shrouds, its ghostly silhouette stood stark and abandoned. On this particular night, the senate building's ominous appearance would match Dracula's mausoleum in Transylvania.

Washington, D.C., was in bed; the night was pitch black with swirling mists of vapor slowing traffic to a crawl; brilliant avenues of blue and orange streetlights were now only narrow circular bands of light reflected back into their source.

A secret verbal invitation to a parley had summoned certain individuals to a conclave intentionally held in the wee hours. Abraham Anselm thought nothing of a clandestine meeting at an ungodly hour. As usual, his tormenting antagonist was Representative Charter Saladin who argued, "Except in wartime, all meetings must be able to pass the light of publicity."

Saladin fought not only members of the Senate, but his own House of Representatives. He admonished, repeatedly, that early-morning meetings were deceitful; that such meetings were sanctioned by an unethical minority of Congress, and that the planned results would bode no good for the American people. Charter, against the pleadings of his colleagues, openly proclaimed,

"Such 'trysts' in the night are always self-serving; Congress has benefited by acting like 'jackals slinking away from the public's ire'; further, guilty parties hold their selfish parleys in the middle of the night because they know the news media and the nation's watchdogs will be sleeping." That quote, alone, caused Abraham Anselm to loathe Charter Saladin like a crazed zealot.

Consequently, the discussion in Senator Anselm's office was no accident. Only the participants could benefit. Anselm knew that the majority of the American people, the "middle-class," would lose more freedoms,…while still footing the bills. The New Yorker didn't care.

Senator Abraham Lieberson Anselm would govern the agenda, and he had already listed the financial rewards. Now he had to sell the others.

The first specter to pass the night guard, and waft down the hallway and through the door was Senator Jacob Bergenfeldt of New Jersey. Then came the firm footsteps of solid leather shoes echoing down the corridor, and Marchen Judisch, Israel's Diplomat-at-Large, entered the office. Ten minutes later the slow, cautious footsteps of Massachusetts Senator Theo Dennahy paused outside the door. Dennahy was peering up and down the dark hall. Abraham Anselm opened the entryway and almost had to pull the reluctant Dennahy inside at 2:00 a.m.

"At least you're here, Theo," said Anselm. "We're expecting one more."

Dennahy was studying his cohort, Jacob Bergenfeldt, and was attempting to place the face of Marchen Judisch.

"Ah, yes. Ambassador Judisch of Israel. Correct?"

Marchen smiled, "We haven't been together since the time we flew down to the Bahamas, Senator Dennahy. It's good to see you again."

Theo Dennahy wasn't too sure. That flight had been in Judisch's airplane, and Theo had been a weeklong guest who appreciated the white sandy beaches, the pure emerald-green waters, fabulous cuisine, and all expenses paid,…with no questions asked. Dennahy kept such gratuities concealed for obvious political reasons. Although not adverse to unrestrained gifts, whether money or favors, Theo just didn't wish to be caught. But, he sat down, accepted a drink, and waited for the intriguing early-hour meeting.

The hushed offices of Senator Anselm grew noticeably noisy due to the nighttime silence when ears tune in to obscure sounds unnoticed in the daytime. A superb Grandfather Clock chimed twice with such rich bass notes that it resonated like the gong of a Buddhist Temple. Crisp autumn winds blew against the windows, and the panes flexed with muted creaks and pops. Whenever a guest shifted his position in his comfortable seat, a protesting groan echoed from each chair. Finally, a door slammed from far up the corridor. Someone was coming. The walk was confident, as if the person knew exactly where he was going. And—he did.

Secretary of Trade Mangel Mayer Mirish strode into the room. The other guests were dumbfounded. They knew Abraham Anselm was powerful, but none ever thought his sphere of influence extended to the President's cabinet. The tempo of the sleep-robbing meeting increased with the sudden interest. A drink was handed Secretary Mirish who gulped it appreciatively. Everyone had his glass refilled and sat back as Abraham Anselm cleared his throat.

"Gentlemen, we are here to decide whether or not we can put together an unobtrusive league of American businessmen accustomed to doing commerce in the nation from Capitol Hill. I may organize a core of tight-lipped men who have legislative experience; men who are familiar with the centers of influence that move Congress; men who want to assist certain world leaders so that we can maintain peace and protect the American public."

So far, Anselm had appealed to the patriotism of the visitors, and had stressed each man's importance to the league. After such an ego builder, this parley clique smiled in tandem. Anselm grew bolder.

"We might represent Arab nations, Palestinian territory, and certain Zionist groups. They are anxious to receive a 'Welcome Mat' that will give them an acceptable image...an enhanced image...in Washington."

Senator Dennahy spoke loudly, "Do you mean to do business with those damned Mid-East tyrants who surround Israel? Israel, our last resort over there?"

Secretary Mangel Mirish jumped to his feet, "You mean support those blood-sucking b————s who have kept our defensive Navy in the Mediterranean and Arabian Seas? Senator, that's un-American and traitorous."

Anselm quieted the group with his hands. His expression showed he had not finished. "Gentlemen, **it is <u>American</u>**. I said PEACE. Working quietly behind the scenes we can do more in a year than the Western powers have done the past decade. After all, they are leaders of their nations. We may disagree with them, but they also disagree with the United States. In no way do we adopt their methods or customs. It's the other way around: If they wish to have anyone assist them in removing their stigmata, then they will have to do what WE say. We will be responsible for promoting peace and bringing them to our table for a dialogue of common grounds."

Such a statement was idealistic, perhaps even noble, and the visitors only grumbled. Anselm had not been shouted down. The New Yorker said, "Gentlemen, if we accept this challenge, there is one major benefit that will accrue to every one of us."

Eyebrows raised, and heads cocked just a little. More than one mind was thinking, "Here it comes...the cost, the royal shaft, and the ruinous publicity when the Washington Press finds out. Trade idealism for disgrace?"

Anselm acted concerned. His chosen gang leaned forward from the edges of their chairs. They never dreamed what he would say next.

"Fellow 'Patriots', I have had forced on me...an actual fortune...which I have refused. However, several governments, several of the ruling class in the Mid-East have informed me that if we help them in their quest to receive assistance from the United States, every congressional and administration participant must be properly rewarded; it is the custom of their countries—to refuse would be a supreme insult—and the worsening of relations in that part of the world."

Senator Jacob Bergenfeldt leaned farther forward, a quizzical look on his face. "Abraham, just what in Hades is this 're-ward' we must accept by helping them?" Bergenfeldt quickly caught himself, "I mean if we help them?"

Abraham Anselm inwardly smiled. His confederate of 20 years had already joined him. Get a few more...and he could name his 'patriotic partners.'

"Men, over there they have vast sums of money from oil income; money from trade—export and import income; mining income from precious metals and industrial ores for building; gems, coal, and, so far, additional discoveries we know nothing about.

"They appreciate your abilities and earnest efforts so much that they have insisted there can be no arrangements unless we allow them to compensate us for our troubles.

"I have been sworn to secrecy. But, I have promised them that I would advise each and every participant that he will receive princely sums in such amounts that every man here tonight will be a multi-millionaire by the end of this year.

"The good faith of our Mid-East friends will be evident because each of you will have your own untraceable private account in a gold-backed bank in Zurich, or Grand Cayman Island, whichever you wish."

A dead silence was the response to Abraham Anselm's address. The heavy sighs and furrows etched on the brows of the visitors showed some deep thinking. Anselm could almost hear the brain-gears grinding.

He had appealed to the hidden morality and creed of every man: Idealism—the never-ending search for peace. Goodwill—that we are brothers-under-the-skin, and must work together for better world understanding. Personally-first, if the interests of the United States might be compromised, WE will name our terms, and the Mid-East collaborators will have to "go along." Second, they will pay us for our successful efforts. We don't have to take the money. We can give it to charity. After all, we do have an obligation to our constituents back home, and…the money…the money…. Hmmmmmmm, yes,—the money."

Abraham Anselm studied the faces and the body English of each guest. He walked softly among his visitors, refilling their glasses with double shots of alcohol to make them relax. It also made their true selves start to emerge. And Anselm missed nothing. He was reading them as if each man were a book.

In a soft recliner chair, Mangel Mirish was leaning back, his eyes closed. His memory brought back the years of public service and how little he had to show for it; how little he had been able to provide for his family. His mind threw thoughts like confetti in a stiff breeze.

"For the first time in my life, money. With money comes acquisitions. With money comes power. All my life, I've had very little. Now, by joining this league—an unlisted lobby—I'll have the power to do, the power to influence, the power to command.

"I can send my children to any school I choose. I can give my wife diamonds and furs. And all because of this money. In less than a year…I'll be a millionaire. And why not? I've worked hard. Who else deserves it more? Besides, no one need know. I'll play it cool. Anselm will know how. And with knowing…I'll have all that money."

Secretary Mangel Mirish of the President's Council had done an excellent job of rationalizing his greed. Money, . . lots of it, would become an easy substitute for honor and integrity. Also, it would give him the resource necessary to inflict vengeance for past injustices, real or imaginary.

The New York Senator had an impressive start recruiting the first member of his undercover league. Shaking the hand of Mangel Mirish, Abraham Anselm could parrot what politicians in smoke-filled back rooms had said for decades: HE IS OURS."

Tomorrow there would be jubilation in some Mid-Eastern countries.

◆   ◆   ◆

Jameson Cody Dittus snoozed in a webbed loungechair. Sunlight bounced like a halo off the beautiful rainbow aggregate buried in the surface of his back-yard patio. He was tanning; he was sleeping; he was relaxed. Secure in the knowledge that he would be at his Hidey-Hole Lodge for a long-deserved R & R vacation, Cody was unexpectedly jolted wide awake by the whistle from a turbine engine wailing overhead. He looked up, straight into the face of a helicopter pilot leaning out of the cockpit-blister and was disrespectfully thumbing his nose at Cody.

Cody laughed and thumbed his nose back at the hovering aviator. The flier was the same one who had helped "kidnap" Charter Saladin and Bergan Gruenspan to Hidey-Hole Lodge. The flier was shouting, "Where? Where?" But his voice was blown away in the windy maelstrom of the whirling copter blades. However, linguist Dittus effortlessly read his lips.

Cody ran to an adjacent gravel-covered stretch where a line of trees ringed a circular plot of ground. White pea-sized stones complemented the flowers and lush timberland; yet, Cody had designed his hideaway with such a contingency as this in mind. There had to be another exit from the lodge beside the lone dirt road coming in. A graveled helicopter pad was created, but its appearance masked its purpose. The circle of trees forced a copter pilot to be careful setting his whirlybird down. Moreover, tread marks are obvious when pressed into a cultivated lawn. Yet, any tire depressions left in pea-gravel can easily be raked smooth again.

Cody pointed to that circle, and the whirlybird settled neatly on the circle's exact center. With his fingers clenched and his thumb extended, the helmeted flier placed his thumb in his mouth, tipped his head back, and imitated a thirsty airman guzzling a beer. Cody got the picture and rolled out his portable bar. The day was warm for even an Indian summer, so Cody blended a tall glass of "Old Blockbuster and Tonic" and walked toward the pilot,…who was walking toward Cody with a small string-tied package.

"What is that?" asked Dittus.

"You get it when I get that cold drink…and a soft chair."

"Be my guest," said Cody. The pilot grabbed the drink and added,

"I'll make myself comfortable. There may be an answer required—yes, it is from Oz. I was told to get it to you fast."

Cody Dittus sat down at the table and carefully examined the sealed envelope. Then, lifting his pant leg, he withdrew a wicked dirk from its sheath, and slit the strings and wrapping as if they were gossamer.

"My God." thought the military pilot, "This guy's ready for combat even when he's relaxing. I wouldn't face him in a dark alley with a gun in each hand."

An eerie silence fell over the patio. An occasional westerly zephyr caused forest leaves to whisper to the clandestine agents below. The whirlybird pilot said nothing. Only the clink of ice cubes in his glass disturbed the quiet. And from the background came the sound of hot metal cooling as the stilled helicopter turbine protested with a "tink, tink, tink." Halfway through the communique Cody gasped and fell back in his loungechair as he reread the message. Oz had surprised him again. He had expected information on Marchen Judish, the Israeli Diplomat. The surveillance team of Oz agents had lost Marchen in spite of watching him 24 hours a day. There was no evidence that Judisch was in the country. Although he was **not** seen leaving the U.S.A., he had dropped from sight. As Cody read on, memories squeezed out all thought of Mark Judish.

Cody Dittus had never learned why Danvier Dyan had so ruthlessly tracked him down and mistreated him so viciously; he never understood why Dyan had obviously decreed an agonizing "Death to Dittus" by torture. Now the stunning facts were spilling out of the letter from Oz.

At one time, the highly specialized Office of Strategic Services had installed the first American-made computers. The machines were slow; primitive with their fragile radio vacuum tubes; and, the heat generated required a large air conditioned room. Nevertheless, the OSS organized the first cross-reference on each agent's career, and had printed the original history of every known enemy agent, or suspect, in the world.

Now, with fantastic minuscule-voltage transistors, home offices use bread-box size computers which store data, cross-check supposed unrelated items from country to country, and focus on the likely agent involved. Unbelievably, the newest machines can assimilate up to a hundred million bites of information every second.

History records America's OSS was phased out after World War II, but the unknown, highly secretive Oz remained, . . incredibly effective to this day. And, the missive recounted items about the Cody Dittus of 12 years ago.

In the city of Dar-el-Beida, a port in Morocco on the Northwest coast, a young agent, Cody Dittus, survived his first fight-to-the-death and dispatched one of the cruelest men on the face of the earth. The would-be assassin was Druid Kahn Membossie. His headquarters—hangouts—were the bars and brothels of Casablanca. Dar-el-Beida was the Arabic name for Casablanca.

Cody was trailing a Nazi sympathizer, reputedly a trainee with remnants of Heinrich Himmler's murderous Gestapo of 1945. Druid Membossie had absolutely no conscience nor remorse over killing or torturing...be it men, women, even children.

On a moonlit night, Cody Dittus found himself in a littered dead-end street in the brothel district of Casablanca. Realizing he had taken a wrong turn, he retraced his steps to locate a main avenue through the neighborhood. Cody found himself blocked by a bearded man in white Arab clothes. He would have walked around the Arab because he intended no harm to anyone and was only learning the city and its more unsavory haunts.

But, there was no mistaking the foot-long blade, its keen edge turned up, ready to slit Cody from navel to Adam's Apple. He spoke Arabic, emphasizing to his accoster that he sought peace. The Arab closed quickly upon agent Cody Dittus who frantically spoke English, then switched to another Arab dialect...all to no avail. He looked into the eyes of the Arab—the malice and evil in that face were unforgettable. The Moroccan's gleaming blade was inches from Cody's stomach. Cody jumped back and sideways in the one moment left to protect himself and retaliate.

Reaching between his shoulder blades, Dittus yanked out a specially-made steel dirk with a sticky adhesive-tape hilt to prevent it from slipping out of his hand. Cody made two lightning-fast moves: His left hand chopped downward across the Arab's wrist as the assailant thrust his blade at Cody; his right hand slashed down on the mugger's face with the speed of a professionally trained killer.

There were three equal responses by the would-be assassin: The Arab had badly underestimated his adversary—the swift counter-attack was unexpected; the Judo blow across the knife-brandishing arm shattered his wrist bones, paralyzing his fingers. The suffering white-robed attacker now retched with excruciating pain; then, Cody's dagger severed to the bone every bit of tissue and skin from the Arab's temple to his jawbone, and finished slashing his upper chest down to his waist. In a swirling pool of blood, Cody's accoster, ravaged from head to sash, went from pain, to shock, into unconsciousness. He dropped like a sack of fallen grain.

As the earth of the street soaked up the blood, Cody Dittus realized his predicament. He was a white man, a Caucasian, . . actually termed an "infidel" by Moslems, . . whose religion is Islam. A white man who does not believe Islam does not believe in religion. Infidels are hated.

Also, Cody was in one of the worst ghetto areas of the city. Life is least precious here. And, worse, he was an infidel holding a knife, standing beside the body of an Arab in a dark dead-end alley. There would be no time for explanation. Cody's life was minutes away from termination.

He almost ripped his shoes off his feet and ran like an olympic sprinter in the direction from which he came. A smart move on Cody's part. His running feet hardly made a sound on the packed earth.

Only later did Cody Dittus learn from the American Embassy, that a relative of the Iraqi leader, Sadah Diyarbar, had been critically wounded in an assault by Moroccan rebels. Relations between both countries were strained until Morocco assured Diyarbar that the government deplored such aggressive acts and apologized profusely. Moroccan troops launched a brutal search of Dar-El-Beida, Casablanca. The problem was too many suspects who could have murdered an Iraqi named Druid Membossie.

Membossie, incredibly, survived, but only after surgeons stitched and sutured several hundred times to seal his wounds. The knife fight left Membossie's evil face disfigured for life. That incident inspired his nickname, "Kahn the Scarred."

The long-forgotten items merged perfectly and revealed the answer Cody Dittus had asked himself and Oz Directors for a year: Druid Kahn Membossie was tied in—related?—to the tyrant, Sultan Sadah Diyarbar, of Iraq. Further, Jabal and Mohabe Hejira had confirmed Danvier Dyan had bowed and kissed the hand of President Sadah Diyarbar.

Then, Cody finished the last sentence of the communique. "Kahn Membossie is next in line to ascend the Iraqi presidency. Diyarbar's brother is not in favor. In fact, he is lucky to be alive…at this moment. Be advised that the sanctioned one is Diyarbar's <u>cousin</u>, Druid Membossie."

That explained another Mid-East tenet: Why had Cody Dittus been pursued, captured, and tortured? Because an enemy of one is an enemy of all.

Cody was unsettled by the thought. He grabbed a bottle of brandy. It was time for a stiff drink.

14

Sources and Secrets

Leith Ohmstead listened carefully to Cody Dittus. Leith had just driven his auto under the weather-protective carport behind the back of the log lodge. Cody never asked him what he had done this day—nor any other day—both men readily conceding that each never know the other's itinerary; that they be well informed of their respective duties <u>only</u> when working together. That was the prime dictum of **Oz**. In the event of capture, no agent should have knowledge of another agent's assignment or whereabouts.

Cody Dittus' conclusions made sense to Ohmstead. Cody said,

"You are reading Oz's communique to me because you were there,…in fact, you saved my butt when Dyan and his cutthroats were giving me 'the heavy once-over'. I'd be dead had you not come along. So, here's my hypothesis:

"I was discombobulated when the American Embassy informed somebody about Druid Membossie. That somebody was probably an Oz contact, so, by that time, I had been whisked out of Morocco before the U.S. might be embarrassed. Those Mid-East Arabs know ways to make a man talk we've never thought of. Knowing the mind-set of the Iraqis, here's what I surmise has happened.

"Someone from the U.S.A. leaked information to specific parties in Lebanon. I believe, and Charter Saladin also believes, that one of the House or Senate committees has a turncoat supplying vital data about American agents throughout the Mid-Eastern countries…at least those countries paying him or them. Anyway, how Membossie lived I'll never know. They would have had to pump him full of blood. I sliced Druid wide open like a watermelon. I had no choice. If I had missed, he'd have disemboweled me.

"So Druid Membossie lives. Yet, why was no one over there wondering what he was doing in Morocco? It follows he must have been transported back to Baghdad and his cousin, Diyarbar. Back then, both revolutionists, especially Sadah Diyarbar, were plotting the overthrow of the Iraqi government. Less than a decade later, Diyarbar succeeds. It takes 'Kahn, the Scarred' several years to regain his full health, so Diyarbar makes him bide his time. Arabs have long memories and nearly the patience of the Chinese.

"Somehow Sadah Diyarbar enlists a terrorist named Marchen Judisch, a refugee Jew from Germany. Judisch works his way into the Israeli Diplomatic Corps, masquerading as an agent of the Mossad. Mossad feeds him secret data, and Judisch, actually a double agent, funnels it to Iraq's Diyarbar.

"Diyarbar hires Danvier Dyan as a spy and terrorist. Dyan swears allegiance to President Diyarbar by kissing his hand and the Sultan's ring; and,…so does Mark Judisch. Both men, ever since, have pledged their loyalty by kissing their leader's hand every time they meet. Jabal and Hejira have proof positive from photos taken at one of their meets. Okay?"

Leith Ohmstead held up his hand, interrupting Cody,

"Then, tell me, what happened between Dyan and you?"

"That's the easy part, Leith. Cousin Membossie learns from their American spy exactly **who** is the traveling American who disfigured him for life…an American agent. Druid Kahn begs his leader, Sadah Diyarbar, to find where Dittus will be next. O.K., Leith, you're ready to ask HOW?

"Let me ask you—does Mark Judisch keep in touch with the Mossad? Does he have the confidence of some high official…like General Moschi Rubinstern in Tel Aviv? Is it possible the Mossad got conned by their roving diplomat, Judisch? While the Mossad is speculating about agents of the CIA or our Army and Naval Intelligence, Dyan disappears from Israel, . . and reappears as an unidentified courier and a skilled pilot for the Israeli Embassy in Washington, D.C. Remember: An enemy of one is an enemy of all.

"Now, Leith, try this one on for size: Our American turncoat gets another bonus check by letting President Diyarbar know exactly where I'm based, passing as an exporter. The trace is on and—BINGO—Dyan has me.

"Leith, you bring me safely to the good ole U.S.A. to convalesce, and begin your investigation of a 'strongly suspected leak' in Washington. So, warnings are issued by probable turncoats in Tel Aviv or Jerusalem—and I'm betting there's a leak even inside Israel's Mossad—that the whole apple cart may be spilling in Washington. Those threatened with exposure are members of the Israeli Embassy in Washington, the Baghdad strongman, Diyarbar himself, even 'peace loving Syrian soldiers' in Beirut. All have one simultaneous fear: The door may be slammed shut in their faces on secret information from Washington cliques.

"Whoever finds the traitor in Washington, collapses the house of cards.

"That's why you were jumped in your Washington hotel room. You were getting too close and this gang of cutthroats knows only one way to keep Leith Ohmstead silent. Eliminate him. That's when you took your high dive."

"Ya'but, why me, Cody? You and your comrades, Jabal and Mohabe, were the ones unmasking the culprits in the deadly intrigue. I should think they'd do everything to kill you."

"Leith, you're in the wrong hemisphere with the wrong person."

"How's that again? Cody, had any of those cutthroats found you here at this lodge, you'd be a dead man."

"That's right. Yet, think on this. I had escaped. They didn't know where I could be found. That relegated me to being target #2. After all, I hadn't broken or exposed any part of the spy ring over there. Certainly not those in positions where they exercised treason. So far, they're still operating. However, their key man, the Washington informant, got nervous. He learned we were working the same side of the street…but, it was Leith Ohmstead who was right here.

"What I'm telling you, Leith, is that such information, alone, made you target #1. You were getting too close to the source—the one thing Diyarbar and the terrorists could not afford to lose. That's the prime reason for the high dive off the balcony of the Stouffer-Mayflower Hotel. Another rationale is that when our traitor informed them about me, Cody Dittus, they deduced who the other agent must be, the one who got me away from Danvier Dyan. Please recall that someone told our enemies we were working the same side of the street. That would be enough to cause an attempt on your life.

"Someone in, or having contact with, Oz, the CIA, FBI, Military Intelligence, and even The White House, had to be dumbfounded that you survived your fall. Otherwise, how could 'Andre the Specialist', a mugged and fingerprinted international hit man, know where and when to sneak into Washington General Hospital to deliver the coup de gras? How do you like my thinking so far, Mr. Ohmstead?"

Leith nodded very slowly, absorbing the proffered facts and logic of his astute friend, Cody.

"You make sense, Mr. Dittus. We're close to the source, but there's too many suspects. No Congressional or White House aide could direct all that scenario. Our job is all the more difficult because I refer to suspects in high places. Don't flinch at my remarks, Cody. There has to be more than one traitor to maneuver among so many nationalities.

"We're getting there, Cody, but I fear it's a long road ahead."

◆   ◆   ◆

"It is I," spoke a muffled Mid-East accented voice through the phone. Agents Ohmstead and Dittus were finishing a hectic conclave at Oz Headquarters in Washington, D.C.

During the secluded meeting, three of the top directors of Oz had critiqued the exceptional activities of both agents during the past two years. Before the clandestine conference was adjourned, Leith and Cody had been ordered to turn in their Smith & Wesson 9-millimeter automatics. Wonder and concern over such a directive showed on the agents' faces, but they obeyed. Yet, instinctively, both men placed their hands close to their favorite killing knife—located between their shoulder blades, or strapped on the calf of a leg. The Oz supervisors recognized that the agents complied with the order…but that certainly did **not** include their complete trust.

So there would be no misunderstanding, the directors handed Leith and Cody a special package wrapped in oil-paper. Properly stored, the airtight contents would have lasted centuries in perfect condition. Both men carefully cut open their respective package and each found a new S & W automatic.

Ohmstead and Dittus were firearms experts. The caliber had changed.

"What is this cannon?" asked Leith Ohmstead. "This is no 9-millimeter." Cody Dittus nodded in agreement.[1]

"Gentlemen, this is Smith and Wesson's newest super handgun, a 10.0 caliber whose jacketed bullet will penetrate steel.

"The gun's innovative cartridge is immensely powerful, and the next time you practice on the firing range you'll be amazed how the gas-exhaust mechanism has been redesigned to substantially reduce recoil. Accuracy is increased without damaging or fracturing a user's wrist. The other smaller package contains 40 boxes of armor piercing and hollow-nose cartridges. The armor piercing will penetrate anything you wish…except a tank.

"The hollow-nose bullet has a new interior-braced design which will flatten to a half-dollar size blob of lead. Tissue damage is unbelievable. Exiting a human body, it will leave a hole the size of a basketball or larger. Anywhere the bullet hits, it should put even a seven-foot giant down."

"What about a silencer?" asked Leith and Cody with one voice.

---

1.   [Initially, S & W's 10-millimeter automatic had problems which necessitated recall. Corrected, it is a phenomenal weapon].

"It's there. Wrapped with the gun. The new silencer snaps on and off like an air-hose chuck. No more time wasted to screw it onto barrel threads. Smith & Wesson have broken new ground."

Cody Dittus opened the ammunition package and quickly attached the silencer on the large-bore automatic pistol. He practiced sighting the hand cannon on each director one by one. The Oz administrators grew restive. Leith Ohmstead kept his head down, but his body was shaking with mirth.

The Head Director, Jacksonian Tubb, swore and said,

"You think you're damned funny, don't you Dittus?"

Cody Dittus waxed eloquent with poetry,

> "Fie, Fi, Fo Fem,
> I'll drink the blood of athe Ozie-men.
> I see them scream, I can hear their cries
> As I shoot them right between their eyes."

It would be difficult to imagine what tangent the meeting might have taken if not for the interruptive phone call. A sinister-eyed director handed the telephone to Leith Ohmstead.

"It is I," spoke a voice with an Eastern enunciation; however, the tone was decidedly British.

"Keep talking, I can't place who 'I' is?" answered Ohmstead.

"We must get together, Master, you have some Mossad visitors."

The British inflection was unmistakable. "My God. JABAL? Where in Hades are you?"

The highly secret conclave ended. There appeared to be little enthusiasm to continue further talk. Director Tubb said it all—

"Get your assassin asses away from us. You've been members of the 'Dalton-James Gang' too long. By the way, you're getting a hefty pay raise—in anticipation of your finding the traitors in our government. Keep us posted,…and we'll send you every tidbit we know. Now, get back to your Hidey-Hole Lodge and get drunk…or something.

"Yeah, don't look so funny at us. We know all about your lodge in that Virginia paradise. You and your other crazy agent-friends sure put the kibosh on some highly respected Washington businessmen. We had a hell of a time quashing idiotic stories of an unexploded atomic bomb. But, your scheme worked. You own an exclusive tract of land which Washington bigwigs avoid like the plague. If you two weren't so good, I'd shoot you myself. Now, get your 'assasses' out of here."

Thus ended another harmonious venture between management and labor.

The airport was the same one used by Charter Saladin and Bergan Gruenspan. The hour was 0500, pitch black, when Jabal Thej-a-kel and his companions walked toward the dim, fog-shrouded lamp suspended above a hangar door. Always cautious, the reception committee of three stood under the light, their hands inside their coats…caressing their 10-millimeters.

Out of the mist Jabal appeared, then held his hand out and beckoned two faint ghosts to come forward. When the obscure light illuminated the faces, Leith Ohmstead and Cody Dittus gasped. They were unprepared.

Standing before them were the unforgettable Israeli Mossad's General Moschi Rubinstern, and his Chief of Staff, Colonel Marseille LeBourget.

Officers' Rubinstern and LeBourget had no questions about the meeting in pitch blackness, well before the crack of dawn. The handclasps were sincere, but brief. Ohmstead punched Dittus with his elbow, and Cody gave the "go sign" to the pilot. The next instant the pilot was gone. Moments later, from the depths of the cavern of night, came the whine of a jet turbine. The helicopter was warming up, its blades whirling and whistling faster and faster. Leith Ohmstead beckoned with his palm, "this way" and stepped into the gloom. Automatically, Leith and Cody, the General and Colonel, bent over as they approached the whirlybird. Copter blades were not designed as guillotines, unless you ignored them…particularly if you were tall.

The foursome climbed the narrow steps leading inside the copter and were barely seated before the craft took off into the mist. The General and Colonel leaned forward studying the pilot. He paid no attention to the spacious windows, but kept his eyes glued to the cockpit panel. He was flying like a blind man, trusting his instruments to guide him through nothingness to a safe destination. Occasionally, the craft flew past a dim yardlight, barely below them. What an introduction to America—and its technology.

The pilot, checking his dashboard clock, turned his head toward the companionway and motioned to Leith. Ohmstead took a small remote radio from his pocket, pulled up the aerial, and pressed a button. Immediately, a small green light flickered on and off. At the same time, the pilot yelled,

"I got it." And he touched his thumb and forefinger in the sign of the big "O.K." and he expressed the signal several times to Ohmstead. The pilot had a cockpit instrument that was also flashing, its needles slowly merging onto one spot. All sense of forward motion ceased, and the pilot again yelled, "Seatbelts, everybody. Going down—landing in thirty seconds."

Suddenly, landing lights flickered on from the ground. Their brilliance lit up the cockpit and fuselage. The lights reflected back from the pitch blackness and early morning fog. But, the pilot was looking at nothing from his side window. He intently studied the instrument panel until trees and a meadow came into view. Slowly descending, the Oz pilot, still keeping the beacon needles centered on the special instrument, let out a war whoop. The helicopter landing pad lay directly below. With a slight bump the wheels touched down and the motor whined down to a fast idle. Dim interior lights came on, and the four passengers disembarked. Leith and Cody gave a nod of thanks and waved goodbye to the skilled pilot. Moments later the turbine whine increased, the rotor blades swished around with increasing speed, and the copter lurched upward and disappeared into the black hole of a foggy night.

As the whirlybird's sound faded into the distance, Leith punched the button on his remote.

"That turns off the radio beacon. Now, let's just see where we are."

Ohmstead punched another button on his remote and backyard lights blinked on. Another button turned on lights within the log cabin. All the while, General Rubinstern and Colonel LeBourget kept turning in circles, their mouths hanging open as they examined the luxuriant greenery and rustic lodge.

Cody Dittus, staring at Ohmstead, said, "When did you install a helipad landing system, remote backyard lights, and radio-activated interior cabin lights? Better yet, how? We haven't been home during daylight."

Leith quipped, "The local Russian Embassy is remodeling, so I bought their used-parts and had their KGB technicians install the system while we were at Oz headquarters. I got a terrific deal—a lifetime guarantee that won't terminate unless the current is turned on."

Dittus placed his hands on his hips and sluggishly turned, glaring at Ohmstead. General Rubinstern and Col. LeBourget were chuckling.

Leith continued, "Naw, Cody, I lied. Actually, they are usable parts from the Hashimoto Bomb Works of Tokyo…real cheap after the explosion.

"Aw, don't look at me that way. I won't lie to you, Cody. I scrounged the parts off your souped-up Pontiac. Now, when you start your engine, the coffee maker comes on, although I'm still working on getting rid of the gasoline taste. Oh, also, your engine now operates on only three cylinders."

Cody, disgusted, asked, "You're not going to tell me, are you?"

Leith answered, "No, Cody, I'm not."

Cody, walking into the house, shouted, "If you'd said so in the first place, I wouldn't have had to suffer listening to all that bull hockey."

The early morning fog dissipated, and as the sun peeked through the misty hills, the foursome sipped coffee and relaxed. General Rubinstern and Col. LeBourget fell asleep in their lounge chairs on the patio. Both men were seasoned veterans of combat. They embraced needed sleep whenever and wherever they could. The morning was quiet except for the beautiful singing of the woodland birds. The sun shone on a panorama of green that was a balm to the weary men. Rubinstern and LeBourget dozed peacefully...until they heard the slap of 8 x 10 photographs being laid on the table. Then they heard the stern voice of Leith Ohmstead interrupt the serene stillness.

"If these photos don't wake you up, nothing will. I believe the pictures will explain a lot of the headaches you've been having in Israel."

General Rubinstern sighed, stretched the sleep out of his system, and gazed bleary, unfocused eyes on the photographs. He stopped in the middle of a yawn, gasped, and exclaimed,

"Great God. That can't be **he**...kissing the hand of Diyarbar?"

Colonel LeBourget jumped up and, over the General's shoulder, studied the glossy prints. Abruptly, his eyes opened wide, his jaw muscles twitching. Both Israelis turned to one another with sick expressions on their faces.

LeBourget whispered, "Danvier Dyan. Kissing the hand of Sadah Diyarbar. Unbelievable. And who's this chap with the scarred face? He looks familiar."

Cody Dittus answered, "That's Druid Kahn Membossie. I met him argumentatively in Dar-el-Beida. Interesting ancestry."

"How's that, Mr. Dittus?"

"His last name bespeaks African; his olive-skin says Arab; his Christian and middle names are European...or Eurasian."

Marseille LeBourget said, "You mentioned you met him argumentatively? In Casablanca? You had the wrong man, Cody. Membossie's no worry to anyone now. Been dead for a number of years, probably in a revolutionary coup."

Cody replied, I see you know your geography...and history, including Arab-European names of many towns. Dar-el-Beida is Casablanca."

The colonel responded, "We had better know. Israel is an awfully small spot on the huge African Continent."

Just then Leith Ohmstead snickered, "Tell me, gentlemen, how do you account for Kahn Membossie being in the pictures with Diyarbar and Dyan? That dead man looks pretty lively to me."

General Rubinstern interjected, "It's obvious. A mistaken identification. He's dead—the man in this picture is a lot thinner and has a beard. Druid Membossie, as I recall, was clean shaven."

Leith looked at his partner. "You're on stage, Cody. Start talking."

"General, Colonel, the man whose picture you are looking at **is** Membossie...but, a 30-pounds-lighter Membossie. I'm the man who placed him on a permanent weight loss; prompted him to grow a beard; and, put him out to pasture for several years. His beard obscures his scar. So, look closer."

LeBourget squinted at one of the enlarged photos. "Yes, I can see that awful scar through all that facial hair. You sure that's Membossie?"

Cody Dittus filled his cup with fresh coffee. Then he told the story of his deadly fight with "Kahn the Scarred" in Morocco; that The Mossad filed him and his sketched picture in their Rogue's Gallery after his altercation with Cody Dittus.

"He's the only man who ever survived my attack. He should have died."

The general, puzzled, said, "I don't get it. He hasn't shown up anywhere for several years...which would confirm his death. Yet, you say he survived your lethal knife wounds, including his throat you slit?"

"Exactly. Somehow, somewhere, medical attention was fast. I know they had to pump gallons—I mean gallons of blood through him until they sewed him up. That's why he took years to convalesce. We've been told he lost a hundred pounds, suffered hepatitis from some infected blood, and has regained only seventy pounds of his former self."

Rubinstern asked, "Where did you get that information?"

"From Oz, General."

"OH. Har-umph. That's good enough for us...right, colonel?"

Marseille LeBourget chuckled, "The Mossad doesn't know where we are, we're in an undisclosed hideaway, guests of Oz and two of their best assassins; and, you ask me if I agree? Believe me, General, anything Oz says is good enough for me, you, and us."

"Har-umph. Quite."

Cody Dittus rummaged through the kitchen—perhaps ransacked is a better word—and fried, poached, and baked a French breakfast replete with wine, French pastry dessert, and after-breakfast coffee royale.

General Rubinstern patted his stomach. A month of this and I'd top 300 pounds."

"Yes" said the colonel. "And when we get back to Tel Aviv, our army cook will take it off just as fast. General, why don't you transfer him to the tank corps?"

"Because he's already destroyed some of our best tanks—crashes into them—and even drove through the women's barracks when the occupants were bathing."

LeBourget said, "I'll bet that was a terrible shock for them."

Rubinstern replied, "Oh, I don't know. The assembled troops said it was the most enjoyable base parade they'd ever attended."

After the laughter calmed down, Moschi Rubinstern grew serious.

"Tell me, Leith, are you absolutely sure that the man who attempted to kill you, while you were in Washington General Hospital, was the international terrorist, 'Andre The Specialist'?"

"Definitely. We traced his true identity through Interpol. Fingerprints and mug shots were confirmed by Oz. We knew something was fishy when the ID in his wallet showed him to be a Federal Aviation Authority licensed aircraft mechanic in their employ. He operated under the pseudonym of Cash Delway. He died horribly...getting what he intended to give."

The general and colonel merely looked at one another.

LeBourget asked, "How and why in the world was he here? In the U.S.?"

Leith said, "Colonel, he was actually employed by Danvier Dyan, your Assistant Diplomat-at-Large. Delway took good care of the King Air 350 owned by your Israeli Diplomat, Marchen Judisch. Oz had already briefed both of you that it is Judisch and Dyan who fly important American congressional leaders into Lebanon and Baghdad, Iraq."

Rubinstern mused a moment, then turned to the Oz agents. "We'll keep a close eye on Marchen Judisch here. That way, you...WE...will recognize his contacts and shadow him wherever he goes. We can use him very effectively...until he catches on. Then we'll recall him. Don't look alarmed. We are The Mossad, and Judisch knows there's no place to run. Without our approval, he would be dead the moment he tries to cross the African coast."

Cody Dittus asked, "And what about Danvier Dyan? Am I to get the opportunity to even the score with him?"

"In a way, Cody. I'm willing to let you be the instrument of his destruction. God knows you have the right. However, his fate will be even more horrible than at your hands. And you'll do it politically?"

"POLITICALLY?"

"You will plant the seed. Supposed military operations on the Iraqi border by Israel. We will make Sadah Diyarbar panic...and rush his troops toward the border intending to jump into hostile territory so as to defend himself. The United States and NATO Allies will howl 'bloody murder' and the news media will have a field day.

"Iraqi photo reconnaissance aircraft will take pictures…showing nothing. There will be no Israeli Army at Diyarbar's door. We, of course, will know nothing of a planned invasion. In the eyes of Arabs, Sadah Diyarbar will look like a fool. He will suffer loss of support and loss of respect. Sultan Diyarbar could not stand such shame and loss of face. He would blame Danvier Dyan for being a dupe and a traitor.

"I believe you can count on Dyan dying slowly and quite painfully. Would that suit you, Cody?"

Dittus looked at Ohmstead, who returned his cunning stare. Cody was remembering that terrible night in that upper room with the cruel guards, the biting bugs, and the ready instruments of torture. He nodded at Leith.

Both men were thinking the same: Colonel Dyan would experience the ghastly torment meant for Cody Dittus, who had escaped through a tiny window only by enduring the agony of scraping and ripping flesh off his nude body.

There would be no small window and sawed bars for Danvier Dyan.

15

Betrayal for Cash

House Speaker Holcombe Broderick sat exhausted in his ornamental patio chair. This time, even the beauty of the green pristine garden could not soothe and restore the crippling emotions that drained his soul. The cool of an Indian Summer did not invigorate his body as it usually did.

"You're getting old, Holcombe. After 25 years it may be time to `pack it in'. For the first time I've ever known, the in-fighting, the shouted charges and frenzied countercharges on the chamber floor caused such chaos it even shocked the visitors in the gallery. I almost lost control today."

His nodding head jerked upright in surprise as his antique Grandfather Clock chimed 3:00 a.m. through the open windows. Holcombe had been up countless times, unable to sleep. He paced; he strolled through the house; then, alarmed his housekeeper who ran to the kitchen when she heard pans banging on the stove.

"OHhhhh, MISTER BRODERICK! What in the world are you doing at this hour? You are cooking?"

"Relax, Sarah. I couldn't sleep. I'm making several cups of hot milk."

"Here now, Mr. Speaker. You go sit in your favorite garden spot and I'll bring you a pot of hot chocolate. You must get your rest, Sir."

Broderick did as she ordered. What would he do without Sarah? She babied him…for the past 15 years…and he loved every minute of the attention.

On the patio, Holcombe grew pensive. "Let's see, Holcombe, how long has Abigail been dead? Yes, over 15 years. She always thought of you. In fact, Abigail hired Sarah only months before she passed away. Even from her wheelchair, she knew…she knew better than anyone, her time was near. So, she left confidential instructions with Sarah about me. Funny, to this day Sarah won't discuss anything Abigail said to her."

Then Holcombe chuckled. "Sarah always replies the same way to my questions about my wife: `Miss Abigail told me to tell you it was none o' your business.' And that still goes, Mr. Speaker!"

Broderick gave a deep, longing sigh and whispered, "Oh, Abigail, my darling. How I miss you. Oh, how I need you and your wise counsel now."

Suddenly, his reverie was interrupted by the smell and the steamy warmth of hot chocolate thrust beneath his face. Sarah missed nothing. The cup was filled with hot milk chocolate, and on the patio table sat a small silver urn holding more chocolate, heated by candles burning beneath the vessel.

"Sarah, you spoil me, you know. I may even raise your salary."

"I'm doing exactly what Miss Abigail would do. Goodnight." And with a kindly smile, Sarah turned and disappeared into the night.

Holcombe Broderick said nothing. The lump in his throat was too large.

There had been a bill. A defense bill, setting aside necessary millions for a naval fleet and air force assault groups, was established to provide a protective umbrella near Israel because certain Mid-East nations were continually threatening aggression. Passage of the bill was a foregone conclusion. True, it was an emergency measure, but the saber-rattling in that troubled region had reached epidemic proportions. The President endorsed the bill; Cabinet and administration officials who worked closely with Congress wanted it; therefore, the usual vocal outbursts were expected from various members of the Senate and House. Before a vote could be taken, vehement objections came from the powerful senator, Abraham Anselm. Jacob Bergenfeldt of New Jersey followed. Their argument lay in compounding the budget deficit. Many senators were suddenly unsure of their ground—and of their constituents back home.

But, in the House, the consternation brought the proceedings to a halt. Because, unexpectedly, a powerful voice rose: A voice that, until now, had never made waves; a voice normally against conflict and trouble-making; from one who had never accomplished much, if anything, during his tenure in Congress. He only asked Speaker Holcombe Broderick for a few minutes at the lectern. His position in the President's Cabinet almost commanded Broderick to consent.

Mangel Mayer Mirish, Secretary of Protocol and Trade, made a dramatic, impassioned plea against excessive spending, against boondoggle extravagances by the military and its Pentagon war mongers. He insisted that Europe might threaten to let the United States stand alone. The acrimonious buzz among all the House members disturbed Holcombe Broderick.

Suddenly, a crowd of congressmen shouted to be heard; the first representative at the lectern began shouting that Iraq and Iran were dangerous; that it was imperative for us, as leaders of the free world, to act. Another congressman shouted,

"He's right. We must act now. To vacillate by not making a show of force now could result in outright war."

But, that congressman was shouted down. Others bellowed from the House floor, "It's the Jews of Israel trying to drag us into their dilemma; trying to get us to fight their wars!"

The next instant tempers flared, and fistfights threatened. The noisy clamor disintegrated into shouting matches. The din swelled into a roar; the roar almost escalated into a riotous argument. Speaker Holcombe Broderick, astounded, was smashing his gavel so hard on the Speaker's stand that the handle broke in two. The hammer flew through the air somewhere into the unruly mob. Never in 25 years could Broderick believe what he was seeing. And the culprit was standing on the House podium observing his handiwork. Speaker Broderick was an old campaigner. He knew when he had been set up. Too many House members responded to the plea. Effectively done beyond a possible recall, Holcombe realized the move had succeeded boldly. The French Assembly started it long ago, and realistically calls it a "fait accompli."

Holcombe Broderick, furious, left his House Speaker's seat and dashed toward the podium. There was going to be a quick understanding with the culprit, Mangel Mirish. The Secretary had crossed the boundary of ethics.

Holcombe arrived at a deserted podium. Nor was anyone nearby...only the cries and curses of excited congressmen...including those who kept the awesome disruption going.

Broderick frantically looked for Mangel Mirish. He was gone.

The distraught Speaker pushed the button repeatedly. The button summoned the Sergeant at Arms and his pageboys. Broderick also buzzed the Security Guards. His repetitious signals brought an immediate response. Over the raucous bedlam he instructed the Sergeant at Arms and the security people to swing open all chamber doors and "herd the cattle out!" It didn't take the assembly long to figure that today's session was closed and that the motion to vote had been suspended. The following day it was tabled.

In the Senate, the "fait accompli" transpired in a similar fashion. Tragically, the new members of the "PATRIOTS' LEAGUE" believed they were helping America. Even Theo Dennahy of Massachusetts justified the action as a necessary one which could not hurt America. The Senate controlled itself better than the House, but then there were only 100 senators in chamber versus a House numbering approximately 500. And the House took its lead from the Senate because the bill on military expenditures never came to a vote. An alternate motion was made and, after haggling, it carried. That motion tabled the bill...indefinitely.

The Israeli Ambassador-at-Large, the ex-German, Marchen Judisch, had called in his IOU's. His argument to learned members of both houses was that Israel could not afford to antagonize the Arab nations at this particular time. Israel would appreciate American protection, but just not at this particular moment.

Marchen Judisch was most effective. His opinions, and his position in the Israeli delegation, carried great weight. Senators and Representatives both decided to go slowly.

Abraham Anselm rubbed his hands with glee. The way was now cleared for clandestine loading of arms and munitions on certain ships docking at Eastern Seaboard ports. The booty for delivery to Sultan Sadah Diyarbar would run into the millions. Another term of office and he could "retire" a multi-multi millionaire—along with other members of the PATRIOTS LEAGUE.

Marchen Judisch, resting comfortably at the Embassy after a week's work "advising" Congress, would profit immeasurably. He had little fear of disclosure to the press or Secret Service. He was a diplomat living on Israeli soil in their Washington Embassy; it was also politically expedient for any member of Congress to keep mute about his special connections with Israel. Yet, unknown to Judisch was the existence of a shadow. Day and night the Embassy was under surveillance by tapped telephones, parabolic reflectors that could pick up a normal conversation from a mile away, and by rolls of super-sensitive camera film which could equally record faces a mile away…faces lit only by the light from one feeble candle. On alternate shifts, or working together, were two men in nondescript business suits. Their men had flown in quietly. They were pros. And their leaders were a General and a Colonel…of the Mossad.

Holcombe Broderick returned to his home, a refuge among the storms on Capitol Hill. Weary, exhausted, unable to sleep, he drank the scalding hot chocolate which calmed his queasy stomach. He had heard from the President.

"Holcombe, what the hell did you do to me today? Do you realize how vulnerable we are in the Mid-East? Without a ready military force in the Gulf, Israel can be surrounded on three sides, the ocean to their back, within days. Some of those warlike countries are nuts! Imagine what would happen if they merged those huge armies. My God, Holcombe! Why? WHY?"

Broderick answered, sick at heart, "Mr. President, it was that damned jackass, Mangel Mirish. I don't understand either. You appointed a Jew, but why he was **against** the Jews in Israel is beyond my comprehension. Why…"

The President interrupted, "Yes, I'll admit it sounds unbelievable that he would do that to me…my own cabinet man, but he has assured me that a group of the representatives jumped into action on his words; that he never had a chance to explain what he was proposing…an alternative. Damnit, what's worse, we had briefly discussed such a plan where we might have used the money for the U.N.!"

"Mr. President, what alternative? What U.N.? He never mentioned anything else at all."

"Holcombe, if there was a lot of fallout, we would approach the protection issue by using Canada, England, and other U.N. armies. Secretary Mirish says House members began shouting at him and that, when he turned around, you were glaring at him. He told me, to avoid embarrassing me, he ran from the chamber and returned to his office. The last thing he saw was you blowing your stack and pounding the smithereens out of your gavel. His running doesn't surprise me, but I've never known him to lie. So, just what the hell really happened?"

At that moment Holcombe Broderick knew he had been royally set up. He stammered into the phone, "I…I'll have…have an…answer for you…in the morning, Mr…Mr. President."

"I can't tell you how disappointed I am in you, Broderick. This is the first time you've let me down…in fact, let your country down." The President allowed no more conversation. He hung up.

Broderick was now so exhausted, he could barely stand. The President had never called him by his last name. His longtime good friend always called him "Holcombe" or "Mr. Speaker." Now, Holcombe was physically ill. The President had been taken in, too—beautifully hoodwinked. There was a turncoat in his Cabinet.

The Speaker sat in his garden sipping. His despondency was a black hole. "Dear God, what to do? Earlier the Senate Majority Leader had called. His doctor had given him a hypodermic shot to ease an excruciating migraine headache. Broderick perceived that the leader of the upper house could also suffer. This day both of them had taken a beating.

"I wonder what the President said to **him?**"

Holcombe's head dropped to his chest. He dozed, then slept soundly. A half-hour later he awoke, startled by a crash of breaking glass. His trouser leg was wet. He had dropped the cup of cocoa which broke in the crash onto the concrete patio. Suddenly, he was no longer alone. A woman's voice spoke,

"Gracious goodness, Mr. Speaker. Now you've made a mess. Don't bother; I'll clean it up; but, you put those pants in the clothes hamper. Now, Holcombe, you get to bed. You need sleep. Perhaps you'll follow the yellow brick road and sleep in the land of Oz."

Sarah rarely called him by his first name, but Broderick laughed, "Sarah, you're a genius right when I need you. You are absolutely right. Let the mess go, brew me some more hot chocolate, then get back to bed. The clock just chimed 5:00 a.m., and I've got some phoning to do."

"What? Phoning at this hour?"

"Yes, Sarah. Now leave me alone and get the hot cocoa, you sweetheart."

Sarah left, carrying the urn which, by now, needed new candles. She was muttering, "Five o'clock in the morning, happy as a lark, wanting another urn of cocoa, and he calls me 'sweetheart'. He's been on that Hill too long."

Broderick, nodding in satisfaction with his decision, punched an open line on his patio telephone, dialed that highly confidential number, and heard a soft click on the other end...but no voice.

"Oz? Fast as possible. Get your envoys, Ohmstead and Dittus, here to my house, immediately! Then contact Congressman Charter Saladin. Get him to my house pronto, too. That's all."

He hung up. He knew what was the best cure for himself. He'd drink more hot milk...or hot chocolate...and sleep with a pillow behind his back right there on the wrought-iron bench. And, he wouldn't go to the Hill tomorrow either. It would be Friday, and he'd use it and the weekend to recoup. He would recharge his batteries, then go on the attack.

He shouted, "Sarah? I'm hungry, too. Bring me a bucket of sandwiches."

◆   ◆   ◆

Charter Saladin, groggy, almost allowed his head to fall back on the pillow. Had he done so, it would have been the most restful sleep of his tossing-turning night. Abruptly, his eyes popped open and he realized he had barely spoken to Speaker Holcombe Broderick.

"My God! What a dream! The hour hand is barely past 5:00 o'clock and I could have sworn I talked to.... Oh, good Lord! Charter, you're supposed to be at Holcombe's home now. Take a fast shower and run."

The cold water, spewing from the shower head, struck him like a frozen blow. He gasped, hollered from the shock of icy water, and grabbed the soap. Saladin moaned with exasperation. He was trying to soap his body through his pajamas. He almost tore the buttons off getting out of the P.J.'s, while he turned the air blue with his cursing,...when he heard the scolding voice of Elena Imadie Saladin speaking to him.

"Now, Charter. Turn off the water; get out of those wet things; wring them out; and, neatly hang them over the towel racks. Do I have to do everything, my husband?"

Charter sighed, "No, my dearest, your wish is my comman-...." Charter's voice choked. Even from her grave Elena was with him, guiding, comforting. Charter Saladin leaned his head against the tile and sobbed. He wrung his pajamas damp-dry, then carefully hung them on a shower-room towel rack. Elena's presence filled him; her absence crushed his heart. Wistfully, he turned the water to warm, soaped thoroughly, toweled down, and only when he was fastening his tie did he discern he was dressed in one of the suits Elena Imadie had chosen for him.

Charter remembered nothing of getting up, showering, nor dressing. Walking down the stairs to the foyer, he felt a wondrous sensation, . . the specter of his departed wife hooking her arm around his and lovingly escorting him, once again, toward the front door. As had been his custom, he turned and gently kissed Elena goodbye. The door latched behind him. Only when he strolled down the front steps did Charter comprehend he was alone and had kissed the air. But, had he? Even now he smelled the scent of Elena's perfume. His heart was overflowing with a love that refused to die.

What was that saying Elena had expressed over and over?

Charter's firm voice broke the stillness of the inky night.

"Ah, yes! 'There are more unexplained things on this earth than the Angels have ever thought of'."

In the blackness of the imposing tree-lined street, two ominous figures merged with the foliage. Without a word both fell in step with Charter. There was one man on each side of Congressman Saladin, and each had a firm grip on the congressman's arm. They steered him to a waiting black automobile. Unexpectedly,

Charter was shoved into the driver's seat while the other man started the engine. Then, both accosters climbed into the back.

"You drive, Mr. Congressman. We'll tell you where to turn. Our orders are to take good care of you."

Saladin laughed, "You can't hurt me. Elena Imadie Kassam and I have been together this morning. I'm ready. In fact, I'm eager to join her. Have at it now. I'm not the least bit afraid. Do your worst, punks!"

A puzzled man in the back seat turned and whispered to his companion,

"Well, this is a one whale of a comedown since our last meeting. Who's Elena Imadie Kassam? Hollywood starlet?"

"No, Cody. It's his deceased wife. The one who was shot. Remember?"

"Mr. Saladin, please turn down Wisconsin avenue, drive onto Dumbarton, then hit Olive and 29th Street."

"Hey, that's Speaker Broderick's home. You going to kill him, too.?"

Saladin only heard whispering. "Hey, Leith, this guy is still asleep. Didn't Holcombe phone him?"

"He told Oz he'd take care of it. Broderick's pretty reliable."

This time Saladin yelled, "I said, 'Do you plan to kill him, too?'"

"Damnit, Charter, don't you know us?"

"It's after 5:00 a.m., pitch black, no streetlights around this auto, both of you behind me holding guns, and you expect me to identify you from the back of my head?"

"CHARTER! It's Leith Ohmstead and Cody Dittus!"

"WHO?"

Exasperated, Cody Dittus ordered, "Pull over to the curb Mr. Saladin. You're only three blocks from Holcombe Broderick's house. Drive there and park. The Speaker is waiting for you."

Saladin was amazed. "You're letting me go? Alive?"

Leith Ohmstead was chuckling and shaking his head. Cody Dittus wasn't.... when he said, "NO! We'll walk to Broderick's house. Then we'll recommend that he shoot you himself."

"You're not going to kill me?"

"We don't shoot dumb animals! Drive on, Charter. Keep your eyes open." The automobile drove off. Leith Ohmstead had a thought.

"Cody, that's your Pontiac hot rod. What if he puts the pedal to the metal? With that engine power he'll probably wreck your car."

"Just whose side are you on? I can't believe he didn't recognize our voices. He and Bergan Gruenspan only spent a whole day with us."

"We'll see when we get there. Probably some coffee will wake him up. I'm convinced he's asleep on his feet. I'll bet he doesn't remember talking to Broderick. Yet, he had to, because he was walking out his door dressed."

Cody increased the pace as they walked toward the House Speaker's home, "Man! I sure wish I could sleep like that."

"No you don't, Cody," said Leith.

"And why not?"

Leith Ohmstead pointed to Broderick's porch light. It was on. He answered Cody. "Because, my friend, you wake up at the slightest, strange, out-of-place noise. Ordinary sounds, common to the locale, don't bother you. But, the moment you miss hearing a peculiar noise, that is the moment someone will walk up and blow your head off, or slit your throat. Think about it."

Cody and Leith walked up the steps to Holcombe Broderick's residence. Cody, quiet, was digesting Leith's words. Solemn, he only said, "Yeah." They knocked softly on the front door. It opened immediately, and Broderick's strong hands pulled both of them in.

"Welcome, Gentlemen, we have lots to discuss."

"Not until we get some coffee in us, Mr. Speaker. Dawn is just now breaking, and we left our getaway so quickly we had no time for breakfast. By the way, we're sure Saladin will fall asleep unless you get something in him. I don't see him. Where is he? His conversation with us, if you call it that, was akin to the Mad Hatter at Alice's tea party."

Holcombe replied, "He's in the den, sitting in the upright chair...snoring. He walked past me without a word. Reminded me of the President."

Dittus and Ohmstead laughed. The President's ability to slight people was well known. Just then Holcombe Broderick yelled up the kitchen stairs,

"SARAH? SARAH! We need a lot of coffee, toast, and doughnuts!"

◆   ◆   ◆

Congressman Saladin walked briskly through the greenery of Broderick's courtyard garden. Between deep breaths he gulped generous swigs of coffee. As he emptied his fourth mug, he strode past Agent Ohmstead and broke the silence with a "Good morning, Leith."

He continued on his invigorating walk while the agents and Speaker talked in low tones. Broderick said, "I know, from my House spies...er, sources...that Saladin has spent a week tearing apart inequities in several Senate and House bills.

The man built up a sleep-debt because he has been working well into the A.M. hours. My early urgent phone call must have been the final straw."

"Then, you did phone him?" asked Leith.

"Yes, but I ended up shouting. I was sure he had gone back to sleep with the phone at his ear. Watch it, here comes the speed demon, again."

Saladin almost galloped by as he said, "Good morning, Cody Ditto."

"That's DITTUS, you drowsy Arab!"

The next time around, Charter Saladin stopped, huffing and puffing, and poured himself another coffee. "O.K. I'm ready for the meeting. Where's the doughnuts? I'm hungry as a horse!"

"You've sure been acting like one, too," answered Cody.

"How's that again?"

But Dittus, Ohmstead, and Broderick were already walking back to the den. Not without smirking a bit, however.

"My sources," said Broderick. He stopped talking when he looked up to see raised eyebrows on his three guests, especially on the faces of Cody Dittus and Leith Ohmstead. Holcombe grinned and began again,

"Since we're among friends,...my SPIES tell me..." Speaker Holcombe noted Ohmstead and Dittus were making the big 'O' with their thumbs and forefingers. Both spoke as one,

"Right on!" Holcombe chuckled because no one could ever delude the two pros from Oz. They saw things in black and white.

"My spies tell me that there was an early morning meeting..."

Cody Dittus interrupted, "What time?"

"2:00 a.m.—in an office of the Senate Building, held by Abraham Anselm and some mighty influential men; all but one from Congress...and the Administration."

Leith Ohmstead sat bolt-upright. "From the Administration? Who?"

Holcombe Broderick said, "The Honorable Mangel Mayer Mirish of the President's Cabinet, our Secretary of Protocol and Trade."

Cody Dittus whistled. Charter Saladin gasped and slapped his hand to his forehead. He looked at Broderick, and softly asked, "Who else, Sir?"

"My informant tells me they were...they are...The Israeli Ambassador-at-Large Marchen Judisch; Senators Abe Anselm, Jacob Bergenfeldt, and—Theo Dennahy."

It was Charter Saladin's turn to whistle. "No wonder he hates me; bad-mouths me to the President; and, literally froths at the mouth when my name is mentioned. That was the same time I gave that ethics speech in the House. I warned everyone that secret meetings were out; that, if the parley can't stand the light of day and publicity, it would be a dishonorable meeting that would hurt this nation. And leading it? Anselm, that corrupt S.O.B.!"

"How reliable is your, er . . source? Meaning, could he testify?"

"Absolutely, he's the chief Senate Building policeman who schedules the Senate security officers."

"A civil servant who could get into lots of trouble with these politicians? How did you get him on your spy team?" asked Cody.

"I got him special medical aid for his wife who ailed for years; I also get him tickets to the Washington Redskins' football games. He's been secretly reporting to me for years."

Leith shook his head, "Hell, even Oz can't get us tickets to the Washington Redskins. How do you do all these things?"

Holcombe answered quietly, "I've been setting up this one-way pipeline for a quarter-century. I helped the Redskin coaching staff one time when there was a possible scandal and..."

Charter Saladin snorted and asked, "Have you done anything for the President...surely you're holding some of his I.O.U.'s?"

"Not yet, but I'm diligently working on it. Don't be so impatient."

The room exploded with laughter. Broderick wagged his finger and said,

"Remember what people have said for years. I'm a ruthless, scheming, egomaniacal tyrant who is mad for power."

Three pair of eyes studied Speaker Broderick. The room was silent, and the Grandfather clock ticked loudly. Charter Saladin spoke first.

"I believe you are one of the greatest patriots in this country today." Leith Ohmstead almost whispered, "Do you realize we have become a nation where patriots are disappearing?

"Excluding this man and a mere handful, the patriots are going; before long they'll be gone!"

Representative Charter Saladin contemplated that discomfiting thought. Rubbing his chin he pondered, then said,

"Hmmmm, let's see. At the 'Hidey Hole' we saw Mohabe Hejira's secret photos of the Basra, Iraq, rendezvous between Senator Anselm and 'El Presidente' Sadah Diyarbar. That evidence was damning; the secret meeting in his Senate office may have been outright treason. But, I do remember Jabal's statement when he said, 'Hejira thinks the pilot's name was Mark or Marchen.'

Didn't your Oz associate, Jabal, believe it was Marchen Judisch? Don't you have a picture of him kissing the Sultan's hand?

Leith answered, "Mohabe Hejira's hearing is suspect; certainly not admissible evidence. But, the photo of Judisch kissing Diyarbar's hand is damning…and heavy artillery for the Justice Department. Yet, we can't prove Anselm did anything illegal. We've had Anselm under 24-hour surveillance this past month. He's been mighty quiet. Nothing suspicious."

Charter asked, "How about circumstantial evidence? Could we hurt him, even indict him, that way?"

Broderick replied, "Only if the evidence is so strong that refuting it would only open a new can of worms—cause a new investigation. That would ruin his credibility and his reputation."

"Then," Charter Saladin almost yelled, "I have damning evidence."

Cody Dittus leaned forward. The conspirators—Anselm, Diyarbar, Judisch—all tied one way or another to Danvier Dyan. That theme echoed over and over through Cody's mind. Colonel Dyan almost ended Cody's life, . . painfully. And Dyan was a brutal henchman for all these individuals. Cody, leaning directly into Saladin's face, almost commanded him,

"What evidence could you, a congressman on Capitol Hill, get on Senator Anselm that is not available to other congressmen?"

Charter stared right back at Cody. He knew Dittus was not one to trifle with. Charter took a deep breath,

"Just hear me out. Remember, I'm from New Jersey, right next door to New York. A third of my people work in or for New York companies. A close supporter, and a confidant, is Executive Vice-President of Chase Manhattan. He's a shrewd banker, highly regarded; privy to **lots** of inside information."

Cody, suspicious, queried, "WHY? How could he help us?"

"Because others need information this banker has. It's reciprocity—you scratch my back and I'll scratch yours. And he got an extremely confidential six-month bank record belonging to Senator Abraham Lieberson Anselm. It amounted to many thousands of cash flow dollars, as much as any successful, influential senator might have. The deposits and withdrawals were consistent, like those over the years. Except one time! Briefly, for a two-day period, Anselm's account ballooned by two-and-a-half million dollars."

Cody exhaled with a gasp. He fell back in his chair. The questions rolled across his brain like a movie projector. And Charter answered them.

"It was a transit error; an electronic goof in Iraq using the wrong fund transfer account. The recipient was correct—Anselm. But instructions from the Baghdad bank urgently requested immediate transfer to another bank."

Leith Ohmstead was electrified. "Where did the two-and-a-half million dollars go from Chase Manhattan?"

"To a secret numbered account in The `Suisse Bank' of Zurich!"

Holcombe Broderick clapped his hands together and cried a fervent,"Hallelu-jah, Lord! Here's to clerical errors...Hallelujah!"

Leith Ohmstead looked at Dittus, whose eyes were twinkling, "Well, Cody, it's BINGO time,...again!"

16

Flight to Sanctuary

For the first time, among the clutter of suspicions that lacked explicit proof, the congressmen and Oz agents had finally touched the fringe of intrigue. Not that the pictures of a U.S. senator and Israeli diplomat, kissing the hand of the leader of an unfriendly nation, proved that the two men had committed wrongdoing. Such greetings are the custom of many peoples in the Mid-East, so the photos only proved that an American and an Israeli had kissed the hand of a foreign leader. Any court would have thrown out charges alleging traitorous conduct. So far, gathering incriminating facts, with proof-positive verification, had been almost impossible because covert activities had been effectively cloaked through assassination, imprisonment, or insufferable torture.

But now? Cody Dittus was wearing an ecstatic smile when he asked Charter Saladin, "Could you provide a copy for Leith and me?"

Saladin grasped folded papers from his inside coat pocket and handed them to Cody. The sheets tabulated statements of Abraham Anselm's checking account for the past six months; there was another account, a small savings, but its balance remained small and had changed little over the years. While Charter's confidant confirmed that Chase Manhattan had rarely transferred monies to Anselm's savings, the six-month statements also verified there were no withdrawals or transfers to any banking competitor. However, one entry had resulted in raised eyebrows, then a secret security-monitored phone call to Charter's executive banker friend.

There, on the last page, were entries posted for the previous ten days. Prominent among the transactions was a deposit of 2.5 million plus a bank executive's urgent note, "Transfer to 'Suisse of Zurich' immediately!"

◆   ◆   ◆

The ruse employed at Frederick Municipal Airport, Maryland, was one for the books. Upon orders by General Moschi Rubinstern, a young ex-platoon leader promoted to company commander, was assigned to Mossad's elite surveillance team and flown to the United States. Capt. Gursten Wollenski felt privileged to be selected, because he envied the professionalism of the highly regarded, super-secret organization called Oz. Wollenski had already met the impressive team of Ohmstead and Dittus—the hard way, looking at cocked 10-millimeter Smith & Wessons pointed at him—right in the Tel Aviv office of the Mossad's Commander-in-Chief, General Rubinstern.

In that office, Gursten Wollenski learned that the old OSS (Office of Strategic Services) was thought to be buried. OSS quietly became Oz, the Phoenix which rose from the ashes, and brilliantly championed intrigue, retaliation, and obstruction of enemy strategy; even the toppling of hostile governments. Wollenski wanted to be as shrewd, clever, and competent as Agents Leith Ohmstead and Cody Dittus. However, today he discovered that his heroes weren't the only masters of craftiness.

◆   ◆   ◆

In the blackness of the early morning, a telephone call to the Israeli Embassy interrupted the sleep of Danvier Dyan. Thanking the night guard, Dyan, groggily picked up the phone and heard, "Danvier, go to scrambler!"

Dyan was jolted awake as if a bucket of cold water had drenched him. He switched on the scrambler which alters any voice to gobbledegook over the phone wires. If the caller does not have a descrambler to convert the gobbledegook back into proper English, he continues listening to gibberish.

"Dan, they're on to you. You're being watched day and night by Mossad."

"WHAT?" How did they find out? Who talked?"

"You heard of Oz?"

"Yeah! Some supposedly secret society that performs wonders. Russian KGB friends kept talking about Oz. Sort of a legend created by the international undercover agents with too much time on their hands."

"It's no legend! It's real. Oz has a dossier on you so thick that they filled in the gaps for Interpol (International Police Cooperative). You can stay and face the music or run to a safe haven. But, your work there is finished. I'll bet you're not doing anything there, now. Right?"

Danvier Dyan paused. He'd done nothing recently. No aircraft flights, not even carrying messages around town. Then he said,

"How do they know about me? I've never done anything to merit notoriety; I've always carefully covered my trail to avoid any possibility of suspicion. I've been hiding in the shadow of the Israeli Ambassador, so who spotted me in this hemisphere? My operations have always been the Mid-East."

"Think back, Dan. During your terrorist raids did you meet anybody suspicious? Did you fight against anybody who might recognize you?"

Colonel Dyan thought a long minute. Finally, he had a thought and almost groaned in his reply, "Hmmmmm, There was one, just one. He led a company of Israeli soldiers against me near Jerusalem's Golan Heights. He fought me to a standstill!"

"Know his name? Ever meet him again?"

"Ohhh, yes! We tangled several times. He almost got me. Hell of a fighter and leader. He did more with fewer men than any unit I've ever come up against. He was a captain. His men followed him without question. Ah, mmmmmmm...name sounded like Zinski...his men shouted to him sometimes to clarify orders. Yes, that's it. Zinski."

"How about Wollenski? Gursten Wollenski?"

"Lord! That's it! Several of his soldiers warned him about me trying to flank him and they yelled, 'Gar', or 'Guard.' Until now the best name I could make out was 'Gar Zinski.' Damn! Is he over here...in D.C.?"

"We don't know. It's possible. Our men in Lebanon tell me he's disappeared; and, no undercover Palestinian has seen him. Left no trace. What other non-Arabs have you fought with?"

"Well, of course, I've fought the Jews of Israel for the past 10 years. When Wollenski was able to identify me, you notified me because of your Mid-East contacts, and I flew to America...to join Marchen Judisch. Since then I've dyed my hair and grown a mustache."

"You ever run into a Britisher...or an American? Like when you ran that terrorist brigade of peace-keeping Syrian soldiers in Beirut?"

"Absolutely not...why,—."

Suddenly Dyan stopped, his breathing audibly louder over the phone. Like a patient coming out of deep anesthesia, Danvier Dyan suddenly remembered. He had begun growing his mustache before he captured the American. After all these years, could that guy still be able to finger him?

"Sir, it couldn't be. The American we captured was a scared rabbit running for his life in the market square of Beirut. We thought him a spy; so, frankly, we beat him until he was unconscious, then imprisoned him in a bug-infested room. If he were a spy, the torture we planned for him would have found out the truth."

"Planned?"

"Unbelievable! Somehow he wiggled through a small window after sawing the iron bars. His escape had to be painful. He ripped and tore his body on the stone window and the stubs of the iron bars. Next, he fell from the second floor to the stone steps below; that should have killed him it didn't. Worse, he killed my First Sergeant before he escaped. Cut his head off. We found the head lying in a corner.

"Then, running naked down the street at night, he met two of my toughest troopers who were on patrol. We found their bodies, heads blown off, but no one heard a sound. That fellow was the only man ever able to elude me."

"Dan, your pigeon had help! If naked, he certainly didn't have any concealed weapon, and the silent shooting of your soldiers tells me a silencer was involved. Ever figure out his nationality?"

"Said he was an American in the import business. I didn't believe him. Since coming to the U.S., I now realize he spoke with a midwestern accent and used American slang. Yet, I'll never understand how he could silently massacre my men, then escape without a trace. No one's ever done that to me."

"Dan, you remember when Judisch brained an investigator with a sock full of silver coins, then threw him off the balcony way up on the Stouffer-Mayflower Hotel? He was getting too close to exposing me. Well, that man was an agent of Oz. Like your importer, he was as tough as nails. Somehow he survived the fall. So, we sent 'Andre, the Specialist' after him right into his hospital room. And, from his bed, that agent dispatched Andre; used Andre's weapon, too; and, our international hit-man ended up on a marble slab. Judisch now looks continually over his shoulder."

"What's that got to do with me and that American in Beirut?"

"That Oz agent has a partner—has had one for years—and this partner specializes in Mid-East trouble spots. He speaks fluent Arabic."

"What are their names? I probably know them."

"Don't waste your time. Nobody knows them. Those who might identify them are dead! These agents are the ones who clued in the Mossad; General Rubinstern is diligently cleaning house; that means getting rid of you! Get the Hades out of the United States! You've been warned. So, good luck!"

"Thank you so much, *Senator.*"

"Damn you, you stupid idiot! You and your `Big Mouth'. I'M GONE!"

There was a noticeable "click," and Danvier Dyan's phone went dead.

Colonel Dyan trembled. The Mossad knew, and they were here. His protector had called, and in gratitude Dyan had unwittingly used the esteemed "Senator" title. Suddenly, Danvier realized how precious life is.

He had to move immediately; else, the Mossad would eliminate him. Frantic, the sweat of fear dribbling down his body, Colonel Dyan packed and armed himself. In 10 minutes he was ready. Panicky, he fled through the night in a black auto, its lights off. Only on the super highway was he forced to use headlights. He stomped the accelerator. Frederick Municipal Airport would be the last piece of American soil he would ever stand on.

◆   ◆   ◆

Captain Garsten Wollenski almost missed the black car rushing through the Israeli Embassy gates. On a cloudy, pitch-black night the ebony auto blended perfectly with the dark. Half asleep from another unproductive night of surveillance, Wollenski jerked wide awake due to the unexpected roar of a racing engine. If the car had quietly passed the gate, Wollenski would have continued snoozing. Now, however, the Mossad Captain realized a furtive weasel was escaping from the henhouse. He followed, although his windshield framed only inky surroundings.

The captain reasoned that the driver of the fleeing car would have to use his brakes which would flash. When the culprit hit the main drag of a highway, his headlights would have to be turned on to prevent a collision. That chain of events is exactly what happened.

Wollenski followed the occasional blinking red brake lights, then entered a main artery from Washington and saw the fleeing auto's headlights go on. The time was 3:00 a.m., and those sealbeams shone like beacons. After a half-hour high-speed drive, his quarry turned onto a smaller highway. Two road signs intrigued Garsten Wollenski: Frederick, Maryland, and Frederick Municipal Airport. Within minutes Wollenski was on the darkened airfield.

Cursing the inky darkness, Garsten could see nothing but the dim blue lights of the runways. Near the middle of the field a small beacon rotated, piercing the night with alternating colors; first, a shaft of white light; then, a ray of green. Just a brief glance at the airport beacon handicapped Captain Wollenski's vision. For a minute or two he could see nothing but the tower light and runways. In between, the field was pitch black. He could not even see the parked aircraft and padlocked hangars. He dared not turn on his headlights which would guarantee night blindness. Finding it too dangerous to drive blind on a strange airport, a desperate Garsten Wollenski jumped from his car to pursue his quarry on foot. He averted his eyes from the interior dome lights which came on the instant he opened his door. Unfortunately, the blaze of brightness also alerted the fleeing culprit that he had been followed. Frustrated, Wollenski again cursed the darkness. No doubt the escapee was delighted with it.

The Mossad Agent began running. Where, he did not know. But, he skidded to a stop on the concrete just before a silver wingtip would have bashed his head. He could see the shiny aluminum, but other aircraft, painted in the darker reds, blues, and grays, merged with the night. He finally found a vacant taxiway and walked carefully toward the runways. Surprised, he walked right up to an abandoned black automobile.

That was the moment Garsten Wollenski knew he had been chasing someone skilled in deception and cunning. There was a sudden cranking, then the roar of an engine; then more cranking, followed by a burst of power from a second engine. Somewhere, out there, an airplane had come to life. But where? He couldn't see a thing.

Colonel Danvier Dyan had spotted headlights of a car far behind him on the highway. The lights remained the same distance away, never approaching nor dropping back from his car. His pursuer was no neophyte. The Mossad agent, whoever he was, had seen him leave the embassy during a dark, overcast night; somehow caught a glimpse of his almost invisible auto; and, did so at a late hour when, normally, he should have been dozing. Yet, the "tail" had stayed right with him. In his haste to flee the country, Danvier had not taken time to disconnect the tail and brake lights. That oversight was a mistake. But, on the airfield, he threw caution to the winds.

Danvier Dyan had flown from the airport so often that he could draw a map of it blindfolded. He used this knowledge to great advantage. His pursuer, he correctly assumed, did not know this municipal airport at all. While Wollenski bumped, staggered, and felt his way through the labyrinth of parked aircraft, buildings, and taxiways, Colonel Dyan was running quietly in tennis shoes toward the parked King Air 350. The feel of a familiar key brushed his fingertips and his cadence never skipped a beat when he touched the cabin door. Inserting the key, he unlocked the door, closed and latched it softly, and strode through the fuselage's dark interior into the pilot's compartment. Another familiar key quickly turned the ignition switch "on."

Smiling, for he knew the panel switches by heart, he closed his eyes and pictured the toggles he wanted. First, he snapped on the instrument lights. Soft red and blue lights illuminated the instruments and key operating switches. Dyan had no worry about using radio because this was a Unicom System on Frederick Municipal Airport which did not have an FAA authorized control tower. Danvier cracked open the throttles, advanced the fuel mixtures to rich, set both propeller pitches to fine, and punched the automatic prime buttons. He turned the ignition switch to left engine. The starter cranked the motor. The motor burst into life. Then he turned the ignition to right engine, and it, too, roared. He released brakes and advanced both throttles.

The King Air sped down the taxiway toward the runway. Quickly, Danvier Dyan snapped on his landing lights. The powerful beams picked out a windsock which was hanging limply. Winds were still, so he could take off in any direction he chose. Laughing at his pursuer, who must be screaming at him by now, Danvier firewalled the throttles. The wheels screeched as they swiftly turned onto the runway. Gaining speed like a frightened rabbit, the craft rocketed down the concrete ribbon and became airborne. Moments later the wheels thumped into their storage wells.

Colonel Dyan, a superb pilot, craftily flew on instruments through the darkness until the field was left far behind. Only then did he turn on the outside navigation lights and flashing strobe light so that other pilots could see him miles away. His course was the usual one, a direct line to Canada and the next airport in line for refueling and Newfoundland. Swapping planes, he would jet across the sea.

Captain Gursten Wollenski raged in fury. He never saw the bright flames from the engine exhausts until his quarry opened the throttles wide. Yanking out his Uzi 9-millimeter automatic, he never had time to use it. In the extreme darkness just before dawn, he was unable to target the airplane for a well aimed shot. Too far down the runway for even a lucky hit, the aircraft climbed into the night and the sounds of beating propellers dwindled into silence, leaving only an occasional whisper of wind to sweep the runways.

He had been outfoxed, outsmarted, and cleverly deceived. Worse, he didn't even know who the fleeing culprit was. By now, Wollenski only prayed he had not followed a decoy while the real quarry got away.

Gursten almost cried with humiliation. His first step would be to inform Mossad. Next, he would face General Rubinstern and Colonel LeBourget.

◆   ◆   ◆

Gursten Wollenski literally crawled into the sequestered Washington office of Gen. Moschi Rubinstern. If the young captain would have had a tail, he would have curled it between his legs. The chastised, contrite officer didn't even notice Agents Ohmstead and Dittus seated on the far side of the general's desk. Colonel LeBourget cleared his throat.

"Ahemmm, cough, cough. It is the decision of this execution squad...er...I mean...this Summary Board that our American comrades administer the proper justice. Gentlemen, if you will?"

Immediately, Leith Ohmstead and Cody Dittus began arguing. Cody said,

"Let's stretch his neck. Death by hanging. I'll spring the trap door and you can have what's in his pockets."

Leith instantly objected, "But, I wanted to spring the trap door. I love it when his neck goes 'Crraacckkk.' You can have what's in his pockets."

Cody disapproved. "This isn't working. We'd both enjoy watching him drop through the trap door. Sayyyyyy, how about slitting his throat?"

"No way," countered Leith. "That's too fast. He must suffer awhile."

"How about a garrote? We could have him use a saw-toothed cable on himself. He could saw right through his own neck. It'd take a while, too."

"Naw, Cody. He'd get sick and faint."

"Yeah, but Leith, when he wakes up he has to start sawing again. Why, it might take him half a day to cut through that Israeli neck."

"Yabut, Cody, we'd waste a good steel sawing cable. It would start rusting from all that blood and gore. Ever consider **a** dull guillotine?"

By now, Captain Wollenski was standing, his face red from a slow burn. He started to speak, but Leith and Cody ignored him completely.

Cody snapped his fingers, "I've got it! We'll use him for bayonet practice at the nearby Green Beret camp. The medics could treat him between stabs, and he might last a whole week. It'd be painful, a long period of suffering, and good training for the boys."

"I LIKE IT!" said Leith Ohmstead. "And after a week, if he's still alive, we can use him for grenade practice."

"Yeah, yeah!" agreed Cody Dittus, gleefully rubbing his palms together.

The Mossad general and colonel were smirking ear-to-ear while the Oz agents were slapping each other on the back and chortling.

"Yeah! That's the way it should be. He'll be serving a useful purpose when he's tied to a post with all the other straw dummies."

Wollenski was fuming. His slow burn increased to rage. "You guys think you're funny! After what I've done, I don't find any humor in your remarks. Furthermore,..." Gursten Wollenski stopped in mid-sentence and turned toward Marseile LeBourget. "Colonel, did I hear you say 'execution squad'?"

Colonel LeBourget smiled. He walked from behind the desk and laid a fatherly hand on the young captain's shoulder.

"Gursten, it's not as bad as you think. First, you followed the right man. The fleeing man was Colonel Danvier Dyan. He ran because someone warned him. He's heading back to the Mid-East for sanctuary, but we're going to give him an unexpected welcome. Second, there was no decoy. Following him was the correct procedure. Leith and Cody will explain the facts of life to you."

Wollenski sat down in front of Ohmstead and Dittus. Both Oz agents leaned forward for some serious talk.

Cody spoke. "Gursten, Leith and I would have had trouble catching Dyan in the middle of the night. He was in his territory, Frederick Airport...which he knew like the back of his hand. You met a master of deception and have learned how he thinks. You were lucky!"

Wollenski blinked quizzically and uttered a brief question: "Lucky?"

Leith Ohmstead explained, "In the past five years we've had three...yes, three...agents who each made a mistake. That mistake cost each man his life. Cody and I are no different. We stay only one or two jumps ahead of our adversaries. Fortunately, those dead agents never exposed Oz, and their captors never knew enough about Oz to ask. The captors believed they executed a Berliner, a Londoner, and a Rhodesian. After all, the British and Germans have been in the Mid-East a long time. So, our Oz agents were so good that no one suspected they were Americans. Just keep plugging away. Let's hope your next mistake is similar to this caper; you'll still be alive. Cody and I don't think you fouled up. We believe you made the best of a poor situation. Frankly, I'd probably have missed the black auto sneaking out through the Embassy gate."

"So would I," added Cody.

General Moschi Rubinstern stopped the conversation with a wave of his hand. "Gentlemen, I close this inquiry. There's nothing against Captain Wollenski. In fact, his lengthy surveillance brought us surprising results. I want you to listen to this tape over one of the Embassy phones."

Leith frowned and asked, "YOU have the Embassy phones bugged? Anyone doing that can cause an international incident. You, the Mossad, tapping your own phone lines? That's incongruous! General, I believe you have put the United States at risk with Israel. Relations between our countries are strained enough as it is. Your ambassador could make our President squirm."

"Leith, Cody—We don't tap phone lines."

Ohmstead and Dittus looked at one another with disbelief. Both were too wise to take issue with the general. Yet, Rubinstern missed nothing.

"Ozmen, Israel now taps the frequencies of multi-cabled phone lines. From a concealed spot nearby we beam a parabolic induction ray through a phone cable and tune to the various phone line frequencies. We can, like radar, pick up the impulses like those you get through an induction coil. Instead of entering a junction box testing each line by clamping on alligator jaws, we use induction to pick up the multiple signals."

Cody looked aghast, "Impossible! That would be a development that outmoded every wiretap system and procedure in the entire world."

General Rubinstern looked disgusted, "You Americans! You believe only you invented electronics and computer circuitry. Let me advise both of you that Israel has some pretty good inventors, too. I assure you this tape was obtained with our induction system. I admit that it takes a 4-wheel truck to transport the gear. A few more years and we'll reduce it to lap size. I thought you Ozmen should hear this one. I've played it only once."

The general nodded at Colonel LeBourget and he placed a tape player on the desk and pushed the button. What came out was garbled gibberish.

"Now, gentlemen," advised Moschi Rubinstern, "We'll feed the output into this enigma machine." Rubinstern flipped a switch on a typewriter-sized mechanism and the scrambler gibberish converted to clear English.

"These scramblers/descramblers are ours. Israeli made. Yet, the caller had to have one when he talked. His scrambler was programmed for the same type scrambler we have at our Embassy. You're going to have to figure out the caller's identity, while we figure out who gave an enigma machine to him."

The men in the room were electrified at the conversation coming out of the enigma. The instant the name, "Dan," was spoken every agent…Oz and Mossad…knew Danvier Dyan was answering the phone call. On hearing the reference to Cody's escape from Dyan (with Cody's identity still unsolved), Dittus glanced at Leith Ohmstead with a puzzled expression. Then, when the caller mentioned Leith's plunge from the Stouffer-Mayflower Hotel, plus knowledge of an unknown partner who may have been in Beirut, a startled Leith Ohmstead looked back at Cody Dittus. How did the caller know so much about them and the super-secret Oz?

But when the caller blew his stack at Dyan, everybody knew that Danvier's colossal goof pointed right to Congress. Dyan definitely said,

"Thank you so much, **Senator!**" The investigation suddenly focused on Washington, D. C., and "Senator" was an important title on Capitol Hill.

Agents Ohmstead and Dittus adjourned to a corner of the roomy office.

"What's the form, Leith?" asked a concerned Cody.

"You and your blasted British colloquialisms, Dittus."

"All right, Leith. Then, 'Vas ist los, mein Herr'?"

"Now what, you damned linguist!"

"That's German for 'What's the matter, Mister'?...or else, 'What's up, Master'? Now, if you like Arabic...."

Leith Ohmstead growled, "Shut up, Cody. In plain English, we'd better inform Speaker Holcombe Broderick immediately. You concur, Cody?"

"I'm no cur, but I agree!" Ohmstead's response was an obscene gesture.

Cody Dittus said, "Remind Broderick to inform Congressman Charter Saladin. Charter has personal pipelines into the Senate. Besides, when it comes to Senator Abraham Anselm, Saladin will dog him like a bloodhound."

Ohmstead whispered, "Like me, you believe that caller was Anselm?"

Dittus' answer was a shrug of his shoulders. Cody was honest: He didn't know. So far, evidence against Anselm was circumstantial. Even a voice identification analyzer, with its court-approved, speech-pattern printout might be worthless. A scrambler can alter voice patterns.

Across the room, General Rubinstern, Colonel LeBourget and Captain Wollenski were in a huddle. Rubinstern said, "Well, gentlemen, our friends, the Ozmen, are planning their American strategy. No men of their caliber like to discover that a high official is shadowing their every move. They haven't said so, but it's logical they're worried about treason on Capitol Hill. In the meantime, what do we do?"

Captain Wollenski answered with conviction, "Sirs, it's time to implement Operation Wipeout. We can't let Colonel Dyan seek sanctuary with our enemies. He's confirmed our suspicions that he is a traitor to Israel. We must act!"

Colonel LeBourget said, "You're pretty sure of your decision. I can't exactly recollect Operation Wipeout. The General's eyes are twinkling, so he knows it thoroughly. What do you know of it, Captain?"

"Colonel, Sir, I'm the man who thought up and implemented the plan, especially if it involved the terrorist, Dyan. I met him in combat too many times. I have men standing by in Quebec, Danvier Dyan's favorite stopping place...he speaks fluent French you know—and those French Canadians protect their kind from the English. I have spotters in St. John's, Newfoundland, and even Sandwich Bay, Labrador. He'll fly his own long distance jet to the Mid-East from one of those places. I then alert our air force and army regiment. They'll scare the Hades out of Iraq's Sadah Diyarbar who should race to the Saudi Arabian border to prevent an Israeli invasion."

"Captain, you're going to have us blitzkrieg through Jordan to the Iraqi border? King Hussein of Jordan would attack with his army and the U.N. would be up in arms. Uncle Sam wouldn't be too happy, either."

"Colonel, we've got C-130's and 141's. Our tanks and special equipment can intentionally create dust storms visible a hundred miles…by air. Dyan will be 'herded' by our Israeli jet fighters till he passes right by the troops and tanks. He'll think it's several divisions, and he'll run home to papa. Or should I say Sultan Diyarbar? Our combat radio frequencies will 'just happen' to be the same as those on his aircraft. The script is already written. Dyan will make an urgent report of impending war to Diyarbar.

"Within minutes of Colonel Dyan's plane disappearing to the Northeast, our tanks, troops, and special machines will be back on the giant transports and out of Jordan before King Hussein can mobilize. That's when Operation Wipeout will go into effect."

LeBorget almost shouted, "THAT'S when 'Wipeout' goes into effect? What the heck do you call combat troops, tanks, and planes in Jordan?"

"Only the window dressing, Colonel."

"Where do we implement Operation Wipeout?"

"We don't, Sir. President Sadah Diyarbar implements it!"

"God's Sake, Captain! What does that mean?"

"Simple. Diyarbar 'Wipes Out' Danvier Dyan. Painfully, we hope."

17

War That Never Was

Leith Ohmstead and Cody Dittus had quietly listened to the explanation of "Operation Wipeout." Leith, however, look perturbed.

"Tanks, troops, and planes are an expensive method to get rid of one man! Clever and well thought out, Captain, but awfully expensive."

"Not so, Leith, Cody. The plan protects both of you and Oz. You see, if we, the Mossad, were to capture Danvier Dyan, the news media would get hold of the story. Colonel Dyan would, of course, have to stand trial…before he was executed. Our way, in the final analysis, is rather cheap. Dyan simply disappears. President Diyarbar will allow no publicity, whatsoever. His ruthless code of vengeance should guarantee nothing but silence. His justice will be swift, probably a torture-laden death, with an even faster burial. No one will ever hear about it. Dyan will just disappear like your female American pilot, Amelia Earhart. The last sighting known of Dyan will be his flight northeast into Canada. See the benefits?"

Cody Dittus frowned, "No. I don't understand, nor see any benefits."

"Cody, we are having security problems within our government and the Mossad. You have your problems in Oz, perhaps leaks within other government agencies, and certainly within congress itself. If Israel apprehended Danvier Dyan, the rats would start fleeing the ship. The guilty would cover up every back-room deal, quit betraying their country, and you'd never find the leaks.

"Our way, Operation Wipeout, lets Diyarbar do to Dyan exactly what we want him to do, . . minus the notoriety. When Diyarbar rushes troops to repel an invasion and finds his border an empty desert, the whole world will have a field day. The U.N. and U.S. will object and Sultan Diyarbar will be accused of initiating a Mid-East war. He'll look like a fool before the eyes of the world, and he'll lose face among the Arabs. He can't stand being ridiculed and laughed at. He should go wild with fury. He will accept no excuses for such an error. Sadah Diyarbar would never be able to forgive his loyal and trustworthy follower, Danvier Dyan. Dyan will suddenly disappear into the African wilderness, never to surface again. Meanwhile, the guilty parties in the Mid-East and America, under threat of exposure, will breathe a sigh of relief. Soon after, when things calm down, they will continue their illegal, treasonable acts. Then, when they commence operations anew, we'll be watching. And waiting.

"General, may I initiate 'Operation Wipeout' immediately?"

General Rubinstern gave a vigorous nod. Gursten Wollenski headed for the Mossad's "Doom's Day" telephone, the red one which made things happen. "Excuse me, Ozmen. I have to put Col. Danvier Dyan out of business."

◆   ◆   ◆

From out of the sand dunes of Saudi Arabia appeared a four-wheeled Jeep. It was the dawn of another day and both intruders were heavily bundled against the chilling cold of the nighttime desert. The driver was a skilled veteran assault soldier. Anchored from the rear floor, the butt of a machine gun touched the backbone of the driver. He could man the fast firing weapon in an instant. There was no windshield. Each man traveled with black hoods that blended with the dark. In front of the goggled driver lay a rapid-fire 20-millimeter cannon. The driver was an expert in its use.

The driver, Eric Fogelmann, was an American soldier-of-fortune and a key instructor at the advanced infantry tactics school. His exploits and proficiency in combat were evident by the plethora of medals awarded him by his grateful adopted-country, Israel. His assaults on enemy fortifications earned him the reputation as a one-man squad or even a platoon.

Riding beside him was another highly trained soldier—unique in his qualifications: On the parade ground he could have loaded his tunic with the wings of a paratrooper, senior jet pilot, glider helmsman, helicopter pilot, and command navigator. Eric's sky-seeking companion was the renowned Sinbad "Sailor" Dynamit, an Austrian emigrant. He was famous as a fifteen-year-old paratrooper in Israel's six-day war with Egypt; he helped lead the infamous raid on Entebbe, Uganda, against Emperor Idi Amin; and, he commanded the forces that achieved permanent possession of the Golan Heights against Palestinian rebels and terrorists.

Casualties were atrocious, but Israel now controls the high ground above Jerusalem. On Golan Heights his pinpoint accuracy with mortars and his ability to throw hand grenades remarkable distances earned him the nickname, "Sailor." (It was said, "He could toss grenades across The Dead Sea.").

Using a red flashlight and red goggles, which protected him against night blindness, "Sailor" Dynamit studied a strip map of the Saudi Arabia-Iraqi borders. Topping the highest sand dunes, Sinbad Dynamit checked the map to verify its reliability with that of the quartz display screen on his celestial navigation computer. The computer, plugged into the Jeep's special 24-volt cable, was a lap-size navigation system. He knew the unit was turned on only by the quiet humming of tiny high-speed motors which spun the gimbaled gyroscopes inside. Regardless of where Eric Fogelmann drove, the quartz display gave the exact latitude and longitude to the navigator, Sailor Dynamit. The machine's accuracy was claimed to be within two feet anywhere on the globe. In other words, Sinbad and Eric knew precisely where they were, even if subject to discovery and death by both countries, Abruptly, still scanning the celestial navigator, Sinbad's hand gripped Eric's right arm. Thinking as one, neither man moved as the jeep slowed and stopped. The silence intensified the men's awareness of their own heartbeats. The hissing rush of cold night air became audible, beating on their eardrums. Both men jumped when they heard the cry of a nearby animal. Its pained squealing disclosed the ancient never-ending ritual of a small desert rodent being crushed between the jaws of a desert predator. Fogelmann observed Dynamit flicking a small toggle-switch. A faint amber bulb began blinking. The box was an ultra high frequency radio transmitter, its two-foot antennae pulsing a beam to a flight of aircraft already winging their way from Israel. Flying at dangerously low hedge-hopping altitudes, Israeli pilots would operate below unfriendly radar.

Sinbad the Sailor slid from the jeep, dug a hole in the sand atop the high dune, and buried the transmitter, with only the short antenna showing. Its signal could be heard a limited distance of only six miles; it was up to the Israeli pilots to fly precise navigation so they could "home in" on the faint signal. "Sailor" Dynamit smiled. He wasn't worried about his navigators. He trained them, and he graduated only three out of every ten.

A moment later the Jeep motor growled softly again. The exhaust system was practically noiseless. Eric drove a straight line indicated by Sinbad. Three miles later the second ultra high frequency transmitter was turned on and buried. With the second antenna above the sands, the "landing field" was now directional and the runway was the firmest ground with the fewest rocks. Pilot and plane had to land quickly, land short, then make a short takeoff.

Their task completed, Eric Fogelmann and Sinbad Dynamit awaited the arrival of the C-130's and C-141's. As dawn lightened the horizon, the assault group arrived. Twelve giant cargo planes skimmed the surface of the sands, landed, and ground to a halt. In moments tanks, troops, weapons carriers, and "Startrek" half-tracks spewed from the open maws of the aircraft. The outer-space caterpillars held huge fans—making them look like super swamp-buggies, the type that cruise the Florida/Georgia Everglades. Only these swamp buggies with the enormous propellers would be able to fly or else level every sand dune in the Mid-East.

An officer, recognizing his commander, Colonel Sinbad "Sailor" Dynamit, waved to him and Eric Fogelmann. He pointed to a monstrous C-5 jumbo cargo plane that had just landed behind the assault group. A crew stood ready to load the Jeep. Sailor and Eric stepped out of the small auto and it was driven down the massive throat of the C-5 fuselage. Both men gaped when the Jeep disappeared far away into the rear of the craft.

Major Fogelmann asked, "I can't even see the Jeep. This plane is so large you could hide a tank."

"The officer pilot answered, "Six or eight of them, depending on their size, plus a battalion of soldiers…with full equipment."

Sailor Dynamit asked, "Lieutenant, where did you store the Jeep? In the men's room?" He laughed at his own joke. But, he gasped at the reply.

"No, Sir. We stored it in the rudder."

Colonel Dynamit muttered, "They're taking the fun out of war, Eric."

Terrorist spy, Colonel Danvier Dyan, was beginning to relax. His twin engine private jet, cruising at 520 miles per hour, was flying at 28,000 feet with flight clearances from the coastline almost due east to Baghdad. Another hour and he would be landing…safe among his friends. Suddenly, the breath gushed from his lungs. Terror constricted his throat, and his mouth went dry. Pacing him, directly off his left wing were three Israeli jet fighters. And they were new models, because Dyan didn't recognize the fighter craft. He did know, however, that whatever the Israelis made, it would be extremely good, but, bad for an adversary. And Danvier knew where he stood.

The flight leader motioned with his gloved hand. The sign language was unmistakable. "That way! Turn about south southeast." To make his order more understandable, one of the planes dropped back and held his position 20 yards behind Dyan. One short blast from his 28-millimeter cannon…and, goodnight! Danvier broke out in a cold sweat.

As he obeyed, carefully turning to his right, he almost retched. There, off his right wing, flew another trio of Israeli fighters. He had no idea where they were taking him. He had flown the direction ordered only minutes when his radio cackled, "Joseph, what's that tremendous cloud of dust on the horizon? Sand-storm?"

"Don't know, Major, but we'll soon be there. Looks like…like…By God! They're tanks, and, and…Man! It's an army. Looks like they're crossing the border of…."

"Shut up, Joseph. You're broadcasting."

A stern voice came through their earphones. "We see you up there and received your IFF (Identification: Friend or Foe). We're crossing now, and want air cover. Come down and cover our advance. Who's in that plane and why are you escorting it?"

"We don't know, General. He indicates his radio doesn't work. We were going to make him land at an abandoned airfield south of here."

"Dammit, let that private plane go. He can't hurt anyone. Get down here and help US! Understand?"

"Understood, Sir. Tango Flight coming down. Over and out."

Aping a prisoner who just received the governor's reprieve from the hang-man's noose, Danvier Dyan, crying with relief, pushed down the nose of his air-plane and dived toward the earth five miles below. He would hug the earth and make it difficult for any fighter to find him. He firewalled his aircraft, pounding the throttles in a frenzy, trying to extract the last ounce of speed from the plane. He had seen the tanks, the troops, the terrible dust cloud they raised—hundreds of tanks, probably a hundred thousand troops, or more, ammunition carriers, and now squadrons of attack jet fighters. He'd heard them admit they had crossed the border…and they were coming from Saudi Arabia. Were the Saudi's with them? He pounded the throttles.

A high flying Israeli jet tracked Colonel Danvier Dyan with his radar. He "locked on" and turned away only when Dyan was approaching Baghdad Air Control. At Mach 3 speed it wouldn't take long before he could radio "mission accomplished" to the army columns below. Less than an hour later, the Israeli cargo planes were fully loaded and taking off. Their fighter planes saw to it that the transports returned safely to Jewish soil.

That same afternoon a special reconnaissance plane confirmed that the Iraqi army was moving southward. Before dusk, Iraq had brought charges of military aggression by Israel; the United Nations frantically scheduled an emergency session for midnight; and the United States sent a tongue-in-cheek warning to the Prime Minister of Israel.

The message began, "My Dear Prime Minister—." It caused no rippling of the waters in Tel Aviv. England investigated by using photo recon airplanes over the territory supposedly occupied. The pictures, flown to London's War Office and England's Prime Minister, showed only a thousand square miles of hot desert sand.

Within three days the European and American newspapers proclaimed, "The Frenzied Fight of the Phantom Forces." Television crews had a field day showing miles of empty desert. Earth-circling satellites, shared by television networks, showed the Iraqi Army halted to a standstill. That night, when Diyarbar's army could not be observed by the news media, the Iraqi army turned and retreated back to their bases and hidden bunkers.

President Sadah Diyarbar refused to be photographed, and angrily rejected requests to be interviewed. When Barbara Walters called for an exclusive, he exploded. Diyarbar still had his television—channels piped in from all over the world—and he found himself the butt of countless jokes. Australia called his military personnel, "Diyarbar's Dingoes." Late night television shows referred to Iraq and "Sherman Sadah's March to the Sea...of Sand." Sultan Sadah Diyarbar found no humor in the news coverage.

Colonel Danvier Dyan was never seen again. Dyan's Interpol dossier, gathered by France's Surete, America's clandestine Oz, and England's covert MI-6, went into an inactive file where it yellowed with age.

◆   ◆   ◆

Congressman Charter Joseph Saladin had received anonymous phone tips on the whereabouts and whyabouts of members of both houses. Senators were political centers of power. But, certain representatives, after continued reelection, developed foundations of power themselves. After a required period of service longer than many influential senators, a representative could build a foundation of legislative dominance that made senators walk softly around him. Such a man was Charter Saladin.

He was noted for his Saladin Symposiums. Like the ancient Greeks, his meetings were by invitation, and invariably entailed joint discussions of a particular subject; however, often one guest would be drawn aside for consultation in a private room. Few invitees ever refused a Saladin Symposium. The word had spread for years of his magnanimity...as well as his displeasure if you walked on his bad side. Charter was in an omnipotent position to help people; he delighted in doing things for the "Capitol Hillers" (as he liked to call them). Conversely, if he grew angry with any member of the Upper or Lower House, he could act like a wounded elephant; he had a long memory, and he relished doing things to "Capitol Hillers."

Once he believed he had been lied to, cheated, or been used, he would set his own steel trap: The time might be a week, a month, many months, or even a year or so, but once he maneuvered an opponent into a propitious situation...SNAP! Jaws would clamp down in a death grip. No victim ever forgot Charter Saladin when he evened the score.

Such was the relationship between Congressman Saladin and Senator Abe Anselm; only the legislative alliance was Anselm's choosing: Animosity!

Charter Saladin had remained disturbed from the moment he viewed the secret photographs taken in Iraq by Mohabe Hejira, an undercover agent and adopted son of the royal personage, Jabal—Jabal, the jackal. Mohabe Hejira remained in Baghdad as a merchant, and kept himself busy, and suspicion-free, with frequent merchandising trips to Beirut. Both cities were hotbeds of intrigue, and he minded his own business while awaiting further assignments through Jabal.

At the rustic Hidey-Hole, the hideaway of Cody Dittus and Leith Ohmstead, Charter had first viewed the astonishing photos of Senator Abraham Lieberson Anselm warmly shaking the hands of Sadah Diyarbar. What was confusing was the association with Marchen Judisch, a key diplomat from Israel. The pilot, who obviously revered Sultan Diyarbar, was, supposedly, also Jewish, and his adoration for the ruthless Diyarbar was even more baffling. The Sultan, President of Iraq, openly hated the Jews and, if he'd had the power, he would have driven the Jews into the Mediterranean long ago. But, there...outside Basra, Iraq, fronting Saudi Arabian territory, an American Jew senator joined known Jewish personnel of Israel's Embassy in the United States. All were mysteriously conniving with an Arab enemy.

Keen minds often think alike, and House Speaker, Holcombe Broderick, was akin to a father to the younger Saladin. When the phone rang in Saladin's office, his receptionist immediately put the call through to Charter.

"Hello, Mr. Speaker," enthused Charter Saladin. "Holcombe you must want something because my intuition tells me this is going to cost me. Am I invited to one of your famous 'receptions', or are you looking to raise Hades at one of my symposiums?" Saladin ended his question with a chuckle.

"Frankly, Charter, neither," said Broderick. "Actually, I've seen you quite concerned about something for several months. I thought you'd visit me at my chambers, or else at home. But, you've never phoned. You've got to unwind a little. It's only been a year since Elena Imadie's untimely death. Why won't you let me help you?"

There was a pause. Holcombe Broderick knew he had not been disconnected because of somewhat labored breathing coming through his earpiece.

After several, "Well?…well?…WELL?" forcefully spoken by Holcombe, Charter finally broke his silence with a plea.

"I must speak to Oz; those fellows, Leith and Cody. You know, Ohmstead and Dittus. It's important."

"You know I have no way to contact them, Charter," said Broderick. The Speaker heard only a despondent, "Oh."

"Now, doggonit, Charter, hold your horses! I can notify Oz, and they can have one of them phone you. Does that help?"

"Immeasurably!"

"Good Lord! Does that mean 'yes' or 'no'? I'm just a country boy, you know; raised in a log cabin, walked barefoot to school ten miles through thirty feet of snow. Why, I even…."

Charter Saladin moaned, "Holcombe, why don't you go to…."

Speaker Broderick laughed. Saladin only spoke to him like that when he was feeling good. Holcombe hung up, but not before he said,

"Be at my home this evening at 8:00. I'll have guests."

The overcast sky made a black, rainy night. Broderick's porch light was off; the front yard lamppost burned dimly in the gloom. A car door slammed, and an aged couple emerged. A tall distinguished gentleman walked with a stoop, his cane necessary for a gimpy leg. His wife moved slowly, bracing each step with her aluminum walker. A doctor would have diagnosed the two as a man with a curvature of the spine, probably osteoporosis; the woman with a severe joint disorder, such as arthritis. They slowly stumbled up the stone steps and clumped their way to the front door.

Charter Saladin watched through the ornate glass window as they approached, "My God, Holcombe, here comes the blind leading the blind. We should have gone out to help them."

"You don't know the half of it, Charter. Offer to put them out of their misery after they get inside." Charter looked at his mentor with surprise.

Speaker Broderick opened the door and guided the couple inside, as he almost shouted out the door, "Welcome, Ginny. Come in, Noble."

When the door closed, the bent-over gentleman straightened up with a groan, "Another five minutes and I'd have broken my back. Lord, how this beard itches. Cody, look beautiful for Charter Saladin."

Saladin's mouth dropped open with astonishment. Leith Ohmstead stood to his full 6' 6" height, and carefully pulled his beard off his face. Holcombe Broderick handed him a towel and Leith, splashing on a gum remover, wiped his itchy face clean. It was Cody Dittus' turn.

"First, out of these heels. My calves ache, and these shoes are killing me. Brother! It's a pleasure to get out from under this hot wig, and the makeup and lipstick make my face break out."

Cody also washed his face and lips with makeup remover. When Broderick offered both agents a brandy there were no complaints, just sighs of pleasure. But, Charter Saladin's expression made Leith and Cody roar with laughter. Holcombe was not far behind. Saladin was stunned.

"Fellas, I thought this was done only in the movies!"

Cody answered, "Congressman, we sometimes visit a scene of operations many times. Foreign country officials aren't stupid, you know. Many of them are damned clever. To avoid being observed as the same person time and time again, we appear in different guises. It's a life saving procedure. You either get good at it, or you die...sometimes quickly, sometimes not. Now, kiss me, you fool!"

Leith and Holcombe guffawed, but Saladin still stared in wonder.

The speaker grew somber. "Fix us all another drink, Leith, and let's get down to business."

Cody Dittus jumped up. "I'll do it. Leith is beat. He got the once-over from the Oz bosses today. Things might be coming to a head in Washington and the Mid-East. And soon, too."

The foursome adjourned to the den where they sat comfortably in a circle. Holcombe pointed, indicated Charter. "Tell us what's bothering you."

Charter Saladin spoke hesitantly. It was from a long habit of organizing his thoughts into a concise, understandable presentation.

"I don't know where the beginning lies. This time either now or when I end my talk, so here goes: I hold what is now being called 'Saladin Symposiums', and many congressmen and their staffs consider it almost like Speaker Broderick's coveted receptions. Not on the scale of our esteemed Speaker, but more informal...being a man of the people I put most of my guests to work. I don't have my parties catered."

Speaker Broderick snorted, "All right, Charter, knock off the bull-hockey and get on with it." But, Holcombe chuckled along with the rest.

"What's significant is that Senator Anselm has twice refused my invitation so that we might 'mend fences'. My newest employee is now my key advisor. Via courtesy of Speaker Broderick, the great attorney and strategist, Mr. Bergan Gruenspan, is chief of my staff. Gruenspan had been with Senator Abe Anselm a year ago when he went to work with Congressman Broderick. Bergan is no fool, and, after twenty years of close association, can play Abraham Anselm like a steel guitar. Strum Anselm gently and he'll sing beautifully—up to a point that might incriminate himself.

"Anyway, after my last invitation, Gruenspan asked Anselm why he wouldn't come; that the Senator could learn even more from me than what Gruenspan was already feeding Anselm. I believe it was then that Anselm made a blunder…perhaps a confession. Senator Anselm answered Bergan saying, 'I don't want a thing to do with that Jew-hating Arab-American; I especially don't want to face the ghost of his assassinated wife!'

"Gentlemen, Bergan and I discussed that remark a lot! First, I do not hate Jews. I hate power-mad egotists who righteously believe the people must live their way, . . that is, he knows what is best for the people. Yet, he can't tolerate me fighting him over anything he does. At last, I finally realized his bizarre hate for me is primarily because my ancestry is Arab. That's what doesn't make sense. We know he's unusually close to Sadah Diyarbar, the most cruel, ruthless Arab in the Mid-East."

Cody Dittus injected, "Charter, I've been there more than any other Oz agent. I speak their language and many of their dialects. You've got to remember: You are here—America—and Diyarbar is an Arab—in Arab country. Diyarbar is making Anselm a wealthy man. You are not. The New York senator is doing what the Romans do when he is in Rome. Anselm does not have to live there. He does here! To him you are an Impediment. Diyarbar is Cash."

Charter nodded, comprehending Cody's every word. He said, "That brings us to Abe's statement about 'not wanting to face the ghost of an assassinated wife'. Bergan Gruenspan and I are convinced that Anselm had something to do with Elena's murder. Inside the law's inner circles there has been suspicion that my wife's murder was a deliberate assassination. The lipstick remark on the House bathroom mirror stated, 'We hit exactly what we aimed at'. The FBI and the best Washington PD detective team have quietly mentioned the theory of assassination. They just don't know why…and neither do I.

"Why would Anselm detest my home? Would the presence of Elena Imadie's photographs, her woman's touch—the layout of the home, her spiritual presence in the house, make Abe Anselm flinch just being there?

"No, Bergan and I now believe Anselm is involved in Elena's death. Outside of the lawmen, Mr. Broderick, and myself, Anselm is the only one to mention, or even think, assassination. That word was never used in the newspapers or on television,…not even on The Hill. The word, 'murder,' was. Bergan knows Senator Anselm like his hand. Bergan says its the cry of a guilty conscience, and an accidental confession by a conspirator."

The room grew quiet. Leith Ohmstead puttered among the ice cube trays and the drinks he was mixing. Leith sighed, then impulsively doubled the ingredients and concocted a dynamite cocktail for each person. The potent drink would mask the unavoidable pain of liberated emotions. Nobody was holding back. Honest thoughts were being expressed, probably for the first time since Charter Saladin collapsed after his loving wife's death. Charter, engrossed, continued despite tears in his eyes. "My telephone pipeline informs me that there are problems on the New York waterfront. Liberian ships are involved."

"Liberia?" echoed Broderick. "That little nation hasn't been heard from since we nearly scuttled our merchant marine."

Leith Ohmstead laughed bitterly as he recalled, "Our merchant marine. WHAT merchant marine? Since the 70's, when the cold war was damned hot everywhere, Liberia bought, traded, and contracted a fleet of cargo ships that outfreighted Japan and Europe. They are crewed by Cubans, unfriendly South Americans, East and West Germans, Greeks, Japanese, Chinese, Indians, and even mercenary Americans. If we knew the tonnage shipped under that flag, we'd be stupefied. We'd also be astounded at the phenomenal amounts of money someone received. Anyway, what did your telephone tipster tell you?"

"He suspected. It was the dogs that confirmed the suspicion."

Cody Dittus sat bolt upright. "Charter, you've got my full attention."

"One dog sniffed and sniffed. He'd whine, but that was all. His police handler told my tipster that it was the only time he couldn't understand his dog. This time the patrolman regretted his dog couldn't speak English."

Holcombe Broderick said, "So, he gave up. There was no heroin."

"No, Sir. Believe it or not, the dog wouldn't leave. He was smarter than his master. The bloodhound kept whining and trying to drag the cop back to the ship…even though the leash was choking him. That was when the policeman finally understood him."

"Understood what?" asked Ohmstead.

The cop put in an emergency call. That dock was flooded with police cars…and two more dogs, specially trained police dogs."

Holcombe Broderick was almost falling out of his chair. "Go on, Man!"

"Well, Sir, the dogs went back to shipboard, below decks, and through the holds. They weren't sniffing for heroin or cocaine."

"WHAT? Damn you, Charter!" hollered Broderick.

"I didn't know it, myself. They have special dogs for the largest shipping center in the U.S.A.—New York City. These dogs can smell two molecules out of a hundred thousand. And, they went crazy!"

Leith Ohmstead smiled. "I was told about this: Gun oil and gunpowder!" Charter Saladin smiled, too. "Absolutely right, Leith."

Cody Dittus whistled and said, "Damn! Munitions! That right, Charter?"

Congressman Saladin only needed to nod, "Yes."

Leith asked, "What was the ship's destination?"

"A small, but highly mechanized unloading facility at Al-Faw, just northwest above Khawr 'Abd Allah, at the northern end of the Persian Gulf."

Cody Dittus slapped his hand to his forehead. "I know it well—almost didn't get out—killed two men—that region is Iraq!"

Leith Ohmstead said it all: "There's a fortune being made. Munitions! There'll be shiploads of them. Under a false flag, they'll try sneaking more weapons to Sadah Diyarbar. People lie. Those special dogs don't.

"As for the gallant men and women of Operation Desert Shield? The same old corrupt, fainthearted politicians stopped you too soon. Baghdad still lives!"

18

Strange Bedfellows

Marchen Judisch jogged early in the morning. His tennis shoes beat a steady tat-too on the quiet road circling the Israeli Embassy. Marchen, a man who prided himself as a fine physical specimen of manhood, lightly pounded the macadam pavement and escaped toward the rock-laden trails laid out in the hills of the dense timberland.

The first inkling of a missing cog in the operating gears of his furtive spy net-work came later when, on this Saturday morning, he endured a stressful drive to Frederick Municipal Airport.

But, now, Marchen was startled by another pair of feet softly pacing his steps. He turned from the macadam road and ran up a rocky trail, a steep climb which ended only when a runner, or backpacker, reached a level bulldozed plot of ground on the summit of a wooded hill. The exertion and stamina required to reach the pinnacle without slowing would tax the strength of a novice runner. Judisch's physical condition made him arrogant. Always before, companions who had run with him had fallen far behind. This time he was humbled.

A stinging hand slapped his rump and a voice urged,

"Faster, faster! You're ruining the rhythm and slowing me down! Go!" Angered, Mark Judisch poured on the coal and dashed toward the summit of the alpine prominence. During his final sprint to the peak, Marchen experienced the discomforting sensation of his buttocks being slapped as that same voice urged, "Faster, dammit! Faster!"

Judisch stumbled to the manmade plateau and fell against a hackberry tree. A sweet scented aroma mollified his nostrils while he gasped and his lungs heaved from the exertion. That same voice said,

"Hey, Mr. Ambassador, try some of these berries. Hmmmm, good. These sug-arberries are good for fast energy and they're quite tasty—sweeten your breath on an empty stomach."

Marchen was stunned. This stranger knew him and knew he was on the Ambassadorial Staff. Inwardly, Marchen was searching his memory and asking, "Just **who** is this man? I've never seen him before!"

Judisch, exhausted, looked into the face of a 6' 6" hunk of muscled manhood with long legs and arms. No wonder the guy could run. Whoever Marchen's butt-slapper was, he was a superb example of manhood. His leg muscles were knots of sinewy bulges cloaking tremendous power. Marchen's "not-by-choice" running companion had a slightly flattened nose—obviously, he had taken a few face-changing blows—only Marchen was betting the tall man had distributed a destructive return, about ten times the amount dished out by his antagonists. The man's hair was thick, slightly wavy, with a red sheen within the brunette coloring. The eyebrows were jet black…a contrast to his hair, but his wide cheekbones paralleled a block-shaped jaw that said, "No nonsense tolerated."

It was the man's eyes that chilled Ambassador Judisch. They were hazel and green, with flecks of gold. Those eyes pierced the soul. No one could long return this stranger's penetrating stare. Women would have found him fascinating…an object of extreme curiosity…and curiosity meant they would fall all over themselves to command his attention. But, to a fighting man like Marchen Judisch, a cold dread gnawed his insides. Suddenly the man smiled, and Marchen relaxed.

"My name is Leith Ohmstead. I enjoyed our little jaunt."

Judisch was churning inside. Mentally he reviewed the unscheduled contest: "Little jaunt? This stranger literally ran me into the ground!"

"Really, Marchen, you should try these sugarberries. You'll feel a new burst of energy and **really fly on the downside run back to your embassy**." Marchen blanched at the thought. What he didn't know was that Leith Ohmstead was doing an incredible job of calming a thundering heart and gasping lungs that begged for air. He had sprinted Marchen Judisch, staggering, into the hackberry. Now he had to convince Judisch the exercise had barely made him break into a sweat. Fortunately, his ploy paid off.

Judisch replied, "I've just gotten out of a sickbed. I'd be foolish to overdo. I'll do a brisk walk back because I mustn't overwork my physical condition. Few men can keep up with me, but…if I hadn't been sick today…I'd have left you behind."

Leith Ohmstead laughed, "I'm sure of that. But, the real danger is finding that you have been left behind…by your comrades."

Judisch started to skip down the path when he suddenly slowed,

"How's that again? You mean **you'd** leave me behind?"

"Not at all, Ambassador Judisch. Your physical condition is magnificent. I meant you are alone now...left behind. Your pilot friend, Danny Boy, has split and left you holding the bag. The `Senator' warned him. Are you just finding it out from me, now? The "Senator" never called **you**?

"It will take some convincing, but we might be able to help you. But, the Mossad won't wait, you know. You've learned how things are in Washington. What's one more body among the nightly killings? `**They**,' the Mossad, like to do their victim in the dark. Quick, gone, and undiscovered until daytime."

Ambassador Marchen Judisch halted so fast that his tennis shoes squeaked on the asphalt. He whirled, glared at Leith, and shouted,

"Who in the hell are **You**? What senator? What Danny Boy? What Mossad? Are you saying you intend to kill me? Is that what all of this is about?"

Leith smiled and assuaged Marchen's anger with a soft reply, Of course not, Mr. Judisch. You have diplomatic immunity in this country. That's why "The Wizard" suggested I tell you, and offer you our services. Your questions and denials are expected. Your first mistake was the lie you just told me. Since when does a Jew know nothing of the Mossad?"

"Damn you! Who do you think you are? Talking this way to an Israeli diplomat?...an ambassadorial delegate? And what the hell is a `Wizard'?"

Leith said it concisely, "Sir, the `Wizard' is the head...the director...of Oz. You've heard faint allusions to `that organization'? Let me tell you, Mr. Judisch, **Oz is**!

"We've shadowed you here, in Tel Aviv, Beirut, Iraq...particularly, Basra. Mr. Ambassador, **we have you cold**!"

Had Marchen Judisch run full tilt into a tree, the shock could not have been greater. This man who calls himself "Leith" knew too many things. Marchen's supposed ignorance of the Mossad held no credibility. After all, he was from the Israeli Embassy. What shook him to the depths was the mention of Basra. In Basra, it was **he**, Danvier Dyan, and Senator Abraham Anselm, who had met and made ovations to President Sadah Diyarbar. Did they...that is...the Oz organization, know that he and Danvier had kissed the Sultan's hand?

Completing his run, Assistant Ambassador Judisch turned, left Ohmstead, and walked across the street to his embassy. Judisch never heard the horn that tried to warn him he was about to be struck down. He didn't hear the car braking with a screech. Like a zombie, Judisch walked through the Embassy Gate to his office. He ignored the curses from the exasperated driver who had saved his life.

Judisch only knew he had to get away and think! In his chamber, he yanked down several stored suitcases.

Fifteen frantic minutes later, Marchen, in his Mercedes, raced from the Embassy toward Maryland. Frederick Airport was waiting. So was his airplane.

◆   ◆   ◆

It **was** a strenuous drive to Frederick Airport; in fact, the stress agitating Marchen Judisch made him beat the steering wheel in frustration; the usually enjoyable trip to the municipal airport changed into a slow drive to a crucial destination that seemed a thousand miles away. Suddenly a sharp curve jumped into view and Marchen's auto careened, tires screeching, around the rapid bend of the road. He skidded off the road toward a deep ditch and stopped, hovering on two tires, the auto balancing on them, suspended in the air. Narrowly avoiding turning over, the car re-stabilized itself and thumped back onto all four tires. The near-disaster brought Judisch back to reality.

"What a panicked nut you are, Marchen. Now you're trying to kill yourself before you've even gotten away. Slow down. It's not far, and the escape plane is waiting."

The moment Assistant Ambassador Judisch drove to his aircraft's parking area, he realized a cog was missing from the gears of a smooth spy operation. "Had that butt-slapping Ohmstead been right?" Marchen broke out in a sweat.

The parking space was vacant! His King Air 350 airplane was missing!

◆   ◆   ◆

A thick stand of bushes and trees on a hillside overlooking the Israeli Embassy concealed an automobile. Leith Ohmstead dressed automatically, never taking his eyes off the Israeli compound while he changed from his jogging clothes into casual slacks and a short-sleeved shirt. Before dressing, Ohmstead had poured an emollient of water and liniment from a large canteen over his body, and had washed from head to foot. He dried himself vigorously with a rough cotton towel. Whether Leith was dressed or standing naked among the cloaking greenery, his training would never allow his eyes to waver from the area under surveillance. Had Marchen Judisch run for cover, Leith Ohmstead would have immediately followed him, undaunted…in his car…driving in his birthday suit.

Suddenly a black Mercedes roared from the compound and dashed toward a highway leading out of town. Leith was just tucking in his shirt when he spotted his quarry. In one swift motion he fastened his pants, buckled his belt, slid into the driver's seat, started the car's engine, and, quickly, was only a block behind his victim. Judisch was driving his German import like a madman, but, excluding an Indianapolis Speedway racer, there was no auto that could run away from the powerful Oz-engineered motor that powered Leith's chase car.

"Well, Judisch," mused Ohmstead, "Where are you headed in such a hurry? You won't mind if I stick to you like glue, will you? Maybe your day of reckoning has arrived. I still recall that you're the guy who used silver coins and your aircraft's pitot tube cover for a blackjack. You put me in the hospital for quite a stay—and I'll never forgive you for that!"

Leith growled like an angry bear as he remembered the attempts to assassinate him: Marchen Judisch had engineered Leith's long dive from the hotel. Judisch had never considered the protective garbage that had cushioned and subverted the death plunge; then into Leith's hospital room came the terrorist killer, "Andre the Specialist," paid by Marchen to administer the coup de gras.

The ensuing fight to the death caused such a trauma to Leith's terribly battered body that it compounded his wounds. The lethal struggles prompted a delay in healing, and critically lengthened the time of Leith's convalescence. Yet, Ohmstead knew he had not reached the top rung of the enemy network's ladder. He was close, but affixing guilt on **the** party responsible for giving the order to kill him only made Leith grind his teeth in futility.

"I know Judisch is obedient to, and takes orders from, President Sadah Diyarbar of Iraq. But, who's giving orders over here? Is the guilty party, or parties, . . on Capitol Hill? Is Judisch protecting him, or protecting them, even at the cost of his life?

"Well, Leith Ohmstead, you know your suspicions don't count in a court of law. Why, even Cody Dittus is stymied. He wants to obliterate Sultan Diyarbar, but that solution only removes one head of the Hydra serpent. Cut off Diyarbar's head, and two will grow back. Let's see, who **would** be the successor? After Sadah there's his cousin, Druid Kahn Membossie. He enjoys killing more than Sadah Diyarbar. Next in line would be Diyarbar's sons…he has more than one son hidden somewhere. Probably tending sheep in the desert. That's another method used by Diyarbar to protect his backside. No, Sir, Cody is wrong. The head may be in Iraq, but the coiled snake is here."

Leith Ohmstead braked heavily. Ahead of him exploded a cloud of dust. From out of the dust appeared a Mercedes convertible. It was driven back onto the road slowly, carefully, completing a hairpin curve which the auto had failed to negotiate. A chastised Marchen Judisch was behind the wheel and he now drove cautiously, oblivious to Ohmstead's car behind him.

"Almost met your maker didn't you, Judisch?" observed Leith. "You might as well keep going. Your airport in Frederick is just ahead. But, you try to escape and I'll drive this car right through the cockpit."

Ambassador Judisch drove to a row of parked aircraft. Beside a taxiway he stopped. He jumped from his Mercedes and stared at an empty parking spot. The tie-ropes lay on the ground. The King Air was gone. Judisch stooped, picked up one of the ropes, and found it had been slashed in two. Someone, in a great hurry, had not even taken time to untie a wing rope.

Marchen heard the purr of a powerful engine. He turned around...and stared into the face of Leith Ohmstead who was sitting in a power-packed automobile. Judisch smiled resignedly. On his left there was nothing to escape with. On his right, effectively blocking access to the airport exit, was that super jogger, the agent from a supposed Oz. Judisch, griping to himself in German, said,

"It's that little 'ole butt-slapper from Oz, Herr Leith Ohmstead! I thought I was free as a bird, until I looked in my rear view mirror. Ohmstead was there. Just listening to his car tells me I couldn't get away if I had a two-day head start. **Oz must be real!** He warned me, but I wouldn't listen. Now, I don't need a diagram to see that I've been left to my fate. What I want to know is **why** was I not warned? Better, **who** warned Colonel Dyan?"

Leith Ohmstead stepped from his car, leaned against the fender with his arms folded, and said. "Nice try! You want to come along easy with me—or do you want to try it the hard way?"

Judisch answered, "You're giving me a choice? I have diplomatic immunity, you know."

"No, you **had** diplomatic immunity. You've broken the law being an international spy; tried to kill me with an eight-story fall from my hotel; put me in the hospital and then tried to have me killed, even there! If my partner were here he wouldn't take you prisoner—he'd kill you right here."

"And you won't? I don't see any gun. Maybe I'll succeed this time, . . and take that hot-rod-bomb you're driving."

"Be my guest, Marchen. Be my guest," answered Leith. Ohmstead straightened and readied himself like a crouching lion.

Judisch asked, "Where's your gun, American? What kind do you use?"

"Marchen, I use a trailblazer Smith & Wesson, a 10-millimeter. I won't need it if you insist on doing things the hard way."

"You think you can take me?"

"Like Sheridan took Atlanta. Better yet, since you are German, I might say 'Like Patton took Rommel—**and** Hitler'. You coming quietly, or not?" Delegate Judisch watched the Oz Agent slowly advance toward him. There was no mistaking the intent showing in the eyes of Leith Ohmstead. Judisch was a great hand-to-hand combat veteran, but Ohmstead's stalking displayed a physical force and training known to few men the world over.

A dominant premonition flashed across Marchen's mind. This man had told him "**Oz Is**"; yet, few people anywhere knew anything about them or their worldwide operations. Not even The Mossad had counseled its agents.

The Mossad! Briefly, Marchen Judisch had forgotten his own organization. He had straddled the line so long working against America **and** Israel that he had forgotten that he was an Israeli Embassy Assistant Diplomat. Just the thought made Judisch break into a cold sweat.

A hand-to-hand fight with Ohmstead meant only one man would walk away…if he could walk. The other would be dead. If <u>he</u>, Marchen Judisch won, The Mossad would be waiting—waiting right behind Oz. And, the Mossad had hounded Nazi criminals all over the world for the past 50 years! Hounded them into capture…or into their graves. Judisch had no options.

He turned around, put his hands behind his back, and said, "You may use handcuffs or take my word that I'll come quietly."

The Israeli diplomat was startled to feel the snap of handcuffs over his wrists. The Oz Agent **had** secured his arms. Then, a similar set of handcuffs…with a longer chain was clamped above his ankles. Leg irons!

"Ohmstead, you've got to be kidding. I told you I'd give you my word."

"I may be unwise, Marchen, but I'm not stupid! You've tried to kill me several times. Only, you didn't know I was a patriot. So, convince me why, of all people, I should trust you! Now, get moving. Into the car."

The blue Oz-engineered auto drove away with its prisoner, the muffled power of the engine echoing off the airport hangars. Behind, parked on a vacant aircraft site, stood a black Mercedes. Abandoned and lonely.

A corner door in a nearby hangar was propped open, allowing the breeze to bring in fresh sunshiny air. Seated comfortably in a lawn chair, blowing American bubble gum like a school kid, was Mossad's Capt. Garsten Wollenski. "Ohmstead! Judisch just missed getting killed. What a hell of an Oz agent!"

◆   ◆   ◆

Speaker of the House, Holcombe Broderick, sat in the shade of his courtyard patio. The evening was cool. Lately, Broderick had left earlier than usual from the bustling atmosphere and burning lights in the Sam Rayburn Building. His weariness had disintegrated into a disease, and he trooped to "The Hill" each morning as if attending his own execution.

Broderick appreciated the setting sun because it splashed ever-changing colors on the patio foliage at sundown. Holcombe found the inner courtyard was the only place he could find contentment, seclusion, and a calm for his arrhythmic heart.

During some House sessions his wildly beating heart almost burst through his chest. Close-mouthed doctors warned him of the consequences of acute stress. But, their medication made him so tired that Broderick refused to take it, claiming that the medicinal cure was as enervating as the medical disease. Once more Holcombe considered retiring from Congress.

The only thing preventing a life-saving decision to retire was the knowledge that two likely successors were "weak sisters", both a pawn of wealthy special-interest groups. Holcombe Broderick was a patriot, while most of the power-grabbing congressional hierarchy were considered "politicians", a name Broderick found more revolting with each passing day.

Silently gliding along the patio walks came his housekeeper, Miss Sarah. How much she was like his dear departed Abigail gone these past 16 years. Sarah set a tea service down by the wrought iron table by his favorite chair. "You need some good herb tea, Mr. Speaker. No caffeine. Good for your heart, Sir. The chamomile is supposed to relax you. You need your rest…and so does Mr. Saladin, too. He looks a little haggard."

"Sarah, why would you mention Congressman Saladin at this time?"

"Oh, he's been waiting in the foyer, Sir. Wants to see you."

"Good Heavens, woman! Charter is like a son to me. Never keep him waiting. Show him in, now! Bring another cup—cream and sugar, too."

"It's there on the tea service, Mr. Broderick. You'll excuse me."

Broderick could only smile. Sarah played him like a violin—she could make him squawk or make him mellow. She was **always** a step or two ahead of him. Exactly like Abigail.

Charter Joseph Saladin walked down the patio, his arms outstretched. Both men gave each other a bear hug. Charter's affection for the Speaker was returned in kind. Holcombe always felt better in his company.

"Holcombe, do you feel like traveling tonight?"

"No, Charter, I don't. Therefore, where are you taking me? If I object, I know you'll kidnap me. Right?"

"Absolutely! But this trip will probably make you feel better. We'll be flying to Hidey-Hole Lodge for the night. The helicopter is waiting."

"How do you know? Who invited you?"

"Oz, Mr. Speaker. Seems they're beginning to trust me. Also, Ohmstead and Dittus put in a good word for me. Of course, they phone me only. You are the only one on Capitol Hill who has their secret number."

"What's this all about, Charter?"

I understand that we're on the home stretch. They've got the goods on an Israeli traitor—operating right here in Washington. We're going to meet friends of Ohmstead and Dittus. They are the chiefs of The Mossad."

"WHAT?" Holcombe Broderick gasped. "We **work** with the Mossad?"

"Leith Ohmstead and Cody Dittus do. They'll lead the 'discussion', but our Oz Directors won't be there. I've gathered that there's a rather cool tolerance between our agencies and those of Israel. Sort of a mutual distrust. Only Ohmstead and Dittus have an in. And, it's solid."

Cody Dittus welcomed Broderick and Saladin at the heliport. Both congressmen were strapping themselves in when the copter took off with a WHOOOOOSH that pushed them back into their seats. The whirlybird was a new model, obviously…but Cody Dittus would only smile at their questions.

The helicopter descended, directly onto a well lighted pad behind the pastoral Hidey-Hole. Within seconds, as the trio disembarked, the copter rose, and with a high pitched whine disappeared into the darkness. Suddenly, Broderick and Saladin were dumbfounded.

Sitting at the outdoor patio table was a shackled individual. Beside him was Leith Ohmstead. Cody Dittus disappeared into the log lodge to prepare a midnight supper and a tray of gin and tonics. A rather unhappy looking man sipped a tall gin and tonic. However, even in this wilderness, in the black hours of night, not having the least idea where he was, the prisoner remained chained. He was manacled at the wrists and ankles. He was going nowhere. He was a "guest" of Leith Ohmstead until further notice.

19

The Squeeze

"Gentlemen, you are looking at the Assistant Ambassador, or **the** Israeli Delegate-at-Large to the Israeli Embassy in Washington, Mr. Marchen Judisch." Leith Ohmstead continued, "Ambassador Judisch is an ambassador in name only, after doing his darndest to eliminate me the hard way…several times.

"Marchen, meet your betters. This is Speaker of the House, The Honorable Holcombe Broderick, and, from New Jersey, one of the elite Congressional Representatives, The Honorable Charter Joseph Saladin."

All three were startled by Judisch's abrupt inhalation of breath,

"Saladin? Whose wife, Imadie, was shot through the heart?"

Speaker Holcombe Broderick caught the inference immediately. He blanched, his skin drawn tight across his face. He knew what was coming.

Charter Saladin gasped. His expression changed as his blood turned to ice. He was barely able to speak audibly,

"Tell me, Mr. Ambassador, just **how** did you know that?"

Marchen Judisch instantly realized he should never have spoken. He pursed his lips in a grimace, clenched his teeth, and looked away from Saladin's face. Judisch's eyes would not meet Charter's. Judisch stared at the table top. He tried to ignore all questions.

"Damn you, you double-crossing b—d. You knew! How did you know?"

There was such silence that the winds could be heard crossing the meadows and swaying the trees. Congressman Saladin sat down, taking a seat directly across from Judisch, and leaned forward,…his face close to Marchen's. Unconsciously, Marchen crawfished, refusing to look into the now-livid face of Charter Saladin. He still refused to answer his question.

"Answer the man, Judisch," commanded Leith Ohmstead. "Answer him now, or I'll bring out two other lodge guests who are most eager to meet you."

Judisch smirked, "You've already introduced me to two people too many. I don't have to answer any questions…from them, **or** you."

Ohmstead grabbed his arm. "Try being a gentleman, and at least tell all of us how you knew Imadi's name, and how she was shot through the heart."

Judisch laughed, "A child could answer that one. I remembered her name from the newspapers and how she had been accidentally killed. I **do** read, you know. It was in all the papers, all the national magazines."

Leith Ohmstead back-handed Judisch right across his cheek and mouth. The blow was powerful, almost taking Marchen's head off his shoulders. A slow trickle of blood spread from the corner of his mouth and dripped on the table.

Judisch glared at Leith. "That was a cheap shot against a chained man. Unlock these manacles and I'll kick your teeth out!"

"Don't tempt me, Marchen. I'd like nothing better. I guess the next best thing is to hand you over to our other guests inside the lodge."

Judisch fumed, "I want one of your American attorneys, and an official from your U.S. Justice Department. All of you are going to find yourselves in a heap of trouble."

"I've a better idea, Judisch. You believe you have diplomatic immunity, but you really don't. Not now. The two men who want to meet you tell me that whatever I wish will be okay with Israel."

"WHAT? Only our chief Israeli Ambassador can make that decision."

Leith softly replied, "Wrong, Marchen. These men outrank even him."

Judisch looked astounded, "Our Prime Minister…HERE?"

"No, Judisch. But, they have the Prime Minister's blessing. Shall I bring out General Moschi Rubinstern, and Colonel Marseille LeBourget?"

One word exploded in Marchen Judisch's brain, and he retched.

"Mossad!"

Judisch knew. As an ambassador and a member of the Mossad, a traitorous Judisch knew that, before morning, he would be talking his guts out to avoid torture. If he refused to cooperate, he would suffer a deliberate slow death. The Nazis and Arabs had perfected unimaginable methods to extract information from their victims. The Jews had become masters of the techniques.

This time, Marchen Judisch looked at Congressman Saladin, then at Leith Ohmstead, and said, "That's all I know. Honest! It was in the newspapers."

Leith smashed his fist on the table. The drinks bounced. Only quick reflexes by everyone prevented the glasses from crashing to the stone patio.

"Marchen, you are a damned liar. Tell him, Mr. Saladin."

Saladin, his face a mask of fury, growled out, "A few newspapers suggested my wife was killed by accident. It was murder, and almost every paper and magazine thought so. The coroner told the news media that Elena was shot. Sharp reporters saw the blood on the pavement before House Maintenance Service could wash away the stains.

"The papers never used the name 'Imadie'. They used her first name, 'Elena'. And, no one, except Speaker Broderick, the medics, a few staff and guards, suspected Elena Imadie had been shot through the heart. The presiding coroner, Dr. Worth M. Grossman, never told anyone about the heart shot. Not even the Washington police. Dr. Grossman only told the media it was a chest shot...into the lungs."

Leith Ohmstead said, "This fact was withheld intentionally. And your inside knowledge of the assassination—and that's what it was—has tripped you up. During your travels from Bosra to Baghdad, to Tel Aviv, to Frederick Airport, to our 24-hour surveillance teams, we have taken telescopic snapshots, certified affidavits by witnesses, recorded wire taps, and filmed you with movies using high resolution tapes. **We have you cold!"**

From behind the group at the table, a voice boomed, "Yes! And your man, Jabal, has just informed **Oz** that Colonel Danvier Dyan implicated Marchen Judisch in front of President Sadah Diyarbar's court. Diyarbar, humiliated by that recent war that never was, had Dyan killed. Danvier was murdered. I might add he died horribly. A traveling merchant in a camel caravan just delivered a microfilmed report. There is even a picture of Dyan's mutilated body. How Jabal does it...and still lives...baffles us."

Stepping out of the shadows into the patio lights, Gen. Moschi Rubinstern, accompanied by his Chief of Staff, Col. Marseille LeBorget, glared at Marchen Judisch. The general said,

"Let us have him, Mr. Ohmstead, Mr. Dittus."

Cody Dittus had just returned from the kitchen. "General, the steaks are on, and here's a tray of my super Mid-East gin and tonics. You and the colonel might as well enjoy yourselves, because we will not transfer Delegate Judisch into your custody. However, that decision will be up to Judisch."

Marchen Judisch looked at Cody Dittus like a reprieved man removed from the hangman's noose. Then, Marchen looked at Ohmstead.

Leith said, "He means **if** you cooperate. Or choose not to."

Judisch, the turncoat ambassador and Mossad agent, hung his head. "I'll do or tell whatever you wish. I'd appreciate your taking off these chains." He sighed deeply, "I have nowhere to go, now." Leith removed the shackles.

◆   ◆   ◆

Senator Theo Dennahy walked along one of the busy loading docks of New York City's harbor. A large unkempt freighter had a crew of Big Apple teamsters working to get the ship's holds filled before dawn. Dennahy shook his head at the rusty hulk and wondered when was the last time the vessel had been painted. He had been chosen to verify the League's shipment. He muttered at the flag rippling in the breeze.

"Whose flag is that? What country? Let's see, a white star and crossed swords? No, those thick curved blades are scimitars. Going somewhere to the Mid-East. It's got to be an Arab country. Lord! You can't even read the name on the bow. How this hulk needs maintenance. I'd hate to kick it at the water line. Might punch a hole through the side."

Theo Dennahy couldn't help but compare the docks of New York to those in his native Boston. He liked Boston better. Regardless, Theo was astounded by the volume of New York's commerce. Hearing shouts, Senator Dennahy looked up and saw the ship's captain hollering from the main deck. The officer was beckoning to Dennahy. Theo waved acknowledgment and walked up the gangplank to meet the swarthy captain who handed him the inventory of the ship's manifest. The authorized papers contained page after page of equipment; the cargo holds had to be packed to overflowing, because the stevedores were starting to chain rolling stock to the steel deck. Every piece was shrouded in weather-resistant canvas.

Theo Dennahy was studying the covered vehicles. He mumbled to himself, "This deck is crowded with rolling stock…probably surplus tanks…**or are they new?**…maybe armored personnel carriers? Perhaps they're caterpillar weapons carriers—mobile artillery? Just what items are **in** these ship's papers?"

The Massachusetts senator thumbed through the pages clamped to the clipboard and immediately recognized, "United States Arsenal, Springfield, Massachusetts." A good boost for his state—lots of new business. He began to understand the influence wielded by the **Patriot's League.** An amalgamation, or "League of American Businessmen," organized by New York's Abraham Anselm, the **Patriot's League** (shortened to **PL** for identification purposes), had a shipping authorization lying on top of the manifest. It was signed by some U.S. Army colonel **at** or **for** the Springfield Arsenal.

Dennahy could not ascertain the colonel's address, but it satisfied schedule requirements for New York Harbor. Theo was surprised at the astuteness of Captain Abdul, the ship commander, who knew him to be a League member. Carefully descending passageway steps that led to the lower decks, Senator Dennahy said to no one in particular,

"Wouldn't you know the Captain had a name like 'Abdul'? Let's see his destination…Hmmmmmm, it's…it's…the port of Al Faw? Iraq barely has a coastline on the Persian Gulf. And now, Iraq has a port on that brief seashore? Well, these Arabs have dedication and strong backs. I'll bet President Diyarbar will have unloading facilities by the time this ship docks.

"Hmmmm, approval by PATRIOT'S LEAGUE? Our League of American Businessmen shipping Springfield Arsenal armaments to Iraq? Man, that **is** up-to-date stuff. That's being patriotic and bringing peace? If Senator Abraham Anselm says it's okay, then who am I to argue? Besides, this **is** New York State. Nobody would dare ship contraband in defiance of our government. Obviously, the U.S. Army brass approves. A shipload of these goods should cost Sultan Diyarbar an arm and a leg. And, the Patriot's League rings another bell on the cash register."

Whistling, but more concerned than happy, Senator Theo Dennahy exited a long corridor that led into the bowels of the vessel. From the steel platform by the door he stared at an immense cargo hold stacked with countless pallets holding wooden and cardboard boxes. Descending to the hold's floor, Theo read the black lettering stamped on each carton. Ball ammunition, high explosive, armor piercing, incendiary cartridges and shells—all in calibers of every size. Long boxes of weighty items were marked, "Vulcan" and "Thor."

From past experience as a member of the military sub-committee of the Senate Appropriations Committee, Dennahy recognized the packing decals of numerous new-technology Gatling guns…multi-barreled .50 caliber machine guns, 20-millimeter Gatling guns, 28-millimeter, 30-millimeter, 33-millimeter…all Gatling guns that fired 3,000 to 6,000 shells per minute.

Several pallets were marked, "Multi-barreled-experimental." Dennahy spoke out loud, "Good God! What caliber would these experimentals be?" Why, we're shipping items our U.S. Army doesn't even have!"

An ex-GI himself, Senator Theo Dennahy knew what fire power was contained in the thousands of boxes. The Gatlings, able to fire **from 50 to 100 shots per second,** deliver a veritable scythe of steel which easily decimates entire companies of soldiers. In just an instant, **slaughter!** Theo tore through page after page, scanning frantically for items he had overlooked. Something seemed **wrong!** Springfield Arsenal deals with firearms. So, what about those motorized vehicles on the main deck? Are there more in the other cargo holds within the ship? With a gasp, Dennahy stopped. He studied the company, routing, and source of the armored cavalry equipment. Shipped from DETROIT! GENERAL MOTORS COMPANY, Detroit, Michigan.

It was motorized ordnance from the Ordnance Depot, and from the Test Center of General Motors, "GM Proving Ground." The GM authorization sheet was also approved by...another U.S. Army colonel, the scribbled name unreadable. Senator Anselm had told the League members they had guaranteed our "new friends" the best equipment obtainable. There were no surplus armaments. They were the latest developments. Everything was shiny new.

"If **we** are promoting Mid East peace, then why are we shipping our best, our most deadly, high-tech army equipment across the world?" shouted Theo Dennahy. The only reply was his voice reverberating off the cargo hold walls. His answer was the creak of flexing metal from a rusty ship at anchor.

Captain Abdul opened the hold's steel door and bowed to Theo Dennahy,

"Has the Senator found the listed materials accurate?"

Theo laughed, "I've been amazed at how much your boat can store. I presume the manifest is correct and to your liking?"

"Yes, Sir, my Senator. First Officer Boudnawbie Smith has completed checking the inventory, found it 100%—in fact, several cartons extra."

"Then, call it a bonus, Captain. Did I hear you say Boudnawbie **Smith?**"

"His ancient Egyptian name is so long, so impossible to spell, that he Anglicized it to Smythe; had trouble pronouncing Smythe, so he Americanized it to Smith. You don't easily forget a ship's officer named Boudnawbie Smith."

Theo questioned, "Can Boudnawbie spell Smith? Has he tried Jones?"

Captain Abdul cocked his head and blinked. Boudnawbie Jones? As Abdul mused both names to himself, Dennahy signed his approval on the manifest, and gladly accepted the inventory verification taken by the first officer. Dennahy returned to the main deck where he said 'goodbye' to Capt. Abdul.

Walking down the gangplank, Theo could hear the captain pronouncing his exec's pseudonym, "Boudnawbie Jones, Boudnawbie Smith." Over and over.

The senator chuckled to himself, "Theo, if you had suggested Boudnawbie Smith-Jones, Abdul would never get out to sea by dawn. If I were captain, I'd worry that my ship might sink before reaching Port Al Faw. What's holding that old tub together is rust and ten layers of chipped paint."

◆   ◆   ◆

From the deck by the wheelhouse of the freighter, Captain Abdul waved goodbye to a prestigious agent for the **PL,** no less than United States Senator Theodore Dennahy. A harbor pilot for the State of New York guided the steamer out to sea. Beyond the crowded waters, a "pilot boat" picked up the skilled pilot, and Capt. Abdul was given authority to begin his long journey. The captain's disposition had changed from that of satisfaction to one of cursing indignation when his Exec informed him that three of his sailors were in sick bay. Such loss of competent seamen from his already meager crew put him in a foul mood. The reason was his new cargo and fire control bosun.

The boatswain (pronounced Bosun) was the best trained merchantman Capt. Abdul had ever seen. The bosun ran a taut ship, and Arab crewmen were noted for lackadaisical obedience to orders. That is, until the bosun, Warrant Officer Ahabe Jagadis, came aboard. A speedboat appeared from a spit of land off New York. The unidentified bosun, his boat pacing the freighter's speed without slowing it, jumped onto a rope boarding net, climbed to the deck, saluted the captain, and handed him official papers from President Diyarbar in Baghdad. Captain Abdul was fascinated with the bosun's olive skin, black hair and mustache. What chilled him was the man's gaze; flares of yellow glittered through hazel-green eyes that stared inside you. The greeting was brief.

"What duties do you wish me to perform, my Captain?" asked the seaman.

"Why, I…." Abdul suddenly had the feeling this Jagadis fellow could do anything. "Mr. Jagadis, you be my cargo and fire control officer."

"Very well, Sir." said the bosun.

"I'll have one of the men show you to your cabin."

"Not necessary, Sir. I know this type ship and will find a place under the quarterdeck." The bosun marched off carrying his garment bag.

Within a quarter hour, Exec Smith informed Capt. Abdul that the new bosun had chosen a cabin held by two ranking seamen. There was an altercation, and the evicted tenants were being sutured by the ship's doctor for bloody cuts and bruises. Soon after, the biggest bully aboard refused an order to tighten certain cargo straps. He laughed when Ahabe Jagadis told him to call him, "Bosun Ahabe, Sir." After the fastest free-for-all the men had ever seen, the bully was carried to sick bay and hospitalized with a dislocated jaw and broken arm.

The new bosun was courteous, fair, but he expected immediate compliance with orders. Also, the men now called him, "Bosun Ahabe, Sir." Discipline was extraordinary. Capt. Abdul and Exec Smith watched in amazement.

The swarthy Arab, in uniform and turban, smiled beneficently at his crew. Cody Dittus breathed the sea air. It was good to be shipboard again.

The lengthy sea voyage was uneventful. Cody Dittus, a/k/a (also known as) Ahabe Jagadis, kept the crew hopping. The dirty decks, gunnels, and railings, were scraped, scrubbed, and painted. The exec swore that if they had not run out of paint, Bosun Jagadis would have ordered the crew to redo the entire ship.

Yet, after completion of their monumental task, "Bosun Ahabe, Sir" commanded all available seamen to tour the decks and wheelhouse. During the evening excursion, Warrant Officer Jagadis kept pointing out the fine work and detail, while heaping praises on the men. The result was not only an increase in respect for the bosun by all the sailors, but an even greater pride in their ship and their own capabilities.

The emotional jolt to Capt. Abdul's sensibilities was tremendous when another fast boat sped to his ship with another request from Sadah Diyarbar.

"Captain, Sir, Mr. Ahabe Jagadis is to accompany us for an audience with the President. Immediately, Sir."

Within minutes the busy bosun appeared, carrying his garment bag.

"I regret my orders will not allow me to pilot your ship into Port Al Faw, Capt. Abdul, Sir. You can do it, but do not forget to reverse engines well before you creep into the wharf moorings. Wharfs can make a lot of splinters and kindling. There will be no tugboats there, Sir. Good luck!"

The Captain grasped Bosun Jagadis' hand warmly. He returned Ahabe's salute, wishing fervently that Sultan Diyarbar had waited until after the ship had docked. Abdul was overwhelmed to learn Warrant Officer Jagadis was also a harbor pilot. His ex-cargo and fire control officer would be irreplaceable.

Bosun Jagadis lowered himself into the waiting motor launch and headed for the Persian Gulf shoreline. When the launch sped behind a rocky piece of shore, out of sight of the rusty freighter, Cody Dittus breathed a sigh of relief. He grinned at the turbaned officer steering the boat,

"Jabal, I was beginning to wonder if you were going to allow me to meet President Diyarbar? With those forged papers I gave Captain Abdul, I might have had a lot of explaining to do."

"As you Americans say, Sahib, `no sweat'. I wanted you to have as much time as possible for your inventory. I presume, Sahib Dittus, you completed your task?"

Cody smiled ear to ear. He reached inside his tunic and pulled out a sheaf of papers. Cody grew serious, and showed Jabal page after page of war equipment jammed into the ship.

"It's the best of our best, Jabal. If they ever get trained men who really know how to maximize the potential of these weapons,…God help our troops if they meet them.

"You'll accompany me back to the States as a second witness to this cargo and the ship used to transport it. By the way, Jabal, did you have a chance to take pictures?"

"Yes, Sahib Cody. I have excellent color pictures of the ship…the name is the only item still painted and not covered with rust. Incidentally, those letters on the bow are old Persian script. Few people in ports around the world can read them. The ship's name is `**Vengeful**'."

Cody Dittus was frowning when he said, "Very appropriate! Someone knows how to tweak Uncle Sam's nose—without him knowing it. Let's get to the airstrip, celebrate our survival in Tel Aviv, then back to Oz Headquarters. The Mossad isn't too happy about us keeping Marchen Judisch under wraps. But, they know we need him to clinch our case.

"Besides, Jabal, you and I have an important meeting with a certain senator from Massachusetts. He's feeling safe now, but these papers should change that."

"Cody, my friend. What if he refuses to cooperate? He's in a powerful position to block any indictment. Can he, as you say, `stonewall us'?"

"Listen, Ozman. This inventory alone? No! Destination, a port in Iraq? That's damaging. If we show a bulging bank account, in his name, in a Swiss Bank in Zurich? That's an act of treason. We have the proof!"

◆   ◆   ◆

Congressman Charter Joseph Saladin had experienced a hard day. The House of Representatives was in another upheaval. Its members seemed to travel a path of crisis to crisis, never listening closely to admonitions or words of wisdom from its sanctioned leaders. Charter found it more difficult, each day, to keep the coalition of newer and younger congressmen in line.

Newcomers to congress were being influenced and coerced by the members of the President's Council, senate leaders, and renegade representatives. If the newer men and women in congress could not remain united as a voting bloc, then their power would dwindle and defer to the senior members of both houses who believed spending sprees were the answer to everything.

Charter stumbled on a lovely Persian rug lying on the foyer floor. He stopped and straightened it...because he suddenly felt Elena's hand on his arm and her haunting voice telling him, "Keep it neat, Charter. You know better than to leave it like that."

Unconsciously, after fixing the rug, he replied,

"There, Elena Imadie, does that satisfy your royal highness?"

Startled, Charter Saladin choked, because he suddenly realized he expected Elena to answer him. Empty loneliness flooded his being, and Charter looked up with an expression of adoring love on his face,

"Oh, . . My dearest Elena Imadie. How I miss you and your strength!"

Saladin, almost crying, slammed the door too hard behind him, and bitterly turned the deadbolt. Elena's presence drove him from his house. Since her death, he had stopped all festivities and parties at his home. Elena's presence was in every room and he had been criticized for holding on to a ghost. But, her ghost was the only thing that sustained him in his frustrating congressional duties in Washington. He almost broke the speed laws driving to the beautiful suburb of Georgetown.

Speaker of the House Holcombe Broderick welcomed his "adopted son", Charter Saladin. He knew that, like himself, Charter found peace and solace among the patio garden greenery. Both men sat on the padded ornamental chairs, sipping cognac and inhaling the fragrant, cool, Indian Summer air. The night was filled with the scents of honeysuckle, cherry blossoms, gardenias, and roses.

Miss Sarah, Holcombe's housekeeper, had phoned both of them earlier at their offices, and told them they would have unnamed guests at 8:00 that evening. Both men were used to such unscheduled appointments, and they suspected that the visitors might bring information about the rumored shenanigans that kept cropping up on Capitol Hill.

"Gentlemen, here are Messieurs Ohmstead and Dittus."

Miss Sarah retired quietly, never explaining how she knew both gentlemen. Nonetheless, by now the efficient housekeeper had long ago proved she had keen eyes, sharp ears, and a silent mouth. Holcombe Broderick often thought she would have been an asset to **Oz.**

Leith Ohmstead opened the conversation by pointing at Cody Dittus. "Holcombe, . . Charter, . . here is the recent assignment Cody just completed. **This** one should wake you up."

And it did! How the Oz agent had cleverly forged papers from Sultan Sadah Diyarbar to a ship's captain named Abdul. Of a hired boat, far beyond the three-mile limit, that put Cody on shipboard; his remarkable impersonation of an Arab seaman; and, the ingenious method used by their old Pakistani acquaintance, Jabal the Jackel, to take Cody safely off the ship and back to America—carrying a complete inventory of the weaponry in the ship's cargo holds.

Both Broderick and Saladin were aghast to learn the "checker" at the New York dock had been Senator Theo Dennahy. Only recently had both congressmen heard about the rumored Patriot's League.

"You mean Dennahy is a member of that league?" asked Speaker Broderick.

Dittus answered for both Oz agents. "Our informant, a chief guard at the Rayburn Building, was the one who told us about that midnight meeting at Abraham Anselm's office. Also, that Dennahy was one of the **charter** members. Holcombe Broderick and Charter Saladin looked at one another. Words were unnecessary. Both wondered what the shipment of munitions would prove.

Cody said, "Such an act, without permission of the State and Defense Departments, is, so far, unknown by even the President. An accusation of such a traitorous deed would hurt Dennahy, but only temporarily. It would not finish him on Capitol Hill. But, gentlemen, I believe this will."

And Cody Dittus handed certified copies of a Swiss bank document to both hosts. "Take a good look, Holcombe, . . Charter.

"It's an authenticated copy from Swiss Treasury officials of Dennahy's gold-backed bank account. The 'Suisse Bank of Zurich', to be more accurate."

Holcombe Broderick gasped, "My God! This U.S. Senator has **millions!**"

Charter Saladin scowled. He spoke through gritted teeth.

"It's starting to come apart at the seams. From Iraq to Washington...we've suspected many conspirators. From Baghdad to Tel Aviv, perhaps Jerusalem, to Beirut, encompassing major American cities, and ending in Washington. And, its beginning to point a finger at New York State."

Broderick first looked astonished. Then he looked physically ill.

"If this can be proven, as you agents suggest, this will break things wide open. It will be the worst government scandal since Watergate."

Leith Ohmstead answered, "Mr. Speaker, this will be far worse!"

Cody Dittus, nodding, regretfully said,

"It will crack the foundation of government. Worse, it will shatter the confidence of the American people."

20

Tightening The Noose

Senator Theo Dennahy, a popular Massachusetts candidate perpetually reelected by a phenomenal margin, sat comfortably in his leather chair and swiveled around from his desk. While looking through his office picture window, he anxiously opened an overseas airmail special delivery letter. He grinned from ear to ear. Here was his share of the recent munitions shipment to the Mid-East.

The confirmation listed a deposit to his account in six figures. Already his account totaled seven—in the millions—and he was wealthy beyond his fondest dreams. In celebration, he lit an expensive cigar, a gift from the leader of the Patriot's League, Abraham Anselm.

"Holy mackerel, this figure shows the price tag on that shipload must be around a hundred million bucks. Just think, Theo. How many of those weapons are high-tech, star trek equipment? And those babies cost a bundle.

"You're already a rich man, Theodore. Yet, when you and your committee visited Iraq, that damned desert Bedouin, Diyarbar, barely received us at his Baghdad palace. He was courteous, distant, **very** brief, and **very** cool. And they say he is our friend?"

Dennahy lapsed into silence. He was remembering that episode involving the diplomatic visit of the Senate Committee in the Iraqi capital. Seeds of doubt gnawed at his thoughts. Dennahy's voice revealed his introspection.

"Hmmmmm! **He** said we are preserving the peace in the Middle East. Obviously, no other Arab nation would attack him. But,…**are** we championing peace in a hotbed of discontent? Or,…"

Theo Dennahy never heard the soft footsteps nor his office door brushing the thick carpet. His contemplations were so focused that the senator didn't hear the "click" of the latch as the door closed. When he repeated his question to himself, it was the unexpected loud reply that startled Dennahy. He sat bolt upright as a strong voice brought him back into "the now."

"<u>Are</u> we championing peace in a hotbed of discontent? Or,…"

"Or, are you promoting conquest? Conquest that overthrows Middle Eastern governments and does bring peace—but, only by the sword!"

Dennahy responded by turning back to his desk...slowly. The hair on the back of his head was standing. That firm voice betrayed one awful fact: The stranger who had invaded his office knew. That disturbing question answering his question exhibited a knowledge of all Dennahy had done.

The Massachusetts senator carefully looked upward and saw an impressive man. He was large; his suit covered an athlete's build; his thick neck supported a head covered with a shock of reddish-brown hair and, his face was a soldier's face—a face lined from the wind and sun; a determined, square jaw under tan skin accented by a scar on the cheek. Undoubtedly a knife scar. A small bump on his nose revealed where it had been broken. But, those eyes! They were the most intense blue he had ever seen. Color? A cobalt blue—deep, penetrating—and they looked at you, studying you. Next, they looked through you. The gaze was not pleasant.

Theo Dennahy had been in combat in Viet Nam. He had been a middle-weight Golden Glove boxing champion at college and in the U.S. Marines. He talked silently to himself while the skin of his neck crawled.

"This guy is no pilgrim! If I met him in an alley I wouldn't last 10 seconds. I was alone. Now, my office is crowded. And with WHAT? And with WHOM?"

Then Dennahy said, "Look, buddy! Don't you start trouble. Even if you are as wide as you are tall!"

"Senator, you should see my partner. He's a 6' 6" giant."

Partner? Dennahy grew worried. "Mister, HOW did you get into this sound-proof office without making a sound? Better yet, WHO are you? What in hell do you WANT? And, I'll tell you this. It's late; otherwise, you'd never get through my staff.

"No one has told you I **am** a United States Senator!"

"I know you are, Theodore Dennahy. And, incidentally, some of your staff are still here. I passed them easily. They never saw me."

"OH!" was all Dennahy could say. His intuition warned, "Careful, this brute is a savage,...a real professional. But, a professional WHAT?" It seemed his uninvited guest read his thoughts. "Relax, Senator Dennahy. You will not be harmed. You can live to a ripe age,...if you have the good sense to cooperate."

"Cooperate? With a stranger? Man, I don't even know you!"

"Maybe not, Senator, but I know you. I know you could make more money on the outside. So do you. I know you need more cash—and you're getting it. I know you're a charter member of the Patriot's League. I know you're cooperating with Iraq and Iran, who are our enemies. I know you meet with Senator Anselm in the wee hours of the morning; you approve shiploads of death-dealing contraband from our New York Port; you receive 'appreciation rewards' from a certain Sultan Diyarbar; you have become wealthy within the past six months; and, a copy of your Swiss bank account is in my hand.

"Furthermore, here's an up-to-date statement from the 'Suisse Bank' which shows a higher balance than the one shown in the letter you are holding. That last cargo earned you an extra bonus you don't even know about yet."

Dennahy jumped to his feet. "Good God, man! WHO the hell ARE you?"

"Senator Dennahy, I am from **Oz.** Hereafter, you'll do **our** bidding."

Theo Dennahy, stunned, his stomach churning, fell back in his chair.

He mumbled, "Caught! By a rumor! But, the rumor **does** exist. **Oz is!**" The invader leaned forward, his venomous eyes paralyzing his victim, "And now, Senator Dennahy, this is what you'll do!"

There was no escaping the force of this stranger. There was no doubt that Dennahy was going to obey. Not if he wanted a ripe old age. Had Dennahy known this spellbinder, he would have listened and forgotten the questions.

Oz had come to Washington, . . with a bang! Cody Dittus was in town!

◆   ◆   ◆

Marchen Judisch, Israel's Ambassador-at-Large, recognized that his title existed in name only. Agent Leith Ohmstead had removed the "ambassadorial" chains,…in the presence of Mossad's leader, General Moschi Rubinstern, and his Chief of Staff, Col. Marseille LeBorget. One word from Leith Ohmstead and the two stern-faced Israelis would have marched Judisch from the peaceful Hidey-Hole into the dense woods nearby. Marchen knew the complications of extraditing a fugitive from American soil; therefore, in the dense unsullied forest, a gunshot might be overheard by that virulent agent of Oz, Leith Ohmstead. Marchen knew that his captors, given the chance, would place a dumdum bullet behind his ear, effectively blowing his head and brain into pieces. Judisch's obvious alternative was to stay with Leith and take whatever medicine the forgiving American courts would administer.

On that basis, Judisch planned a clever escape. On personal parole, his word given to Ohmstead, he wandered the grounds of the scenic, rustic habitation and closely observed the distant roar and vapor trails of passing jet airliners. They continually flew an easterly direction, and Judisch perceptively guessed the aircraft were flying to Washington, D.C. Once able to flee, his physical condition would allow him to sprint his way to freedom. A posse would have problems keeping up with him.

Judisch's spirit wilted. Leith Ohmstead was reading his thoughts. "Marchen, I have some errands to do. Also, there will be a meeting in Washington that you and I will attend this evening. I suggest you enjoy your freedom and salvation while you can. I'll leave another member of Oz here just to keep you company."

"Oh, Cody Dittus will be baby sitting me, eh?"

"Don't flatter yourself. Cody had more important things to do. During our absence, another agent called, `Jabal the Jackal' will keep you company."

The spy, Marchen Judisch, was deflated at Ohmstead's remarks. He started to bluster; then he looked up at a new figure who had joined Leith.

"Marchen, meet Agent Jabal. Jabal, your prisoner, Ambassador Judisch."

"Thank you, Sahib. We will get along famously!"

Judisch looked into the darkest brown eyes he could remember. The eyes did not waver; nor did the swarthy agent smile. Was this man an Arab? Leave him with **this** man? With that face? With that expression? Judisch shivered.

Ohmstead said, "Marchen, under no circumstance should you trifle with Jabal. He is one of two men I would deliberately avoid to preserve my life. Cody Dittus is terrible, but I believe Jabal is worse. Misbehave, and he will mangle you. You've been warned. If you did get away, he would trace you down, stalking you even at night! An angry lion would pale by comparison. You'd be left alive, feeling the pain, but bedridden forever."

The lights in the study of House Speaker Holcombe Broderick were burning cheerfully when the door chimes rang. Miss Sarah, the housekeeper, escorted Oz agent, Leith Ci Ohmstead, and his companion into the brightly lit room. Holcombe stood and was joined by his protege, Congressman Charter Saladin.

"Mr. Speaker Broderick, Mr. Saladin, allow me to introduce the recent Assistant Ambassador, Marchen Judisch. He is under the protection of Oz for the United States government. Right now, the Mossad and the government of Israel want him badly...to stand trial...before they execute him. The verdict by the Israeli Court will be a mere formality."

The Speaker and Congressman looked intently at Ambassador Judisch. What surprised both men was the horror written on Judisch's face as he gazed at Charter Saladin. Judisch, looking at Ohmstead, asked,

"This is Representative **Charter Joseph Saladin of New Jersey?**"

Leith Ohmstead answered angrily, "Ask <u>him</u>. Don't ask me!"

Not understanding the conversation between Leith and his prisoner, Saladin courteously replied, "Yes, I **am** Charter Saladin of New Jersey. You'll have to forgive my memory, but have we met before?"

Marchen Judisch's response was a sob. He recoiled from Charter Saladin, backed into a leather chair, sat down, and covered his face with his hands. Broderick and Saladin, perplexed, stared at one another. After a period of strained silence, Holcombe Broderick queried,

"Leith, is there a reason you brought Mr. Judisch here this evening? And, what do you mean when you say the ambassador is under Oz's protection; that the government of Israel, and the Mossad, want him? After all, he **is** a key staff member of the Israeli Embassy."

"Was, Mr. Speaker. Was! He is wanted for treason by Israel; is a paid spy for Arab interests, primarily Iraq; **and,...he is responsible for the assassination of Elena Imadie Saladin!**"

Ohmstead and Broderick turned to watch Saladin. Charter's face was ashen, and his expression was indescribable. Saladin said,

"You are telling me, Leith, that a known ambassador from Israel, this man, Marchen Judisch, killed my wife?"

Ohmstead answered, "I'm not sure if Marchen Judisch killed Imadie, Charter. I'm only saying that he had to be there."

"How can you know **he** was there?" And Saladin pointed at Marchen with a trembling finger. To Ambassador Judisch the finger was like the barrel of a gun, and the diplomat cowered in his chair, his hands covering his face.

"Charter, a combat team ambushing an enemy normally uses a squad; an assassination team usually consists of only two—the killer and his backup. Didn't you tell the Washington police, **and** Speaker Broderick, that you later recalled hearing the squeal of tires and the roar of an automobile racing out of the parking garage?"

Charter Saladin merely nodded, his stare never wavering from Marchen Judisch. Charter's gaze was fixed upon the Israeli diplomat who was unable to stare back at his accuser.

"Tell me what you mean, Leith?"

"Logical. A well-trained pair can succeed by attacking with complete surprise. Also, just using two men leaves little chance for mistakes or clues. Therefore, Judisch either fired the lethal shot, or was driving the getaway car."

At the incriminating words, Judisch jumped to his feet and hollered,

"I was driving. I would **never, never** have shot a congressman's wife. It was that ruthless mercenary, Colonel Danvier Dyan. He was the one who smeared the lipstick message on the mirror in the House mens' room. He enjoys killing. I was only following orders from…"

Realizing how frantically he was babbling, Marchen Judisch suddenly closed his mouth, sat down, and stared at the floor.

Charter Saladin, still glaring at the Israeli traitor, left his chair and walked toward Marchen. Before he could reach out, Leith Ohmstead wisely stepped between the two men. Congressman Saladin would have committed murder had Leith not intervened. Ohmstead said,

"Not now, Charter. He's more valuable alive! He's only a pawn in this chessboard of conspiracy. You want the head man here! Get him and you destroy the Judases in our government and expose dangerous Mid-East rulers for what they are. Those rulers can't stand the limelight of hostile world opinion. It will divide Arab governments and Arab factions against themselves. They fight for power, distrust each other, and destroy unity. Exposure will increase that mistrust. And **that** will help us, **and** our Israeli allies who stand alone over there."

Holcombe Broderick placed his hand on Saladin's sleeve, "Charter, we've got some traitors we must nail to a cross. Perhaps you should ask Judisch the questions we **all** wish to know. You've earned that right—for yourself…and for Elena Imadie."

Charter began the questioning. "Why, of all people, did you and your soldier/pilot mercenary plot against, and spy against, the United States?"

There was dead silence. Leith Ohmstead bent over Marchen Judisch and sternly said, "You'll tell us everything, answer every question, hold nothing back…or, so help me God, I'll turn you over to General Moschi Rubinstern this very evening."

Judisch begged, "You don't know the power, the vulnerability to assassination even here. There's Mafia hit men and Mid-East hit men who can get you **right in your own home!** All it takes is one order from 'The Man'…and you're dead! My life will be in jeopardy if I talk."

"You'll be **dead** if you don't. The Mossad is patient only because **Oz** has requested patience."

"Oz has ordered the Mossad to keep hands off?"

"Marchen, you don't **order** the Mossad to do anything. You request. Their hit men can train the Mafia. Now answer Congressman Saladin, damn you!"

Speaker Holcombe Broderick interrupted, "We're aware, Judisch, of the long arm of the assassins. I believe one of your men shadowed me in preparation to 'waste me'. He was on my street corner when Oz dueled with him. Your man lost. Another, 'Andre the Specialist,' also lost. For your information, that Oz agent is your captor."

Judisch, startled, looked up at Leith Ohmstead. **"YOU! So, it was YOU?"**

Leith Ohmstead returned his question with a faint smile. Judisch moaned, "Out of the frying pan into the fiery pit. Dear God, I'm a dead man!"

"Perhaps. Perhaps not. You break this case wide open and you will please us. You might even please the big boys in Tel Aviv. It's up to you."

Judisch continued, "The boss hates and fears Congressman Saladin. To kill him would raise too much stink in the capital. The boss is ruthless and vengeful. He figured out the best way to <u>destroy</u> Saladin was to murder his wife. His staff has double-checked how close you two were. He believed Elena was your alter-ego and that you wouldn't make a move on Capitol Hill without her counsel."

"Your boss was right," answered Charter.

"Obviously, your most vulnerable point was Elena Saladin. But, I advised my boss that he was overlooking your own inner strength. But, once he's off on a tangent, he can't be dissuaded. 'The Man' couldn't understand a neophyte congressman being invited to Holcombe Broderick's special intimate dinner party on The Hill. That was the final blow.

"If Elena Saladin were...er, ah...dispatched, it would obliterate Charter Saladin. So, the deed was done at his orders. It worked. Mr. Saladin was out of action for weeks. Surprisingly, when Charter returned to the hallowed halls of Congress before anyone dared expect, the boss decided to drive him out of his mind—a mental collapse or breakdown. When Danvier Dyan put the message on the bathroom mirror, it also worked. He had Saladin out of his way and fully expected Charter's doctors to force him to resign from Congress. That's why Mrs. Saladin was executed. This congressman had stymied 'The Man' too often,...ruined his plans. Saladin <u>had</u> <u>to</u> <u>go</u>!"

Speaker Broderick asked, "Is 'The Man' Sultan Diyarbar of Iraq?"

Marchen Judisch laughed. Broderick continued,

"Are you saying it's an American? Perhaps a member of the President's administration? Even a Cabinet member?"

Judisch laughed harder and louder. "The Boss had more power, money, and influence than anybody you could ever think of."

"How well does this 'Boss' tie in with Diyarbar?"

"Tie in with Diyarbar? Tie in with his vicious cousin, Druid Membossie? Hell! He's a **ruling partner** with them!"

"Surely Iraq is <u>paying</u> him to betray his country. That has to be his source of wealth. Right?"

Judisch roared with laughter. "NO! He's got oil in Iraq and steals more from Kuwait and Saudi Arabia. He's a millionaire and buys more power every day. And he's safe and set for life. He banks it all in Zurich!"

At the mention of Zurich, Switzerland, Broderick and Saladin both jumped to their feet. Leith Ohmstead closed his eyes in relief. Now Oz would be able to move. The lid had just been slammed tight.

Charter Saladin asked the key question in everyone's mind,

"Is 'The Man' a United States Senator?" Judisch barely nodded.

"Abraham Lieberson Anselm of New York? You're saying Senator Abraham Anselm gave the order to murder my wife? Abraham Anselm is behind <u>all</u> of this? You are saying Anselm is guilty of TREASON?"

Diplomat Marchen Judisch said a fervent, **"YES!** Arrest him and you destroy the sinister Patriot's League which gives willful assistance to your enemies. At the same time you'll wipe out the network of spies operating in Washington and in the Mid-East!"

As an afterthought, Judisch sadly added, "And I'll be gone, too."

Holcombe Broderick pulled on Charter Saladin's arm. He motioned Charter to join him in the kitchen. "Charter, get Miss Sarah, my housekeeper, down here immediately. I want all of this written down on paper."

Charter objected, "Holcombe you need an attorney, not a housekeeper. In fact you need a legal affidavit for Judisch to sign."

Broderick chuckled, "Son, Miss Sarah is one of the best legal secretaries you'll find. She can take notes in shorthand faster than you can speak, prepare an affidavit sanctioned in any state, and have it ready for Marchen's signature, plus those of three witnesses, within a half-hour after she retires to her room."

"But, Holcombe, who can type legal forms at this hour?"

"She can. At about a hundred words per minute, . . without errors. Frankly, the way she takes care of me, I don't know what I'd do without her."

"Why don't you make her an honest woman and marry the lady? You should hear the nasty rumors."

"WHAT? What rumors? Who's responsible for starting such evil gossip?"

"Father Broderick, I cannot tell a lie. I am! By stopwatch, it takes exactly 35 hours to travel through Congress before it gets back to me. By then you should hear my story. **WOW!** Our House members can really embellish juicy gossip."

"Charter, if I didn't know you'd bloody up my floor, I'd kill you."

"I admit I may be exaggerating, Mr. Speaker, but my thought about marriage is sincere. Miss Sarah is quite a lady. Highly efficient, too. Just what a lonely House Speaker needs. I'll bet Abigail would tell you to `Go for it'. You've been alone…how long, now?

"Over fourteen years, Charter. Lately, I've been almost at the end of my rope. That's why I want Judisch's affidavit **now.**"

"Why so important to get his name on the dotted line tonight, Holcombe?"

"When you and I, and Oz, get things underway to take the guilty parties into custody, how long do you believe Marchen Judisch's life span will be? At the end of our questioning, he said it all: **'And I'll be gone, too!'**"

◆   ◆   ◆

The following day was a vital one dealing with the internal security of the United States government itself. It was a touchy situation. Politically, it was dynamite. When the word got out, it could bring down an already shaky house of cards—perhaps stagger our constitutional form of government and fell the Administration.

Worse, it would undoubtedly cause the collapse of the party in power. Behind the scenes, the scavengers were gathered, snarling, ready to rip and tear America to pieces. And those wolves would demand a share of the carcass.

As a result, Speaker Holcombe Broderick was intensely agitated because he had to chair the House of Representatives at a time when he should be in a secret meeting with governmental patriots trying to end the intrigue. On this day Broderick was fortunate. The House agenda was slim, and important matters were tabled.

Broderick's conservative nature had long ago forced him to restrain the political ambitions of less-senior associates. Some house motions, even a few bills out of committee, were plain foolish. Meanwhile, the treason would continue until the conspirators were forewarned of their exposure. Finally, able to adjourn by early afternoon, Broderick ran to his office.

"Gentlemen, forgive my tardiness, but this was my first opportunity to get away from congress. Have you ben waiting long?" asked Broderick.

Charter Saladin said, "I ducked out at noon recess, Holcombe. Couldn't you have done the same?"

Broderick sighed, "I wish I could, but the majority whip would chair the session. And that liberal long-eared jackass would even encourage legislation requiring euthanasia for anybody past 60."

Holcombe scanned the close-knit group which included Congressman Charter Saladin and Oz Agent Leith Ohmstead.

"Where's Cody Dittus, Leith?" asked Broderick.

"He's settling things with our cabinet member, Secretary of Protocol, Mangel Mirish. I might add, Cody's companion is a thoroughly contrite senator, Theodore Dennahy, who introduced Dittus to the Secretary."

The door banged! Someone had entered the outer office.

"Got to get that hydraulic closer repaired," mused Broderick. I deliberately let my staff off this afternoon, so now what? Leith, would you please see who's violating my sanctum sanctorum?"

Leith Ohmstead was on edge. Therefore, he was cautiously ready for action. His swift appearance and facial expression told the visitor he was treading on dangerous ground. The visitor was a distinguished looking man, slightly balding, with a look of alarm on his face. He held up his hands like a policeman stopping traffic.

"I regret if I startled you, but I was expecting no one but Speaker Holcombe Broderick. He told me to be here at 4:00 p.m.. I'm a little early. Did I interrupt a private conference?"

Ohmstead said, "May I have your name, Sir? I'll verify your statement."

"Yes, Sir. I am Bergan Gruenspan, counselor to Holcombe Broderick, and a confidential member of his staff."

From the slightly-open door, a voice shouted, "It's all right, Leith. He's my confidant, and Mr. Gruenspan was the one who alerted us to this can of worms. Come in, Bergan, Come in!"

Bergan Gruenspan walked carefully into the Speaker's office. From the corner of his eye he studied the tall giant holding the door open for him. To Gruenspan, it was apparent he was being studied, also. Inwardly, he shivered. The only thought that flashed through his mind was, "What an apparition to meet on a dark night. There would only be two blows—when he struck, and when my body hit the ground. Brrrrrr! Three to one, I'd never wake up."

Suddenly, Attorney Gruenspan snapped his fingers. Without realizing the volume in his voice, he muttered, "Why in hell would Holcombe fool around with **this** musclebound cretin? He'd scare his own mother!"

There was a burst of laughter, and Bergan was looking at the faces of Holcombe Broderick and Charter Saladin. A gentle cough sounded behind him. Bergan turned and found a grinning Leith Ohmstead who admitted,

"My mother always arms herself when she knows I'm coming home."

Gruenspan's embarrassment turned his complexion ruby red. However, when he saw the humor of the situation, he laughed, relaxed, and sat down.

Speaker Broderick said, "Everyone's here of our original group except Cody Dittus. He's testing the waters elsewhere, so lock the outer and inner doors, Leith, and we'll get down to business.

"Bergan, meet Agent Leith Ohmstead of Oz. We talked about `them' at my home last month. That's why I phoned the latest facts of this case to Bergan, and asked him to join us today."

Agent Ohmstead's eyebrows arched in surprise and he leaned forward.

"Now, Leith," Broderick said, "Don't get excited about a possible phone tap. I used one of your **Oz** telephone scramblers. Gruenspan has one, too. We set that up months ago when Bergan joined me as legal council. That's when he learned about Oz,…and the other part of `them,' Cody Dittus.

"O.K., Bergan, you advised that you had important information that might startle our little company. Are you going to tell me you've decided to rejoin Senator Abraham Anselm?"

The House Speaker chuckled, but abruptly stopped when he saw Gruenspan did not smile. Holcombe cringed. Every time Bergan acted this way, it meant unforeseen trouble.

Bergan Gruenspan talked wearily, "Gentlemen, I've been a close friend and confidant of the President for over a decade. In that time he has never refused a favor or an audience with me—in private, too.

"I hate to say this, Holcombe, but attempting to arrange a quiet rendezvous between you and the President resulted in the quickest dismissal I've ever experienced. You, Sir, are going to have problems. That includes Saladin and Agent Ohmstead, too."

Broderick frowned. "Problems, Bergan? Didn't you tell him the meeting would deal with national security? That it involved his own cabinet member, Secretary Mangel Mirish?"

"THAT, Mr. Broderick, is your Achilles's heel. If your intent is to smear Mangel Mirish, you can forget about seeing the President. He personally told me he `has more important matters to tend to'."

"By God, Bergan, he'll listen when Leith Ohmstead and Cody Dittus corroborate the facts. He won't believe such…"

"Dammit, Holcombe, THINK! The President has **never** heard of **Oz.** If he has, it's only a rumor,...a legend. Oz earns its own payroll, and the directors receive funds from the Treasury Department through Social Security. Remember? You, yourself, told me how little <u>anyone</u> knows of Oz."

Charter Saladin interrupted, "Yes, but the CIA and FBI know. They'll back Holcombe Broderick and inform the President that **Oz Is!**"

"No they won't, Charter."

Leith Ohmstead was too calm...almost distant when he asked, "And why do you say they **won't,** Mr. Gruenspan?"

"Because BOTH organizations have a political structure. The top dogs are political appointees. I know...it looks good to the American public that the leaders of the FBI and CIA are the best available, in the Civil Service, and have earned their positions. Those who know the truth bury their heads in the sand. Fact is, the wheels in control stay in control at the sufferance of The President. Regardless, they are still political appointees who can be replaced, and then transferred to Timbuktu. There's always a dozen men and women anxious to take an appointee's job at the drop of The President's hat."

Leith Ohmstead said nothing. He knew that Bergan Gruenspan's assertions were true. Oz operated so surreptitiously that few people knew about it.

A stunned Holcombe Broderick sat down. "Bergan, you mean...?"

"Even your own Oz agents know the score. Secretary Mangel Mirish is 'The President's boy'. He personally selected Mirish for the job; for the new cabinet post The President created. When you disgrace Mirish...expose him as a traitor...you disgrace The President. You insult his intelligence, and you destroy his credibility.

"Putting it bluntly, Mr. Speaker, The President refuses to see you or any of your cohorts!"

The room grew quiet. It remained that way.

21

Rude Awakening

"You, Senator Dennahy, are probably the only member of the Patriots League with a trace of conscience left. Regardless of your good intentions, you know you're a traitor to your country. If you were in a combat zone, you'd be shot by a firing squad; certainly, here in the states, you face federal prison.

"Therefore, you will get me a private audience with the Secretary of Protocol, Mangel Mirish. You'll also provide necessary evidence to indict him in Federal Court on the charge of treason. Frankly, getting caught should almost be a relief. You've been agonizing over the tremendous amount of contraband weapons loaded on that Mid-Eastern ship. Doing business with unfriendly Arabs has made you question yourself. You should.

"I've heard repentance is good for the soul. That's a good point for you. Fortunately, I can verify I heard you expressing doubts and anguish after you realized what you had done. That's why Oz and I are going to let you off the hook."

Cody Dittus now sat on the edge of Dennahy's desk, this time gently explaining what the Massachusetts senator was going to do next. Dennahy's head hung with shame as he asked,

"How can you let me off the hook when you are going to indict me for treason? That'll be the end of me. Worse, it will bring terrible suffering and humiliation to my family."

"You should have thought of that before your greed for the almighty dollar compromised everything you stood for in Viet Nam. It's incredible—you, a highly decorated U.S. Marine, demolishing those principles you've always lived by—for 30 pieces of silver. Think of all your fellow soldiers and marines who might die because of those weapons."

"Dear God! That's what torments me. I must have been insane."

"No, Theo, just human. It was too easy. You made one mistake, but it sure was a lulu! Under the guise of patriotism, you were making big money. But, you sold your soul...your integrity...for a wad of green lettuce. With your contacts and legal expertise, you can make far more money and gain greater respect on the outside. No, you're off the hook, **MR.** Dennahy!"

"MISTER? What does that 'Mister' mean?"

"Effective the first of next month, you resign from the U.S. Senate."

"On what grounds, Mr. Dittus? There's no reason. The news media will have a field day."

"Your wife has been ill, hasn't she?"

Dennahy blinked. "Why...why...Yes! How did you know?"

"You forget. I am from Oz. Your wife is ailing and you wish to be with her; you've been thinking of private practice for quite a while...something that will keep you close to your home. You know the routine! Tell everyone the usual political lies and garbage. Believe me, when industry leaders and heads of law firms hear you're available, you'll be deluged with offers all the way from Boston to Washington. For you the transition should be simple. And it will prove financially rewarding."

Theo Dennahy was frowning at Cody Dittus's remarks. "You certainly like to use the words 'lies and garbage' when you talk about politicians. You don't think much of us in Congress, do you?"

Cody Dittus smirked, then asked, "Theo, if you were in my shoes, would you believe all the bull hockey Washington shovels to the American people?"

Senator Dennahy angrily opened his mouth, but there was no sound. Conflicting thoughts made it difficult to reply. A truthful answer was like a blow below the belt. He could not answer—without telling a white lie. Cody stood up. "At last, honesty—I rest my case, **MR.** Dennahy."

Massachusetts' Senator Theodore Dennahy, signed his letter of resignation that afternoon.

◆   ◆   ◆

Agent Leith Ohmstead, Speaker of the House Holcombe Broderick, and his chief counsel, Bergan Gruenspan, sat cooling their heels in the long corridor outside The President's oval office. They had waited a long time, and an expression of irritation crept over the face of Holcombe Broderick. It is unusual to keep the House Speaker waiting. Bergan Gruenspan sighed and shifted his position in the uncomfortable chair. Bergan leaned forward, and touched Broderick's arm.

"Holcombe, just relax. Look at Ohmstead's face."

Leith sat like a petrified rock—staring into space—his mind far away from the political scene of Washington. Leith knew that they were treading on sacrosanct ground. He also knew they intended to blow the whistle on important, powerful men in governmental circles. The President had enough troubles without splitting apart his administration. Leith expected nothing—but, there were going to be some disappointed patriots.

"What in hell is The President DOING?" demanded Holcombe Broderick.

Gruenspan gripped the Speaker's knee, "Didn't I caution you that The President would not take kindly to hearing the truth from us? Holcombe, I know he has been secretly mixed up in arranging large loans, supplying arms, and making under-the-table concessions to countries like Iran in exchange for hostages or special favors. He's accumulated wealth while thumbing his nose at the words of President Harry Truman."

"Thumbing his nose at Harry Truman? What are you talking about?"

"Holcombe, it was Truman who said, 'You can't make money in politics—If you do, you're a crook'."

"You, Bergan, calling The President a crook?"

"NO, DAMMIT. I'm saying that, following Truman, came Dwight Eisenhower whose West Point training instilled honesty almost to a fault; but, ever since that time in the 1950's, there probably hasn't been a President who didn't make money one way or another. For instance, Ronald Reagan, even out of office, took a gift of **two million bucks** from the Japanese. It was his reward for keeping the free enterprise system wide open on all imports to America—all the while the Japs were beating the hell out of American businesses and bankrupting our economy. Reagan got millions; the Japs got billions…and, the American people are still paying today. Lyndon Johnson could twist arms because he knew where the bodies were buried. As a result, he accumulated a fortune from Texas to the White House,…and Johnson was a political candidate ever since his college days.

"What I'm saying is: Why do you believe **this** President is different?"

Holcombe Broderick grew agitated. He was upset.

Leith Ohmstead was thinking, "Bergan, I thought only agents of Oz were cynical. But, you, buddy, have been around. The victor <u>does</u> get the spoils."

A well dressed man appeared from nowhere and stood before the guests.

"The President will see you now."

Ohmstead rose with the others. He passed the escort who was opening the door of the foyer to the oval office. Ohmstead spoke from the side of his mouth, "Are you a member of the White House Staff…or Secret Service?"

The escort glared—said nothing—just stared.

"Perhaps Army…or Navy. Military Intelligence, right? Tell me, your pistol…have you been issued your 10-millimeter automatic yet?"

As another man was opening the door into the oval office, Bergan Gruenspan asked, "What was that all about? Did the guy answer?"

"No, but I'll guarantee he's wondering who I am. Those new automatics are issued quietly—no fanfare."

Both men, following Speaker Broderick, were chuckling as they walked into the presence of The President. The President cocked an eye at them, then said, "You find something funny about this office or me? Make it brief. I've lots to do. I have little time to spare!"

There was dead silence. There was no invitation for the visitors to make themselves comfortable. Ill feelings smothered the room.

The President remained standing. Therefore, the three visitors did not sit down—nor were they asked to seat themselves.

"Strike three…and Out!" muttered Ohmstead.

"I've been informed by my old friend, Bergan Gruenspan, that we are meeting to discuss MY Secretary of Protocol, Mangel Mirish. So, discuss!"

Speaker Holcombe Broderick started to hand The President a large manila envelope thick with confidential evidence.

"What are these, Holcombe?" asked The President.

"Mr. President, Mangel Mirish has joined forces with a secret society, called the Patriot's League, which is led by Senator Abraham Anselm."

"What's so secret about Mangel and Senator Anselm working together?"

"Please let me finish, Mr. President. They have, in clandestine defiance of foreign policy and federal laws, shipped modern weapons from our Springfield Armory and other arms manufacturers, on Arab freighters direct to Sadah Diyarbar in Iraq. These traitors of the Patriot's League are getting rich. Each member has a secret Swiss bank account and deposits are made in six figures with their bank balances totaling <u>seven</u>. Diyarbar is paying THEM, ignoring us, even though Iraq owes the U.S. and the International Bank enormous debts from past loans."

"And just what do you want ME to do,…. Gentlemen?"

The President's voice almost growled the words. The President was growing madder by the minute.

Holcombe Broderick was pleading, "We must stop these men immediately. Remove them from positions of influence and power, and indict them for working against the interest of the United States. We have proof Senator Abraham Anselm is involved in a spy ring—working against us. We must....."

"THAT'LL BE ENOUGH OF <u>THAT</u> TRAITOR STUFF! THERE'LL BE NO INDICTMENTS—THERE WILL BE NO PUBLICITY. WHAT WE'LL <u>DO</u> IS PUT A LID ON ALL OF THIS!"

There was a pause long enough to enable every person to hear the breathing—heavy breathing brought on by exasperation and frustration. Holcombe Broderick was so surprised at The President's outburst that he stammered for words.

Bergan Gruenspan was a veteran of political infighting, and he tried to soothe the troubled waters. "Mr. President, perhaps you should listen to the evidence obtained by Agent Leith Ohmstead...." The President interrupted,

"You an FBI Agent, Ohmstead?"

"No, Sir. I'm a representative of Oz, a small department of the U.S. Treasury. We..."

"You trying to be funny, Ohmstead?" yelled The President. "Oz? You playing a game with me, and Dorothy, Strawman, Tinman, and the Cowardly Lion? What the hell is Oz?"

"An off-shoot of the OSS, Sir. I've personally found that...."

"The OSS ceased operations at the end of World War II. Congressman Broderick, where did you get <u>THIS</u> KOOK? You've been had if he has convinced you that men of the caliber of Mirish and Anselm are **guilty** of treason."

Leith continued, "Would you, Sir, believe that I've cooperated with the Mossad who can verify that Anselm, a Jew, has worked <u>against</u> Israel and Jewish interests to amass his wealth? That Anselm is working hand-in-hand with Sultan Diyarbar in the Mid East?" The President waved Ohmstead into silence.

"NO! I WOULD NOT BELIEVE <u>ANY</u> OF THAT CRAP!

"Gentlemen," and The President snarled, "You actually expect me to support an open investigation of one of the most powerful senators in America? His influence is international. I'll admit he's sometimes a hard man to deal with, but over the years I've gained his support. **And I'm not going to jeopardize such an alliance for you and any crackpot intrigue promoted by some unknown 'Wizard of Oz'. Understand?"**

Holcombe Broderick stepped forward, leaning over the large desk toward The President who stood stiffly erect.

"Old Friend, you do recall when the wife of one of our most outstanding congressmen, Charter Saladin, was killed in the parking garage beneath the Rayburn building? Her name was Elena Imadie Saladin. You had met her."

The President's tone grew softer, "Yes, I remember, Holcombe. It was a real tragedy. But, what has that to do with this?"

"We have a witness, wanted badly by the Mossad, who participated in the assassination—and that's what it was—to put Charter Saladin out of the Washington scene—He, this witness, will testify that the order to kill Mrs. Saladin **came from Senator Abraham Anselm!"**

Such an accusation landed like a bombshell. For a moment The President's jaw dropped, and he was speechless with a look of incredulity on his face—Then the fireworks exploded.

Never since his military days had Leith Ohmstead heard such invectives. The tirade of curses would have done justice to a top sergeant. The air turned blue with the oaths spewing from The President's mouth. It appeared the meeting was drawing to a vehement conclusion.

"You FOOLS really expect me to swallow THAT crap? Every KOOK walking the streets (and The President looked at Leith Ohmstead), and every CONVICT in the Federal Prison System can provide 'a witness'.

"You want ME to believe that? One of the most prominent and powerful senators in this nation…giving orders to have one of his legislative colleague's wife MURDERED? GREAT GOD ALMIGHTY!

"Holcombe, you need a rest—else you need retirement from Congress. And, by the way, I'm just not sure we're 'Old Friends' anymore. A friend doesn't ask you to ruin a distinguished senator's career; a friend doesn't ask you to crucify one of your own cabinet. Why don't you just legislate your Representatives on The Hill and let the FBI do its own sleuthing?"

The President folded his arms, effectively fencing his visitors out. His facial expression confirmed that his body English showed his disdain. Three words adjourned the meeting—"GOOD DAY, GENTLEMEN!"

The guest trio, thoroughly chastised, walked quickly from the oval office. Holcombe Broderick still held the damning evidence inside the manila folder. He noticed that The President never moved. When last seen, the nation's leader was still standing, still staring—with folded arms.

As the threesome exited from the anteroom into the hallway, Leith Ohmstead said it all when he muttered,

"Someone turn off the stadium lights. This ballgame is over."

◆   ◆   ◆

A surprise awaited Cody Dittus at the Office of the Secretary of Protocol. Initially, the experience was not as rude as his compatriot, Leith, had undergone in The President's office, but it **was** more violent. True to his word, Senator Theo Dennahy had arranged a quiet meeting for Dittus with Secretary Mirish. Yet, somebody had intervened, and the intervention obviously had come from the White House, because two rugged-looking Secret Service Agents stopped Cody in the reception room. They weren't nice, either. Each Secret Serviceman took a firm grip on one of Cody's arms and escorted him, forcefully, from the reception room to the corridor outside.

"Let's see some ID, Mister. Just what were you doing in Secretary Mirish's office? Just who are you? We don't like troublemakers."

Each remark and question was punctuated by a shove from each lawman. Cody Dittus found himself in a squeeze play between the two officers. The scenario was old hat to Cody. It was more obvious that their antics were caused by orders—orders to play rough. What irritated Agent Dittus was that he had done nothing; he had been scheduled by Senator Dennahy for a meeting with Mangel Mirish. Logically, such treatment to his person meant that someone <u>outranked</u> the Massachusetts senator—probably Secretary Mirish himself—or someone even higher. So, why the rough stuff? As usual, Cody grew cold and calm...and bided his time.

"Hey, look at this, Stan. He resides at Hidey Hole, Virginia. Must be some hayseed hick town. Just where is Hidey Hole, fella'?"

"Yeah, and your calling card is...is...WHAT THE—Greg, look at this...an embossed tornado, and his company is...is...OZ?"

And Greg continued the trumped-up inquisition, "What are you, fella', some kind of wizard? Maybe you wear red slippers and call Kansas your home? Just who ARE you?"

And both secret servicemen gave a painful version of a squeeze play with knees pressing against Cody's thighs. Their interrogation plain **hurt!**

Cody, looking scared, began begging, "Officers, please let me go to the bathroom. I can answer your questions in the men's room just as easy. Otherwise, I'm going to go right here on the floor."

The two accosters pushed and shoved Cody Dittus through the men's room door like a battering ram. Cody stepped to the urinal. The agents followed.

Still surrounding him as Cody unzipped his pants, the officers were startled when Agent Dittus suddenly took one step backward, leaving them standing at the urinal.

"Hey, smart boy, what are you trying to pull?"

"THIS," answered Cody. And he whipped his arms around the secret servicemen's heads and locked them in the crook of each arm.

"AND NOW, THIS!" Cody gave a mighty heave of his shoulders and was rewarded by the sound, **"CRAACKK,"** as both skulls rammed together like the smashing butt of a mountain goat's head. Both government agents dropped like sacks of grain on the tiled floor. They were out cold.

Dittus looked up to see an elderly men, mouth agape, who had just come in. "No problem, Sir. Only a difference of opinion. May I recommend you finish quickly? They'll pick on anybody and, after I leave, you'll be the only person here."

"WRONG! YOU'LL BE THE ONLY PERSON HERE. ADIOS."

Cody Dittus was two steps behind the elderly gentleman as he hurriedly left the building through the swinging doors. Cody was chuckling.

It was the first action he'd seen in quite a while. And his monologue was most complimentary.

"Well, Cody. You didn't shoot them, or carve them up using your initials. The leprechauns must be smiling. But, those tough-guy agents won't. They'll have a hard time explaining with such migraine headaches."

He hummed his way to his parked auto. "Ah, the thrill of combat!"

Then, a quick payphone call and the "Good Guys in White Hats" helicoptered their way to a rest at Hidey Hole Lodge. Plans had gone awry; a new stratagem had to be organized, . . because the "Bad Guys" were winning.

22

Crossroad of Justice

The party arrived at sundown. Leith and Cody sat in the shade on the back patio of Hidey Hole, their faces a study of glum discontent. The two were joined by Congressmen Saladin and Broderick, and their legal counselor Gruenspan, who came from the kitchen carrying trays of sandwiches and potent drinks. Conversation was minimal and the five were quiet—each man immersed in his own thoughts—each man guesstimating the next plan of action. Everyone was mulling over the unexpected treatment by the Secretary of Protocol and The President of the United States.

Cody Dittus nurtured his emotional wounds resulting from denial of his appointment with Secretary Mirish. House Speaker Broderick, Bergan Gruenspan, and Leith Ohmstead had been even more humiliated from the harsh treatment by The President.

The weather was hot and humid from a rain that had soaked the fields and woodlands of Hidey Hole. Yet, the air smelled fresh with the scent of new mown grass. As the sun retreated behind the rolling hills, the air turned cool. Mother Nature's bounty brought relaxation and peace to everyone—a noticeable absence of the everyday rat race—while the group munched sandwiches and sipped their drinks.

"Why did Mangel Mirish cut my legs from under me?" wondered Cody Dittus. Leith Ohmstead shrugged, "He didn't. The President probably asked him about the Patriot's League. Mirish denied its existence and any other wrongdoing, and The President bought the disavowal. Although Mirish can get his own secret service escorts, you can be sure The President sent the two agents and told Mirish to cancel the appointment. Senator Dennahy or no Dennahy, Mangel Mirish needed no excuse to avoid facing you, Cody."

"Leith, you believe Mirish **lied** to his own President?"

Ohmstead laughed. "You betcha! Mirish has everything to lose and nothing to gain by telling the truth. Don't forget, Mirish was appointed to the Cabinet by

The President. Mirish can't afford to let The President think he made a mistake. Besides, a couple more years and Mirish can tell everyone to shove it! He'll be wealthy the rest of his life—beholden to no man. By the way, how'd you get away from those secret service men?"

"They're nursing a couple of sore heads. I banged them together, put them to sleep, and called it a day. There's always tomorrow, you know. Now, tell me about your tete-a-tete with The President."

The congressmen looked at Bergan Gruenspan. Slowly, concisely, he told the story verbatim. He left nothing out.

"I wish **I** had been there," said Charter Saladin.

"NO!" said Holcombe Broderick. You would have hurt yourself...and us, too—not that it could have gotten much worse than it was. But, somebody has to stay on the good side of The President. After all, if he wouldn't believe the Speaker of the House, why should he believe you when you mention Elena Imadie?"

The group grew silent, watching the disappearing sunset fade into darkness. At that moment they heard a cough.

Everyone looked up. There, with an apologetic look, stood Jabal Thej-a-kel. The jackal said, "Pardon my intrusion, Gentlemen, but I couldn't help hearing your reports. It is ever so dealing with burros. My father always told me, 'There are more jackasses in the cities than on the farms'."

The crowd howled and Leith Ohmstead said, "Come, Jabal, join us. Have some refreshments and food. Where are you keeping our Israeli diplomat, Marchen Judisch?"

"Thank you, Sahib, I will have a glass of wine. We Pakistanis rarely partake of any alcohol. As to your prisoner, he sits there in the corner. He behaves well, but he has overheard everything since you arrived."

"Leave him be. I'm finding it hard to tolerate his presence," said Charter Saladin. But Leith Ohmstead waved Marchen Judisch to the table.

"Charter, Judisch may have some ideas of his own. I've been watching him and his expression tells me he was not surprised at our failures. He knows his time on earth may be limited and he just might have some ideas."

Marchen Judisch sat down, smiled at Charter Saladin, and quickly grabbed two stiff drinks.

"Had you murdered my wife, Congressman Saladin, I would feel the same toward you. Yet, I had no choice; therefore, I understand your President. He, too, is trapped as to choice—he allows an investigation—your evidence is released to the public—**He and** his party are finished. He allows corruption to maintain the status quo. Is it not always so?"

Saladin jumped up, "This is America! We don't tolerate treason!"

"Sahib?" spoke Jabal. "Our oldest existing democracy, England, has had many revelations of corruption and treason. In the Mid-East such government activities are an accepted way of life. Think for a moment. I know of **no government** that does not show scars."

Cody Dittus was fuming, "Well, we can turn our evidence over to the Justice Department. The Attorney General can assign a cadre of attorneys to go to work; he can involve the FBI; he can..... ."

Leith Ohmstead began pacing. "Not feasible, Cody. The President can sit on the Attorney General. The Director of the FBI might fight The President, but he's subject to orders <u>from</u> The President. Furthermore, enormous political pressure could be brought against the Director."

Bergan Gruenspan asked, "How about the Senate Intelligence Committee? They can stir up trouble and take it to the people on television."

Holcombe Broderick shook his shaggy mane. "Big difficulty! Senator Anselm is ON the Intelligence Committee. He almost runs it. Abraham Anselm is also Chairman of the Senate Investigations Committee—has seniority or control of other powerful panels. He can bottle up all of them."

"Yes, that's why Anselm is so powerful and influential." said Counselor Gruenspan. "Saladin here is one of the few who clashes heads with him. But, he does it from the House of Representatives. And look what Anselm did to Mrs. Saladin. Remember when I first came to you and warned you, Speaker Broderick?" Holcombe Broderick nodded faintly.

Leith Ohmstead motioned for quiet. "O.K., so far we haven't even mentioned Senator Jacob Bergenfeldt of New Jersey. Think The President will protect him?"

"Probably," answered Charter Saladin. "But, Jacob's a follower and not a leader. Indict the others and he falls. However, he'll be gone after this term. I'm going to send him back to the minor leagues. I'll be running for his senate seat next term. I'll beat him, too! So, it's only a matter of time until he's out of government office."

Cody Dittus interjected, "I've got a copy of Theo Dennahy's letter he sent to The President and the Senate Pro Tem announcing his retirement next month. Our real problems are the two powerhouse traitors, Secretary Mirish of the President's Cabinet, and the espionage ringleader, Senator Abraham Anselm of New York. How, by all that's Holy, can we expose them?"

Jabal Thej-a-kel stood and said, "Sahibs, perhaps it is better to ask, 'How can you get to them?'"

Leith Ohmstead touched a switch and the patio lights came on. There was no sound, no discussion, infrequent groans, some clearing of throats; the tinkle of ice from glasses refilled, unusually loud crunching of chips and dip, sighs, an occasional muttered curse. Conversation was stifled.

Marchen Judisch, the German Jew who had betrayed his adopted country, Israel, broke the silence. No one heard him—so it seemed.
"There is only one road open to you. You must kill them!"
Holcombe Broderick, deep in thought, suddenly stirred, shocked.
"WHAT was that you said?"
"Kill them!"
Bergan Gruenspan looked astonished, "Don't be a fool, Judisch. We don't DO that in America."
"In my old country, Germany, I often tramped the woods. The forests hold wild boars, boars with slashing tusks. A boar considers the territory his—when he sees you, he attacks. That wild boar leaves you one choice:
"It's either you or he, so you must kill. I say again, KILL THEM!"

The group lapsed into silence. Disgusted at the men who refused to face an obvious solution, Marchen Judisch snatched his third drink and walked from the light into the darkness. But for his footsteps on the gravel, there wasn't a sound. Holcombe Broderick softly cleared his throat.

"Charter, you know, when you run for New Jersey's senate seat, that Abraham Anselm will put out a contract on you. Senator Jacob Bergenfeldt is a close buddy of his."

"Holcombe, you mean Jacob is a close 'rubber stamp' supporter of his."

"Yes. Yes. Ignoring that,...you can bet Anselm will repeat the same type ambush he arranged for Elena Imadie."

"No Sir, Holcombe. Bergenfeldt's term ends in another ten months. By then his buddy, Abraham Anselm, should be long gone. Anselm will have things other than me to worry about.

"In fact, I plan to call on Bergenfeldt and give him every opportunity to leave office early. The other senator, New Jersey's younger junior senator, has been beating his head against a wall. For years now, both Jersey senators have cancelled out each other. Actually, New Jersey could benefit more with one senator. Those two, being poles apart, have been a disgrace."

Leith Ohmstead interrupted, "I doubt that you'll call on Senator Bergenfeldt, Congressman. At this stage of the game, you need to keep your skirts clean. I believe Mr. Dittus can accomplish a meeting of the minds. Agreed?"

Charter Saladin raised his eyebrows. "What do you have in mind, Leith?"

"Soon you'll know all the facts, and you'll be given copies of all the evidence—you might have to use them someday. You may rock Washington, but you'll do it with your reputation for character and integrity intact. No cloak and dagger stuff. Cody's a natural to do the...er, . . persuasion. I mean...he's unknown except to his superiors and one or two Oz agents: he's untraceable—no known address; he works for an organization that supposedly doesn't exist; he's moving all the time; and he's paid by courier service to a different drop every month."

"How do you Oz agents stand it? No friends, no family—I'd go mad."

"Patriotism, my friend, patriotism. We do more good against enemies of the United States than you would ever dream of. We are well paid, and, if we live, our retirement benefits allow us a fine standard of living. At retirement we begin anew within our own Witness Protection Program using a new name and choice of location. Different strokes for different folks, Charter."

On impulse, Leith Ohmstead excused himself. He walked from under the patio lights into the darkness of the green meadow bordering the rainbow-colored patio. Cody Dittus' eyes followed him. Leith was going to check on Marchen Judisch. Cody's awareness was typical—night or day, Oz Agents watched each other's back.

Leith found Marchen Judisch studying the moon-drenched meadow and rolling hills. Judisch sipped his drink and his thick tongue murmured, "Good evening." He was feeling no pain, but sobriety remained on the surface. Marchen may have been on the wrong side, but his covert training showed.

"You seem to be contemplating tonight, Marchen. Is there anything you might wish to discuss with me? You dropped quite a bombshell back there when you recommended, **'Kill them!'**" Judisch answered with a bitter laugh,

"Wild boars are attacking. You're losing. What other choice have you?"

"Assassination is a dastardly method of elimination, Marchen. Who are we to decide whether a man lives or dies? In wartime, of course, all bets are off, but this is not war."

"Wrong, Leith. It is not war as you Americans view it—but espionage and shipments of contraband weapons are increasing. Both operations are preparation for ultimate war; a war in which American soldiers will die. Some day that war will involve the populace; for the first time in your history, the front lines will be the cities of the U.S.A.. In Germany, we remember well the bombing holocausts."

Leith sighed, "We'll find a legal way to do it, Marchen. These men can be—they must be—stopped!"

Marchen Judisch's answer was a contemptuous laugh; a laugh so belittling that Leith Ohmstead turned away in anger. Suddenly, an unexpected thought struck him. Leith whirled and grabbed Marchen's arm in a vise-like grip.

"Damn you, Judisch, you KNOW SOMETHING! Com'on, spill it. What is it we don't know?"

"If I 'spill it', I'm a dead man!" said Judisch.

"Spare me the hearts and flowers, Marchen. You and I **both** know that Oz is your lifeline. In a few days, my superiors are going to tell me to turn you loose. Then there will be a political fight between Uncle Sam and Israel—Tel Aviv will do their darndest to extradite you home."

Marchen Judisch thought awhile. As he pondered, a ghostly figure materialized out of the night. Judisch never saw him, but Leith Ohmstead instinctively knew it was Cody Dittus.

"Hello, Cody. Welcome to the conclave."

"LEITH OHMSTEAD! How in the heck did you know me in the dark?"

"I could smell you, Cody." Dittus growled.

"Cody, I believe Marchen has something new to tell us. Open the floodgates, Marchen. Spill all of it!"

"You'll recall that I was in the original meeting that organized the **Patriot's League.** Well, the fraternity is growing. Abraham Anselm realizes that the fewer prominent members there are…the less likely the league will be uncovered. Yet, he wants his authority to extend from the Atlantic to the Pacific. He has two economic disasters helping him."

Cody asked, "And what disasters will take his realm clear to the Pacific? He already has the Eastern seaboard."

"He's working on a Texas senator. You might guess who since there are only two of them. But, this one is a wealthy oil man. The oil industry is in deep trouble, as you know. This guy was extremely wealthy—he's just plain wealthy now. If he becomes a member of the league, Anselm will have the Texas Gulf shipping harbors in his pocket, too. That covers the Southwest Sunbelt."

"And the other disaster?" Cody softly spoke.

"The Western seaboard. California or nearby states are implicated. The once-prosperous electronics industries are taking a beating from Japan, Korea, and Taiwan…even Singapore…and China is banging on the door. And <u>they</u> know what cheap labor can do."

Leith Ohmstead said, "O.K., so Anselm wants to tie up the docks on the West Coast. You talking about an industry leader or governor of one of the Western states?"

"Neither! He plans to cover East to West legally."

Dittus snorted, "What's with this **legally**? Is he going to enlist the staff of the American Civil Liberties Union? THAT would be a coup!"

"Gentlemen, it is almost as bad. Anselm's prospect sits on the highest court in the land. He knows that this jurist has lost his shirt investing in the likes of Silicon Valley. He's hurting…and he's susceptible."

Ohmstead gasped, "You mean a member of the U.S. Supreme COURT? DEAR GOD! I knew Anselm was cunning, . . and smart. But, such a stroke, if accomplished, would be sheer genius!"

Judisch continued. "Ozmen, I'm warning you. If Anselm succeeds in recruiting these men he'll be unstoppable. He'll have countrymen in key positions with unlimited influence. He can bounce from coast to coast, finagle from the center of the U.S., and use powerful business interests, plus the Supreme Court, to block any interference with his plans. Once established, I don't know how **any** government agency, not even The President, would be able to quash him. In my opinion, he will make billions—as sure as day follows night, he will lead America into WAR. In a wartime economy he would become the wealthiest man in the U.S.A.. Certainly, one of the most powerful individuals in the world."

Cody Dittus objected, "He'd never get away with it. Not in America."

Judisch guffawed, "Do you remember European history from the early 1930's? What they said about a mustachioed ex-paper hanger suffering with delusions of grandeur? Everyone made fun of him and his name, Schicklgruber. But Europe wet its pants when Hitler came to power. They had reason to!

"It took the combined efforts of the entire world to whip Adolph Hitler. Today, your Senator Abraham Anselm is headquartering his treason, not in a smaller Germany, but in the largest, most powerful nation on earth. Are you so sure he couldn't get away with it?"

Cody looked at Leith. They were both thinking the same thing; their options were diminishing daily. Then, Marchen Judisch asked them a question they didn't understand.

"Why is it that you Americans always have to be so noble? Always play so fair and square that you believe you will win with one hand tied behind your back? So, let me ask you, 'Who am I'?"

Leith said, "You're supposed to be a member of…a part of…the Israeli Embassy. Why you turned your back on your own people is something I'll never understand."

"NOT SO! I am a Jew, a refugee from Germany. Israel is my home. I **never** intentionally turned on Israel. I 'backed' into my traitorous role because of a filthy five-letter word: G-R-E-E-D! It was only a little bit of confidential information; next, just a little bit of espionage against my adopted country; the money **rolled in** and I got my first taste of high living. What I gained in cash I equally lost in integrity. Yet, I couldn't help myself. I backed into a jet-set existence and became a pawn of my enemies. I turned away from everything I once thought dear.

"Regardless, you still haven't answered my question: Who am I?"

Cody Dittus answered, "Frankly, I don't know **who** or **what** you are. I only know you should be shot for treason—a traitor to Israel and a vicious enemy of the U.S."

Leith Ohmstead said, "I believe you and Colonel Danvier Dyan did all you could to murder me. You are a numismatist with a coin collection that is probably one of the finest in the world. You undertook espionage to feed your expensive hobby of dealing in international silver and gold coins. You are an excellent pilot. So, from your horde of coins, you took several rolls of quarters, concealed them within a pitot tube cover, and blackjacked me. You not only gave me a concussion, but you threw me off an eight-story balcony. Fortunately, that pitot tube cover led Cody Dittus and the Mossad to you. If you hadn't collected coins, you undoubtedly would have gotten away with the attack. Then you ordered 'Andre the Specialist' to assassinate me in my hospital room. If you hadn't given us information against these conspirators, I would have killed you. That answer your question?"

"Mr. Ohmstead, this time you are almost accurate about my guilt. I was following orders to get rid of you. I don't know how close you were to indicting Abraham Anselm, but he was worried sick. He thought you were Secret Service. I had nothing to do with Andre the Specialist. That was handled by Anselm. I knew Cash Delway was a superb mechanic, but never learned he was Andre, an international hit man. I guess Andre was keeping an eye on me and Danvier Dyan. Anselm doesn't trust anybody.

"As to who I am…you know I'm living on borrowed time. The answer to my question is: **I am a walking dead man**."

Leith frowned and said, "I'm not sure I'm following you, but you are in no danger from us. Your primary concern is extradition papers from Israel that might be accepted here. Our foreign policy favors Israel, so the U.S. wants to cooperate to the fullest."

"Exactly! The Mossad will be dogging my footsteps the moment your superiors order you to release me—maybe put me on the first plane east. Either way, once I'm out from under your custody, Leith, I will be murdered—right in the U.S.A., or the moment I land in the Middle East. I **am** a walking dead man."

Leith and Cody said nothing. What was there to say? The Mossad never forgets. They've spent a half-century hunting wanted Nazi concentration camp leaders. And they've found them. Marchen Judisch could count his days.

Judisch coughed, then said, "Here's the deal. I'm resigned to meeting my maker. **Let me take Secretary of Protocol, Mangel Mirish, with me.**"

"What do you think, Cody?" asked Leith Ohmstead.

"Let's adjourn to the patio round table. We'd better have a consensus with our congressmen."

"Jabal, too?"

"Especially Jabal. He's cunning, emotionless, and has a mind that faces ugly facts head on."

The trio strolled back to the comfort of the Hidey Hole Lodge.

Holcombe Broderick, House Speaker, asked the key question: "What exactly do you mean, 'Take Mangel Mirish with me'? You intend to do him bodily harm? We won't allow that to happen to a member of The President's cabinet."

Ex-Ambassador Marchen Judisch stood, poured himself another drink, and slowly turned to the troubled group. "Right now I feel like a condemned man tied to a post, smoking his last cigarette, as the firing squad takes aim. My time is short. So, when I rent a two-engine aircraft, capable of long flights, at my old stomping grounds, Frederick Municipal Airport, you can be sure the Mossad will know it.

"A decade ago, I met then-Senator Mangel Mirish when we partied with Senator Theo Dennahy in the Bahamas. My lobbying group was most effective in gaining congressional support for Israel. I saw Mirish again when the Patriot's League was formed. We've communicated by phone a number of times—obeying orders from Abraham Anselm.

"You see, I should have little trouble getting Secretary Mirish to accompany me on a flight to the Mid-East. Senator Anselm has mentioned trips to that region, and I'm banking that Mirish would love to see that portion of the world, too. Of course, a private note to him would emphasize an oil deal will be available that guarantees him a whopping jump in his Geneva bank account. Of one thing I am sure.

"I am positive we will never arrive. The Mossad will move when we leave Canadian airspace and are over the sea."

Charter Saladin asked, "Presuming you are right, just what method would the Mossad use to…ah,…get you?"

"A number of ways: An Israeli Air Force jet striking over the ocean; a ground-to-air rocket; or, most likely, a radio signal will be used to detonate a bomb hidden on board the plane."

Cody Dittus said, "Presuming you do go free…that is, we release you with the understanding you leave the country immediately, what makes you believe the Mossad will know? We won't inform them. Another thing, if you fly at high altitude, a ground-to-air missile would rarely work that distance. We know a patriot missile requires a large firing launcher, a truck full of computer tracking gear, and a sizeable operating crew.

"Also, an Israeli fighter plane, flying in the western hemisphere, might cause a lot of embarrassing questions. And, I don't see how anyone would have an opportunity to get near your aircraft without being seen."

Marchen Judisch smiled, "Nothing will be attempted here in the U.S. or Canada. It's when we leave Canada or Newfoundland, in a fast, long distance jet, that the dirty work will be done. The air routes I'll fly are restricted in some areas. It's required that you file a flight plan for an overseas trip. THAT'S when the ocean-jumping jet is serviced and ready for you to continue your journey. And THAT'S where the bomb will be placed aboard."

"Ridiculous," said Charter Saladin. "It would take too long and attract attention. After all, that's a private charter—a rented plane. It's not like an airline passenger jet where you stow a bomb in the luggage."

Leith Ohmstead answered, "Let Jabal answer that one. Can hiding a bomb aboard a rented jet be done quickly, Jabal?"

Jabal studied the floor, then said, "I can do it—hide a powerful bomb—in three minutes or less. And no one would easily find it."

"HOW?" demanded Holcombe Broderick. "Well hidden in three minutes?"

"Sahib, I would place it in one of the landing wheel recesses. I would not use a radio signal. A timer would do it. When the wheels are retracted into the wheel wells, the bomb would automatically arm itself. An hour later, over all that ocean water? **POOF!"**

Speaker Broderick asked Judisch, "Marchen, what if there **is** no bomb?"

"Then, Mr. Speaker, I would fly to Baghdad for asylum."

"And Secretary Mangel Mirish?"

"He would meet President Diyarbar. He would return to America more money hungry and ambitious.... and a bigger headache than ever for you."

◆   ◆   ◆

Marchen Judisch's words were prophetic. Three days later the Directors of Oz phoned instructions to release Judisch, or spirit him out of the country. Certain agencies were asking questions and applying pressure concerning the whereabouts of Ambassador Judisch. There was danger that the existence of Oz might be revealed. CIA and FBI leaders, aware of the covert Oz agency, were asking questions that were political dynamite. There must be no suspicions that a traitor from Israel was being shielded by the U.S.A.

Early one morning, before the city of Washington, D.C., awakened, a twin engine plane took off from Frederick Municipal Airport in Maryland. The craft headed toward the coastlines of Canada. It landed at Quebec by the St. Lawrence River. Soon after, a twin engine jet flew over the Gulf of St. Lawrence, its course plotted west-southwest toward Africa and the Mediterranean Sea. Then came confusion. In Newfoundland, St. John's radar picked up an aircraft flying east-southeast, a direct heading toward the British Isles. Radio frequencies were monitored, but contact could not be made with the unidentified craft. The pilot had lost his radio,...or was ignoring all calls.

Abruptly, the faint image, now hundreds of miles out to sea, disappeared. The newspapers had a field day. Secretary of Protocol, Mangel Mayer Mirish, had vanished during a goodwill flight to the Mid-East. The President of the United States seemed so overcome that he had difficulty talking with reporters.

But, in private, he was hollering at his aides. "What in hell was Mangel Mirish doing? Where was he going? Listen, we've got to appease these reporters. Just tell them The President had sent Mirish on a goodwill tour of Israel and other Mid-East countries; that he was accompanying Ambassador Judisch, an accomplished pilot, and they flew into violent weather.

"Damn! Doesn't anybody want to keep me in the know? What an idiot stunt to pull just before the elections. Find out what he was doing. Someone has to know. I'll be hanged if I know what he was up to."

The telephone rang in the home of Congressman Charter Saladin. The caller was Speaker of the House, Holcombe Broderick.

"Be at my house tonight at 8:00; the front door will be unlocked. We're having visitors."

Saladin, Broderick, Ohmstead and Dittus, sat around the cheery fireplace which warmed the cold night air of an Indian summer. There came a soft knock, then a ringing of the door chimes, followed by another soft knock. Miss Sarah opened the door and led the visitor to the den.

"Mr. Broderick, here is Major Gursten Wollenski from Israel."

Leith Ohmstead stuck out his hand, "Congratulations, MAJOR. You were Captain the last time we talked."

"Thank you, Mr. Ohmstead…. Good evening, Gentlemen!" After the introductions were over, Gursten Wollenski held his glass high and toasted, "Here's to the men who protect America and Israel."

Cody Dittus, puzzled, said, "I'll drink to that, but what did we **do?**"

"One of you, unidentified, phoned General Moschi Rubinstern about the release from your custody of Marchen Judisch. We staked out his haunts, especially Frederick Airport. The airport authorities, and the Federal Aviation Authority (FAA), cooperated and gave us, of the Mossad, a copy of Judisch's flight plan.

"Our men covered the Canadian airports that Judisch used in his flights to the Mid-East. Sure enough, he rented a jet at Quebec. Mossad wanted no mistakes. Certainly, they didn't want Judisch to slip through our net and get into Iraq. While the jet was being serviced, one of our men…. ."

Ohmstead interrupted, "One of your men, posing as a flight line attendant, planted a bomb—probably plastique—in one of the wheel wells of the landing gear."

Gursten Wollenski blinked. "That's right! How did you know?"

"Jabal told us how you'd do it."

"WHO?"

"Never mind. Please go on with your story, Gursten."

"Approximately a half-hour out of Quebec International, Judisch made a compass correction away from a course that would have taken him to Tunisia. He swung to a more northerly course…directly toward England. We hadn't expected that maneuver from Judisch. Had we not planted a bomb on that plane, Judisch would have escaped into Europe."

Leith Ohmstead said, "I guess the crossroad of justice was reached. Did you have an inkling that the Cabinet member, Mangel Mirish, was with him?"

"Absolutely not! Had we known, we would have called off our dogs!"

Leith smiled, "Don't worry. You did us a favor. That's all we'll say."

Wollenski looked surprised. "We did you a favor? If The President finds out, it will set relations back 20 years."

"The President **won't** find out! If you're curious, ask General Rubinstern. I'll bet he can figure it out."

Holcombe Broderick leaned forward, "Tell us, just how long did it take to conceal and then arm that bomb? Are you sure the downed plane had Judisch and Mirish on board?"

"They found, believe it or not, the rubber raft—inflated—that had been assigned to that particular aircraft. Everything else was obviously blown to pieces and now lies at the bottom of the sea. As to the time it took for our man to hide and arm the bomb? Less than three minutes! When Judisch retracted his landing gear, the wheel, folding into the well, pushed a spring that set the timer. That's why the plane's image was so faint on the long distance scope. About 500 miles is maximum range. And that's when the plane vanished from radar. It had blown up."

Charter Saladin said, "Well, Jabal was right. Incidentally, what type of explosive did you use?"

"A concentrated `plastique'. A little bit makes a big bang!"

Holcombe Broderick exclaimed, "Jabal was right again."

Wollenski asked, "Who or what is Jabal?"

Cody Dittus said, "In your case, you wouldn't want to meet him!"

23

"Twilight of Valhalla"

Bergan Gruenspan swiveled his executive chair away from his desk and stared through the windows into Washington's twilight. This evening, for the first time in over a year, his stomach no longer churned and the stress of a troubled mind vanished. He had almost forgotten what a good night's sleep could do for a weary body. Gruenspan had seen the fates grow angry. He had been surprised when he learned Senator Theodore Dennahy of Massachusetts had resigned. But now he was stunned at the continuing devastation within the **Patriot's League.** He wondered aloud,

"Is it the wrath of God striking those who would turn against their country-men? Or, is it the hand of man?"

There was no answer, so Bergan concluded that both God and man were at work. Within days after that night meeting at Holcombe Broderick's home, Holcombe had personally briefed Gruenspan on all that happened, including Major Garsten Wollenski's confession that revealed that a bomb had been placed. The "why" Bergan already knew. What astonished him was the calm complacency that accompanied Marchen Judisch as he approached his death—taking Mangel Mirish, probably the most politically powerful league member—with him. Judisch's words were haunting: **"There is only one road open to you. You must kill them!"**

The man behind the counselor's desk sighed. He realized that his heart was not racing, not skipping a beat, not thumping so hard that he coughed with apprehension. Gruenspan listened closely. The rhythmic beating inside his chest was slow...and serene. At last, he found himself at rest, not dreading the coming dark and another sleepless night, thanking God that his decision to join the company of Holcombe Broderick had been a blessing. The previous years with Abraham Anselm had given way to depression and loneliness; a situation where, among that large senatorial staff, he stood like a dinosaur—avoided, outmoded, without a future. Speaker Broderick changed it all.

Attorney Gruenspan almost fell asleep in his serenity. Little things, unappreciated for so long, grew evident: The soft hiss of the ventilation system, the unusually loud ticktocking of the Speaker's Grandfather Clock in the next office, the hushed closing of the outer office door.

The closing of the outer door? Was he dreaming? Gruenspan moved his head. He heard faint footsteps brushing the plush carpet. The sound ceased, behind him, at the front of his desk. There was dead silence.

Bergan was intrigued. His composure was such that his heart remained tranquil. He had never been so relaxed. He smiled. He had taken no alcohol, nor any medication. It was just that…he didn't give a damn! As far as he was concerned, the next move was up to the intruder.

The intruder did not speak. After an awkward moment he courteously cleared his throat…gently. A minute passed…an interminable period of time in this circumstance. An unfamiliar voice said,

"Mr. Gruenspan—Bergan?—**Please, I have no one else to turn to.**"

This time it was Gruenspan who raised his eyebrows in amazement. He had not heard that voice in several years. Yet, the tone was pleading, extremely courteous, and almost tearful.

Slowly, Bergan turned around…and stared into the gaunt face of…**Senator Jacob Bergenfeldt.** The face was pale and sweaty.

Attorney Gruenspan stood and proffered his hand in friendship. A hollow-eyed Senator Bergenfeldt was so disturbed he never saw it. Bergenfeldt collapsed into a visitor's chair. Bergan, hand still extended, was shocked at the appearance of the New Jersey senator. Obviously, he was highly disturbed and physically ill.

Gruenspan circled his desk and grasped Bergenfeldt's shoulder.

"I am pleased you remember me, Jacob. I'm further pleased you've come to an old friend who has joined the camp of the enemy. You're quite upset, so I'll tell you that I'll do all in my power to help you. In the meantime, a small cognac is in order."

Jacob Bergenfeldt grabbed the brandy snifter and guzzled the liquid. Bergan blinked when he saw the senator did not choke, so he poured a more generous offering. One more snort like this one and Bergenfeldt would be unable to talk. Minutes passed while Jacob sipped. Finally, he said, "I presume you saw the headlines about Secretary Mirish perishing with the Israeli Diplomat, Marchen Judish? Did you know that I sat with those men in a business meeting only weeks ago? That—"

The senator shivered and suddenly gulped down the cognac. The burning stimulant didn't faze Bergenfeldt's throat or stomach. Gruenspan shrugged, and poured the senator another. Then, Bergan Gruenspan answered him softly,

"You mean during the profitable meeting of the **Patriot's League?**"

Jacob Bergenfeldt gagged. His world was caving in on him.

"My God, Bergan. How much do you KNOW?"

Gruenspan nodded and said, "I know it all, Jacob."

Senator Bergenfeldt drained his glass. He took a deep breath.

"Fill the brandy glass one more time, Bergan.

"I thought I was smart. I realize I'm an idiot. I'm only a rubber stamp for Abraham Anselm. 'Lieb' has played me for the fool. Recently, I've made a fortune by selling out my country. But, I don't understand what's happening. Dennahy of Massachusetts has resigned. I guess his wife's bad health saved him?"

Bergenfeldt looked at Gruenspan for confirmation. Gruenspan did not move nor reply. He waited for Jacob to continue.

"I meant...meant...well, you've seen it in the Washington Post and on television. An accidental explosion in the plane carrying Ambassador Judisch and Secretary Mirish. The **League** is disappearing!"

"No, Jacob. The League's demise is planned. Dennahy is lucky; and he knows it. Had he NOT resigned, he would have gone before Mirish and Judisch."

Senator Bergenfeldt jumped to his feet. "What in hell do you mean...gone before Mirish and Judisch?" Bergenfeldt could not believe the answer.

"Jacob, if Boston's Dennahy had not resigned, he would have been dead long before the ambassador and senator. There was no accident. Every move was planned. What the bomb didn't get...the sharks did. The plans allowed for probable suspicions, but left no way to prove foul play; no evidence should remain. And, that's exactly what's happened."

"I can't believe that. Who'd do such a thing?"

If a special unit of the U.S. Government doesn't accomplish it, then the Israeli Mossad will—and did. And you, my friend, are next!"

Jacob Bergenfeldt gasped and fell into his chair. He was finished!

The evening wore on. Jacob Bergenfeldt sat quietly, ingesting his cognac. The Grandfather Clock in Speaker Broderick's office chimed melodiously. Senator Bergenfeldt gave a deep sigh,

"It's funny how things can matter so much—those chimes, they're beautiful. So rich and mellow. It seems I've never noticed the beauty around me. Or maybe, Bergan, it's the cleansing of a painful conscience?"

"Jacob, it's your release from a slimy quagmire. You've been running a crippling temperature from 'Potomac Fever'. You're feeling better because everything's out in the open. You don't have anything to hide…now."

"I'll have to watch it from now on, won't I?"

There was an awkward silence. The senator, comprehending that there had been no answer, slowly looked up at the features of Bergan Gruenspan. He cringed at the disgusted look on Bergan's face. Jacob could almost forecast what was coming.

"Senator, <u>you</u> are THROUGH! I've already told you that Uncle Sam or the Israelis would decide your fate. Your future was to be decided at your upcoming election. Frankly, a great patriot from your state is going to withdraw from Congress and run for your seat. He'll win it, too."

"SALADIN! Charter Saladin plans to take my place?"

"Gruenspan chuckled, "Don't make me laugh. Saladin intends to represent New Jersey **and** the people. You abdicated that responsibility years ago when you joined forces with Abraham Lieberson Anselm. And you KNOW that! You've gotten rich and should live out your days comfortably…permanently out of political office."

"You're not going to turn me in to the authorities?"

"And prove what? No, Jacob, that would serve no purpose—except to cause more distrust of Congress, distrust of our government. Within a month Anselm will be dealt with. During that time you will begin to suffer blackouts and violent headaches while the Senate is in session. Rumors of serious health problems—rumors spread by your staff **and** your Washington doctor—will corroborate your grievous illness.

"You, of course, will put on Academy Award performances during the sessions. First, you will begin to miss roll call. Then, days will go by when you will not be seen in the Senate or at your office. That will give you time to settle other employment for your staff. After a month you can announce you are 'considering retirement'.

"Jacob, your years in the senate provide you with an excellent pension. With your other assets, you will live the rest of your life in style."

Jacob Bergenfeldt looked like a chastised little boy.

"And if I refuse to go along with this charade?"

"It's no charade, Bergenfeldt. Damn you, LISTEN! The Washington Post would love to spread stories of your treason across the nation. Not only would your own senate body censor you severely, but you would ruin your whole family. The publicity would kill your wife. Oh, there's one other thing."

"One other thing, Bergan? WHAT? What else <u>could</u> there be?"

"It's this: You could be found with the top of your head blown off. History will question whether it was suicide or murder. No one will ever be sure, Jacob."

"The Mossad again? They'll never get away with it."

"You're being the fool now, Jacob. The Mossad takes care of their own problems…those who turn against Israel. In your case, America's OZ will take care of you—believe me, they'll do it without leaving a trace."

"The WHAT? Did you say OS, ODDS, OR OZ? Nevertheless, Americans don't do that to Americans, Bergan. Even the CIA wouldn't touch a U.S. Senator!"

"Jacob, the CIA won't know a thing about this. I assure you, this covert group of hit men, members of Oz, could take out the President, his entire administration, one by one, and never be caught or brought to trial. Believe me, they can make JFK's assassination look like kid's play.

"No, you do <u>exactly</u> as I've told you. You're out of the picture, Jacob. Better yet, you'll be alive, retired, and smelling the roses."

"Quitting politics will mean sending me to my death."

"Senator Bergenfeldt, only your political career is being sent to Valhalla. You'll still be alive to enjoy the twilight of your life."

"As I just asked, suppose I refuse, Bergan?"

"Then, there'll be one big hole right between your eyes. You'll never know where, or when. But, it will happen. I promise you that, Jacob."

Senator Bergenfeldt looked exhausted as he said,

"I see! Well then, before you report back to your group, let me assure you that there will be no mention of Charter Saladin from anyone in my camp. Because of 'doctor's orders', I'll begin missing committee meetings, especially those chaired by Abraham Anselm."

Taking a deep breath, Jacob Bergenfeldt added, "Bergan, will the end of next week be all right for my first disabling headache? I'll make it a point to stagger from the Senate floor."

"That performance would be most timely, Jacob."

◆   ◆   ◆

In the late afternoon the patio of Hidey Hole Lodge was noisy. House Speaker Holcombe Broderick was far from happy when Bergan Gruenspan told about the unforeseen visit of Senator Jacob Bergenfeldt to Gruenspan's office. "Why, of all times, did you tell him we were on to him?" shouted Holcombe. "Saladin was going to announce for his senate seat in six months."

"That's right," agreed Charter Saladin.

Israeli General Moschi Rubinstern said, "You haven't **got** six months!"

"He's right, Gentlemen," intoned Col. Marseille LeBourget. "In fact, for you Americans, I believe you call it 'the eleventh hour'."

Cody Dittus, looking puzzled, quickly asked, "What do you mean, 'the eleventh hour'? We're not at war or in a life-threatening situation."

Colonel LeBourget smiled, "Ah, friend Cody,…but, you <u>are</u>!"

Leith Ohmstead silenced the group with a wave of his hand. "Let's let these Mossad allies tell us what we evidently don't know. Their statements indicate someone left the barn door open. Go ahead, General."

"No, Leith. I'll let Colonel LeBourget explain. He's the one who caught it."

"It?" mouthed Cody Dittus at Leith Ohmstead.

Marseille LeBourget locked his hands behind his back and began pacing as he explained the latest happening to Congressmen Broderick and Saladin, and Oz Agents Ohmstead and Dittus.

"Are you Gentlemen acquainted with the name Druid Kahn Membossie?"

At the mention of Sultan Diyarbar's cousin, every man in the group stiffened, except the two Israelis. Cody Dittus growled,

"If you tell me that Membossie is in this country I want to know where; he'll be dead within hours. I've never known such a beast—that's exactly what he is. He kills for fun, dispatching his victims slowly, torturing them to death. Compared to him, President Sadah Diyarbar is a saint.

"It's a guarded secret in Baghdad, but some say he murdered Hadallah Diyarbar, Sadah's brother. I hope you're not saying Abraham Anselm is collaborating with the likes of **him.**"

"No, but Anselm sent a cablegram to Membossie in BEIRUT! We believe that Beirut is a pipeline to Iraq and Sadah Diyarbar. If Membossie is in Beirut, then you can be sure he's up to no good."

Cody spoke through clenched teeth, "In my old stomping ground, Beirut. Wonder whose throat Membossie's been ordered to slash now?"

Col. LeBourget said, "That's the problem. Beirut's the pivot point for causing trouble in the Mid-East. What we want to know is…are his orders coming from here, Washington, and not from Baghdad? That cablegram from Anselm is, in my opinion, the tipoff."

Leith Ohmstead's face grew fierce as he asked, "The cablegram. Why would you suspect we face an 11th hour?"

"Because, Leith, the contents said, 'Forwarding my trunk within the week. Anticipating lengthy visit. May alter business procedures. Your representative may be needed here. Regards to Professor Ramadan'. And it's signed with initials A-L-A."

Charter Saladin sighed, "Uh huh, the feast of Ramadan. That's in the ninth month of the Moslem year. You can bet there's a hidden meaning there."

Colonel LeBourget said, "I'm impressed, Mr. Saladin. You seem well acquainted with religions of the East."

"My name is Saladin, Colonel. That's quite a name in the Mid-East. King Richard of England found that out. That's Moslem country."

Leith Ohmstead leaned forward, "You agents of the Mossad miss very little. Just what do you believe that cablegram really says?"

General Rubinstern stood. "I can't stand anymore of Marseille's pacing, but he does get to the bottom of things. We've discussed the message and believe it means: 'Forwarding my trunk within the week'. There'll be another shipment of weapons this week. Anselm may suddenly leave the country—'anticipating lengthy visit'—he may run if he can't halt the disasters that have struck the **Patriot's League.** We think the New York Senator suspects he's being set up for a fall. There's 'Regards to Professor Ramadan'. This is September, the ninth month, and the Feast of Ramadan lasts 30 days. Anselm is telling him that, if he runs, he will either leave the U.S. on the 30th, or arrive Baghdad on the 30th.

"Finally, there's 'may alter business procedures'. Anselm may be unable to rid himself of persons hot on his trail—after all, he's lost his killers, Danvier Dyan and Marchen Judisch. Leith, he knows you eliminated his best assassin, Andre the Specialist—so Anselm appears willing to import a real crazy, Druid Membossie, to do his murderous work."

Cody Dittus answered a question in everyone's mind. "Your suspicion of a shipment of contraband within the week seems likely. Yesterday, one of our Ozmen informed me that a rusting Liberian freighter docked in New York Harbor. The Moslem name on the bow is barely readable."

Leith Ohmstead interjected, "That little ole' freighter, 'Vengeful'?"

"You got it, Leith. Want to guess the captain's name?"

"That little ole' Arab, Captain Abdul." Cody grinned.

Leith Ohmstead sat back in his chair. There were no smiles between him and Cody. Leith said, "It **is** the eleventh hour. I've finally come to the conclusion that Judisch was right. You Israelis would be wise to return to your home ground, Tel Aviv. I'm going to get even for an eight-story fall!"

◆   ◆   ◆

The long range transport glided to a stop at Andrews Air Force Base. Its turbo-prop engines idled with a powerful whine. The aircraft, a C-130 Hercules, painted in camouflage colors, was identified by the distinctive markings of the Israel Air Force. Agents Ohmstead and Dittus were saying goodbye to General Moschi Rubinstern and Colonel Marseille LeBourget.

Ohmstead commented on the absence of personnel from the Israeli Embassy. General Rubinstern said, "Leith, the Embassy does their work in the diplomatic sphere, while we...and that means **all** of us...have our work in the military and national security. Our Embassy welcomes us here, but the colonel and I like to work incognito. The less the ambassadorial staff knows about us, the safer we operate. Like you, we work in the twilight zone.

"On your advice we'll soon take off from U.S. soil, and be home this evening. By then, no one will be able to point a finger at Israel or the Mossad. So, Ozman, what are you going to do with the leader of this **League?"**

"I really don't know, General. Anselm had done so much to give aid and comfort to the enemy. He was doing it well before he ever formed the Patriot's League. Anselm left a path through the Mid-East and we were getting close—that path went clear to the United States. Somehow, somewhere, he learned about Oz. The senator was even able to order **Syrian** hit-teams to get Cody Dittus in Beirut. We still haven't discovered how he knew Cody was in Lebanon. Next, assassins almost got me right here in Washington. How Abraham Anselm knew I had been sent to Lebanon to get Cody out of Beirut is only an educated guess."

Colonel Marseille LeBourget looked at Ohmstead and said,

"You can bet Anselm has a high-up contact in the CIA. Your Central Intelligence pokes their nose in everybody's business all over the world."

Leith chuckled bitterly. "Well, Colonel, **you** try to gather evidence against the CIA. They'd protect Al Capone if they thought it necessary. Have you ever heard of an agency of our government tackling another U.S. agency?"

The General snapped, "Never! In covert politics both our governments operate the same way. So, what will you do next, Leith? Criminal charges?" Ohmstead shook his head. "Anselm covers his tracks too well. Some of our evidence is ironclad. The rest of the heap is circumstantial. Normally, it would be enough. But, Senator Anselm wields such power that he could probably halt the Justice Department in its tracks. The fear is that fighting him to a finish might pull down the present administration. Already the people's faith in our present system is about a **5 on a scale of 1 to 10.**"

Moschi Rubinstern agreed. "True. We've experienced the same from fighting the Palestinians. And that's the stuff which breeds revolution."

Leith Ohmstead turned to Marseille LeBourget. "What would **you** do to bring such a man to trial?"

LeBourget answered, "Such a man of power would never face a judge in Israel. I doubt he would even come to trial. In that circumstance, we would have few options. None of them pleasant."

"Meaning what, Colonel?"

"We might have to let him go."

Leith cried, "I could never do that. He's gone too far."

"Then you'd have to remove him from circulation."

Leith grew angry. "There you go, again. WHAT DO YOU MEAN?"

General Rubinstern interrupted. "Colonel, we must GO!" They ran.

The Mossad leaders were waving farewell as the ramp door closed.

Within a minute the C-130 was airborne, disappearing toward Canada.

A quiet Cody Dittus accompanied a morose Leith Ohmstead to the VIP parking lot at Andrews AFB. Cody glanced several times at his best friend. He wisely kept his mouth shut. Both men climbed into Cody's auto and headed toward the exit gate. An Air Policeman, studying the car, waved them to a full stop. The AP, looking puzzled, stared at a clipboard he was holding. "Pardon me, Sirs. Are you the party that saw General Rubinstern and his aide leave on their plane?"

Despondent, Ohmstead didn't even reply. Cody Dittus answered, "Yes."

"Well, Sir, the General radioed the tower and left a message to be delivered at this gate for a Mr. Keith Home-Stead. Is that you?"

Leith answered, "I'm Mr. Ohmstead. What did the General say?"

The AP said, "I can't make any sense out of it, Sir, but the General told the tower you'd understand."

"Read it to me."

"Sir, the message says: '**Bang Bang!**'"

◆   ◆   ◆

The office of New York's Senator Abraham Lieberson Anselm now operated in an uproar. No longer did their boss discuss strategy with key staff members, nor oversee constituents' correspondence through his secretaries. Daily operations moved on a crisis to crisis basis, while all his employees were berated, more often cursed, by the paranoid senator. He ranted at anyone who wanted to quit. His demands approached the supernatural.

There was a reason: Frantic at the dissolution of his highly-profitable Patriot's League and the unexpected deaths of his trusted strong-arm men, Anselm finally, unobtrusively, placed himself under the care of a society doctor who did not restrict the heavy use of tranquilizers. In political circles such medication was referred to as "stress reducers."

The consequence was physiological changes in Abraham Anselm's body that promoted madness. There were pills to calm down, pills to stay alert, pills to sleep, and pills to wake up. The havoc inside Senator Anselm only made his behavior more objectionable to his faithful workers.

When his senate friends quit Congress due to health problems, Anselm suffered a crowning blow. That persuadable dummy, Dennahy, was gone. His puppet, Jacob Bergenfeldt, was collapsing in the Senate, skipping office hours, even failing to return Anselm's telephone calls. The New Jersey delegation was calling for Bergenfeldt's resignation and the election of a new senator. Yet, greed stabilized the ambition of Abraham Anselm.

This time he, himself, had personally checked and approved the cargo manifest of the ship, "Vengeance," and hurried Captain Abdul to load and sail. There were no cronies to obey his orders. Teamster union leaders were astonished that the New York senator was working dockside. Worse, Anselm's treatment of the old union bosses became dictatorial. His medicine-soaked brain was counting the tremendous sums being credited to his Zurich bank account. The only benefit gained by the dwindling of League membership was that Anselm's share of profits from Sadah Diyarbar had quadrupled. Anselm, even by American standards, was now immensely wealthy. A multi-millionaire. His medicines made him hyperactive. Always moving, he could not stand still.

Anselm's inability to stand still created an obstacle for Leith Ohmstead. Anselm never stayed in one place long enough for a confrontation. In fact, Agent Ohmstead could not even find an opportunity to meet the senator. Worse, there was the ship, "Vengeance." Captain Abdul was paying overtime wages to the union stevedores. His freighter would depart New York Harbor within 24 hours. The thought of Sultan Diyarbar of Iraq receiving another immense shipment of modern sophisticated weaponry turned Leith Ohmstead into a wild man.

"Great God Almighty, Cody! That Anselm has reached the point where he's above the law. He thinks he can do ANYTHING!"

Cody Dittus stared at the floor as he quietly said, "Leith, right now he <u>can</u> do anything. He's heading for a fall, but, in the meantime, he can sure steamroller a lot of gutsy officials who might try to stop him."

"Cody, the only thing left open is for the Oz Directors to arrange a meeting between The President and me."

"Forget it, Leith. You're forgetting this is an election year. The President needs all the votes New York can muster. You'd get no help."

Leith hung his head in frustration. "Dear friend, tell me: Is this a government **by the people**...or government **by special interests?**"

"Don't ever ask me that, Leith. My answer would only get you more upset. And, it's growing worse."

"But, that freighter, Vengeance? We've got to stop Captain Abdul and that shipment...and then go after Senator Anselm."

"Ah yes, Capt. Abdul. I've been thinking, Leith. I believe it's time for the reappearance of that turbaned bosun, Warrant Officer Ahabe Jagadis."

The executive officer of the Vengeance, Boudnawbie Smith, strolled the upper deck of the pilot house. He had been at sea too long and sorely missed his family. Anxious to be underway, he enjoyed the cool September air and admired the ever-changing orange and red colors of the setting sun. The ship was tied down tight; the stevedores had finished and gone; and, the dockside lay silent and empty. Only the arrival of a harbor pilot and tugboats were required to set sail. Boudnawbie glanced briefly at the gangplank. Then, startled, he did a double-take.

Strolling nonchalantly up the gangplank was a swarthy, impeccably dressed, ship's officer wearing an immaculate white turban. The officer stopped, saluted the Liberian flag, and stepped onto the deck. There was only one man who lived the code of a strict naval officer and conducted himself with such shipboard protocol. Boudnawbie Smith dashed to the Captain's Cabin.

Captain Abdul was resting, and more than irritated at being disturbed. When his Exec mentioned that a dark skinned naval officer was walking up the gangplank, Abdul snapped to attention. When the name "Bosun Ahabe Jagadis" was spoken, Abdul was already shouldering the door open.

Abdul would have hugged W/O Jagadis if he hadn't sprung to attention and saluted the Captain.

"Sir, I have only verbal orders to join you for the return trip to Port Al Faw. I was in a local seaman's hotel when an overseas phone call told me to report here. It wasn't from President Diyarbar or his aides, but from someone who called himself...Membossie?"

The name was electrifying. Capt. Abdul and Exec Smith looked at one another with the same thought. Related somehow to Diyarbar, Membossie was pure poison…a psychopath who killed members of his own staff for the sheer joy of the kill. Capt. Abdul said,

"No problem, good fellow. You are a member of this ship's company forever. Glad to have you aboard. I presume you want your old quarters?"

"Are they available, my Captain?"

Boudnawbie Smith answered, "They haven't been occupied since your last voyage. Frankly, nobody would dare."

At 3:00 o'clock in the morning, a figure stood on the fantail of the Vengeance with a miniature radio handset. The night was black and the freighter was long past Long Island Sound. Sailing toward Rehoboth Seamount, whose rocky crag lay 1,235 feet below, the ancient freighter groaned and popped as it labored through the swells of a restless ocean. The figure flipped a switch on the handset and sent a continual signal into the ether. Within moments a voice said, "I have you, Sahib."

"Here comes the blinker. Let me know when you have me in sight."

For the next quarter-hour, Cody Dittus, alias Ahabe Jagadis, sent infrequent signals. His efforts were rewarded with,

"Sahib, I see the outline of your ship. Give me a white."

Cody Dittus, shielding the flashlight with his body, blinked the white beam twice. No one on shipboard would suspect someone was on the ship's stern. Cody blinked again and again.

"I have your position spotted. I will maintain this distance until you advise. When will you flash again?"

"Stand by! I should return in fifteen minutes." Cody went below.

By 4:00 a.m., his work had been done, and W/O Ahabe Jagadis flicked his flashlight again. "Come get me. I'm ready to abandon ship. Confirm!"

"I have you, Sahib. When you see the red beacon, take your swim."

The ship's bosun, Ahabe Jagadis, was never seen again. But Cody Dittus tightened his life preserver, tied the radio and beacon light to the vest, and hooked a thin steel cable over the stern railing. Using a small hand-operated cable clamp, Cody slid down the cable into the Atlantic Ocean. His breath came in gasps. The Atlantic was COLD. A man would not last long with the heavy swell slapping and numbing his body. Dittus "flicked" the cable several times and, suddenly, the specially-designed hook released and the cable fell into the sea. Cody switched on the radio beacon and the flashing strobe light. As he floated, he wound the cable around a spool and carefully placed it in a vest pocket. He heard the approach of the Coast Guard motor launch.

Agent Dittus grabbed the long pole shoved at him and felt himself pulled to the gunnel. Strong arms yanked him aboard the launch. The night breeze whipped through his clothing and he shook from head to feet, his teeth chattering.

"Drink, Sahib." Cody's clothes were removed and he was rubbed dry with a coarse towel while almost drowning in hot coffee. The coffee was laced with…brandy?

"No, Sahib, it is rum. It's an old sea custom. I presume your assignment has been successfully completed?

Cody Dittus, ex-Warrant Officer Ahabe Jagadis, begged,

"More rum, Jabal. I'm freezing."

Excluding Leith Ohmstead, Jabal Thej-a-kel, alias 'The Jackal', was one of the few individuals Cody Dittus would trust with his life. And this time he did. The Atlantic at early morning is black, cold, with towering waves that conceal a person overboard at sea. Jabal and the Coast Guard Captain had done a professional job. Cody had spent only five minutes in the ocean.

Dittus ordered, "Jabal, get a radio message to Leith Ohmstead. He'll sleep better now. Tell him the Vengeance will sink slowly tomorrow. The crew will have time to abandon ship."

At noon, while officers and crew ate lunch, a powerful explosion shook the vessel. The outside steel plates, shielding the engine room, buckled and water flowed into the compartment. Minutes later the bulkhead doors were slammed shut and locked.

Executive Officer Boudnawbie Smith said, "Captain, we've contained the water. The bulkheads are holding, but we're developing quite a list. The radioman is sending our position and asking for assistance."

"Good!" shouted the Captain. Have we found Mr. Jagadis?"

"No, Sir. He's nowhere. His satchel is in his bunk…only clothes and a shaving kit. But, he's not been found."

"Allah! Such a man. Such a great seaman. Do you really think he fell overboard during the night, Boudnawbie?

"Yes, Captain, I do. I believe he was struck from behind and thrown overboard. Somebody set the explosive by the engine room and he's still among the crew. Remember, Captain, Membossie sent Jagadis here."

"Membossie? Kill Jagadis and sink Diyarbar's ship?"

"Wouldn't that hurt Diyarbar? Captain, who would succeed Diyarbar?"

THE SECOND EXPLOSION WAS WORSE! The deck bent and the Vengeance almost broke in half. The Atlantic poured into the cargo hold forward of the engine room. It was a death blow.

From the intercom, Abdul heard his Exec, Smith, say,

"No use, Captain. We've sealed the bulkhead door and braced it. But, this hole in our hull is too large. With two holds under water, the ship will lean port until it rolls over. And soon, Captain, it will sink stern first."

"Tell the crew, 'Abandon Ship'. Get up here with me and man the boats."

The ship's stern began to sink; the bow rose into the air. From the lifeboat, Abdul and Smith scanned the crew. Which one? Who set the bombs? "Membossie?" asked Smith. "Membossie!" said Abdul.

With a hiss of escaping air, the crash of shifting cargo, and the groan of buckling steel, the 'Vengeance' capsized and sank beneath the waves.

◆　　◆　　◆

Leith Ohmstead, after a sleepless night, was smiling as he talked long distance by radio-phone. Good old Jabal—what a friend to have on your side. Always dependable, extremely capable,…and always dangerous. What an enemy to have under **any** circumstance.

"Sahib Leith, your seagoing problem is gone. It rests in 200 fathoms."

"Survivors?"

"Everybody. The first bomb went off at lunchtime. It flooded the engine room. A half-hour later, the second one ripped open the adjacent hold. That did it. Abdul and Smith manned the lifeboats. Also, Sahib, they think a crewman killed Bosun Jagadis. They blame Membossie. Cody fooled them all."

◆　　◆　　◆

It was late evening. The dapper gentleman walked down the Senate Building corridor, swinging his umbrella in circles, his briefcase handcuffed to his wrist with a security bracelet. He knocked on the locked door to a senator's office. Attractively painted on the opaque glass was the seal of the State of New York.

Above it, in prominent letters were the words, Abraham L. Anselm, United States Senator. The visitor knocked again, . . forcefully.

The door opened slowly. Obviously, at this hour no one was expected.

Yes, Sir. I regret that Senator Anselm has gone. Will you come back tomorrow, or may I tell him who called?"

The individual denying access to the Reception Room was stylishly dressed. The visitor knew immediately that he was an aide to the senator; the other member of the staff rose from a chair across the room. This man, with tight lips, was edgy. His physique was 5' X 5', and his coat bulged. And he didn't care who knew it.

The tall visitor couldn't help thinking, "This character thinks he's really something. He'd beat up his own grandmother; and that bulge is from a long-barreled cannon, probably a .44 Magnum."

The visitor smiled, doffed his derby, and held out his card.

"I regret, Gentlemen, I must remain here…even until morning. My name is Noble Bare, special American courier for the Swiss Embassy in Iran. The Swiss represent the United States in Teheran. The President has ordered me to deliver important documents into the hands of Senator Anselm immediately. The senator **is** Chairman of the Senate Investigations Committee, isn't he? You may tell him I just flew in from Teheran."

Any other words used by the courier would have made no impression. But, like Sinbad's `Open Sesame', special courier and Iran made the senator's aide blink. He muttered, "Iran? **Now** what has Abraham got his fingers into?"

"Please be seated Mr.,…er, ah…Bare. I'll see if the senator may have returned."

The well dressed man entered the senator's office and closed the door.

The senator's tough guy said, "Where you from, Mr. Bare?"

"Teheran, Iran. I sometimes stop in Washington, but I travel over the world for the Swiss Government."

"Speak some Swiss to me?"

"I beg your pardon."

"Speak Swiss to me right now or I frisk you from head to foot and take a good look inside that briefcase. Understand, buddy?"

The 6' 6" courier did a slow burn. He stared at the bodyguard and said,

"YOU go ahead and speak Swiss. I speak German and English. The accepted language of the world is English, and my Swiss superiors are fluent in it. Next, you have my card and you may check with The President if you wish. But, you will not frisk me; more important, you will **never** poke you dirty hands into my briefcase."

The bodyguard, looking nasty, stood up. He began walking toward the visitor when the senator's aide returned. "Senator Anselm will see you now."

"This is most private. We are to be alone. Can that be arranged?"

The aide replied, "Mr. Bare, the office will remain closed and locked. But, **we** will be in the outer office. Senator Anselm's chamber is soundproof."

The Swiss courier, still glaring at Mr. 5 X 5, stood.

"Wait a minute, buddy," said 5 X 5, "You're not going anywhere. Get it?"

"NO, tough guy! I don't get it. But you <u>DO</u>!"

In one swift movement, the steel-tipped umbrella lifted toward the assailant, and the threatening silence echoed with a distinct 'HISS'.

The stocky bodyguard was awestruck as the thud of a small projectile struck him in the chest. He grabbed for his gun, but his powerful body was suddenly racked with choking coughs. He clutched his chest while the young staff member stared in horror as a bloodstain spread cross the bodyguard's shirt. He stepped backward, fell into his chair, and gazed across the room at the umbrella-wielding courier. His eyes did not blink; nor did he move.

The shocked aide pleaded, "Please...don't kill me. I won't make any trouble. I'll say nothing...if you just let me live, I'll..."

"SHUT UP!" The visitor pulled a small radio from his pocket, and extended a small aerial. "Jagadis, there's a young man coming out the front door. Meet him in the corridor. Escort him to his car and on his way home. If he makes any effort to do **anything,** waste him!"

The aide heard the radio's reply. "You want him alive? Or otherwise?"

"Naw. He hasn't hurt anyone...YET!" The aide was almost fainting. "Please, Mister. I have a wife and children. I..."

"Listen to me, boy. I'm going to let you live. You haven't done anything to deserve killing. You'll meet a man in a brown suit carrying a silver embossed cane. Go home. He'll follow you. You'll be smart to take a couple of stiff drinks and go to bed. You may want to come in tomorrow morning, but if I were you, I'd be studying the Want Ads. Whatever you do, don't screw around with the man with the cane. He eats people like you for breakfast. Understand?"

"Oh, yes Sir, yes Sir. Thank you, Sir. I . . I...don't believe I'll come in tomorrow. I'm not feeling well." The aide peered once more at the body slumped in the chair. The blood spot now covered the white shirt, but the wearer didn't mind. His eyes were still open, unmoving, like his body. Almost sobbing, the aide rushed out the door and down the hallway.

Leith Ohmstead checked the door lock and turned out the outer office lights. The New York Senator's office was closed.

As Leith Ohmstead entered Senator Anselm's expensively decorated sanctum, he rose to shake Leith's hand.

"Ah, Mr. Noble Bare. A peculiar name for a Swiss courier."

"Of all people, an **Abraham Lieberson Anselm** should not have said that."

Anselm snarled, "Just who the hell do you think you are?"

"Senator, don't you wish to see what I have in this embassy briefcase?

"I should think that an arrangement with Iranian leaders-with me representing the Swiss Government that controls Swiss bank accounts-could only prove profitable for you. Perhaps even greater than your Iraqi deal?"

Abraham Anselm's face paled. He reached into his desk drawer and popped several pills in his mouth. He washed them down with bourbon.

"Senator, that's quite a combination. It might kill you. Aside from your drug problems, we must figure out how to resurrect the Patriot's League."

Anselm jumped to his feet. "I said who the hell ARE you? How dare you speak to me like that? I'll have your job—Damn you, I'll have you thrown out of Switzerland. You'll never work in the United States again!"

"Senator, Lord John Acton of England was right. `Power corrupts. Absolute power corrupts absolutely'. Think of the good men, maybe weak men—still idealists—you have contaminated. Even coerced them into committing **treason!** What a ruthless bastard you've become; the people you've had MURDERED! What did Charter Saladin ever do to you except stress integrity and keep Congress scrupulously honest? To destroy him, you had his wife, Elena Imadie Saladin, assassinated; and that evil job was done by traitorous Hebrews like yourself who turned against their own people, even Israel. God! What a sick, filthy bastard you've become! Limitless Money and Endless Power—you're too evil to live!"

Anselm, his face livid with rage, screamed for his henchman,

"VANDETTI! GET IN HERE. BEAT THIS MAN TO A PULP. SMASH HIM, YOU HEAR? THROW HIS CARCASS IN THE GARBAGE! VANDETTI? VANDETTI, WHERE ARE YOU?"

Leith quietly answered, "There's no one there, Senator. Nobody alive!"

Agent Ohmstead, handcuff still locked on his right wrist, was reaching into the briefcase when Abraham Anselm yanked open a desk drawer and grabbed a pistol. But, Anselm froze when he looked down the barrel of Ohmstead's 10-millimeter automatic. The senator was no fool. He recognized the cylindrical tube of a silencer attached to that Smith & Wesson.

With courage born of desperation, Anselm swung his gun toward Leith Ohmstead. **Anselm never heard the "WHIPPP" as the bullet drilled a blue hole between his eyes. The body flopped into the executive chair. Anselm's head fell back on the headrest. His eyes gazed emptily at the ceiling.**

There was no wasted motion. Leith replaced his weapon in the briefcase and removed the handcuff. He took the pistol from Anselm's hand and removed the clip. From a small pocket-tool kit he took pliers and clamps. Carefully infolding a cartridge with cloth so as to leave no marks, he twisted the bullet out. He patiently drove a special patch made of gunpowder down the shell casing and replaced the cartridge in the revolver's cylinder.

Ohmstead clamped Anselm's hand around the gun butt, then held the barrel against the senator's forehead. He pulled the trigger.

The gun blast was tremendous. Leith was thankful the office was soundproofed. Although he had made a "blank bullet," the patch of gunpowder evaporated with the detonation of the cartridge powder. No evidence of foul play remained. Arms experts had seen to that. The shot left extensive powder burns on Anselm's forehead, but that was all. Leith let the pistol drop. The senator's hand still clasped the gun. Only Abraham Anselm's fingerprints would ever be found. The other five shots were still in the pistol cylinder.

The radio message said, "Now! Bring in the new rug."

Cody Dittus, in work clothes, long hair, and a handlebar mustache, walked down the corridor. His nondescript companion was dressed in similar "fashion." A knock on the door, and it opened quickly. Without conversation, the two workmen rolled the bodyguard, Vandetti, into a bulky Oriental rug. The small caliber pellet, coated with poison and fired from the umbrella gun, had killed swiftly. The tell-tale blood had only soaked the front of Vandetti's shirt. No stains or evidence lay elsewhere.

Ohmstead locked the Senator's office; then locked the entrance door; and escorted both workmen outside one of the back entrances to a panel truck. The rug was placed in the back with a guard; the other two men sat in front. Fifteen minutes later they were on a highway into Virginia.

Banner headlines proclaimed: **"PROMINENT SENATOR COMMITS SUICIDE."**

A prudent aide left town. He told police he had been on vacation.

Washington, D.C., police were baffled. But, Lt. Priscilla Kozac had a theory: Again rebuked, she was passed over for her Captaincy. She dropped from sight.

◆   ◆   ◆

The cycle for the "living in the now" continued. The huge splash of news about Anselm's suicide sputtered into obscurity. Sputtered because important happenings dealt with the living: New celebrities, newer scandals, and the ever who-did-what-to-whom clutter which typifies a voracious media.

Meanwhile, Speaker of the House Holcombe Broderick and Charter Saladin spent several days at Hidey Hole Lodge with Leith Ohmstead and Cody Dittus. Jabal Thej-a-kel relaxed, too. When Charter asked the imperturbable jackal where he had been, Jabal smiled and said,

"I have been handling Oriental rugs, Sahib."

In a quiet ceremony, Speaker Holcombe Broderick found new happiness and an end to his loneliness by marrying Miss Sarah. His ex-housekeeper could now spoil him in the manner of Abigail, his deceased wife. Sarah was a worthy successor to Abigail. She steadfastly refused to disclose the private discussions between herself and Abby. Unknown to Holcombe, Abigail's instructions to Sarah were bearing fruit. Sarah became a phenomenon in Washington, D. C. She saw much, heard much, said little. She was the perfect mate. The Speaker of the House acquired a new lease on life—and in so doing, shattered the dreams of key members of Congress whose sordid ambitions placed self above country.

Charter Saladin grew. Highly respected by both sides of the aisle, he became Majority Whip. The father-son relationship with Holcombe Broderick endured, to the everlasting benefit of America. This time, however, they would safeguard both upper and lower houses of Congress. It was Senator Charter Joseph Saladin, now.

The Directors of Oz had sentinels reporting from everywhere...especially in the U.S., and definitely Washington, D.C. A worried caller rushed to the phone. He ordered an unexpected visit by a whirlybird to Hidey Hole Lodge. A weary Leith Ohmstead groaned. Cody Dittus said,

"This one is mine. You take your well-earned rest. After all, I'm only your carpet carrier." Jabal, sipping an enjoyable coke, chuckled. But Cody was serious. Something was wrong. Jabal said,

"Sahib, would you like company? I am restive."

"Not yet, Jabal. In a few hours I may need you. Right here."

"Ah, so it comes...even to Hidey Hole!"

Cody Dittus did not answer. He was striding toward the helicopter.

First Lt. Priscilla Kozac was tired. She almost staggered into her kitchen, looking forward to a cold glass of wine. Her weariness came from a mental depression that sapped every bit of her strength. She pulled open the refrigerator door, its light illuminating her face. She inhaled deeply, then perceived an indistinct form watching her from a seat at the table.

Quickly walking to the backdoor light switch, she flicked it on and grabbed her pistol. Priscilla Kozac froze.

The man sitting at the kitchen table was grinning. Priscilla was peering down the large bore of a cannon. She had never seen a handgun like that. Held in the intruder's other hand was a silencer. The opening dialogue was one the Lieutenant would never forget.

"I can make a big BANG, which might disturb your neighbors. Or...I can make a soft `Phhhtttt', which certainly would disturb you!"

Priscilla's answer was classic, "I prefer not to be disturbed at all!"

Her visitor roared. He flicked the automatic's **safety** on, and laid the gun and silencer on the table. "Your wine is domestic, Priscilla. Please, join me with this bottle of imported `bubbly'. We must talk."

Lieutenant Kozac slowly walked to the table, her hand still on her revolver. She looked into the intense blue eyes of the man. He was poised like a cat. She had an odd feeling that if she could draw her gun, she would never get the chance to pull the trigger. She wisely sat down.

The wine was excellent, tasty, and...intoxicating. Priscilla's tongue grew thick, but she was relaxed. Cody Dittus started talking. He was an excellent salesman. Dittus confirmed that Lt. Kozac's theories were correct. She had been tying together an old crime, the abduction of a man from the eighth floor of the Stouffer-Mayflower Hotel. Somehow she knew it was tied to the "suicide" of Senator Abraham Anselm. But, as usual, she got nowhere with her hunches. She had stepped on too many toes. She would retire a lieutenant. A Captaincy would give her too much authority.

For the next hour Cody told it all—Oz, Agent Ohmstead, Agent Dittus, Congressmen Broderick and Saladin, the traitors who killed, were killed, traitors who resigned from government service, and the Patriot's League. Between gulps of wine, Priscilla Kozac's jaw hung open in astonishment.

The next hour Priscilla spent packing. The rest was left behind for midnight movers. Oz would pack her personals, but her furniture stayed behind. Oz would buy her new. Cody did not have to transport her to Hidey Hole Lodge,…where she would have met Jabal. The hard way.

Priscilla Kozac had become an agent of Oz. She would train, then reside in Europe. At last, she was accomplishing something. Oz listened to her. Days later, concerned Washington Police found her house abandoned. Except for old furniture, everything, including Police Lt. Priscilla Kozac, had vanished without a trace.

The Anselm case was history. The investigation, already at a trickle, stopped after the investigating officer disappeared. Priscilla Kozac had dropped from sight, and the hierarchy of top law officers and city commissioners grew nervous. The rumblings inside said she had gotten too close to the truth; that she had been deliberately squelched; that her caseload of crimes might give clues to the why of her sudden disappearance. But, this was an election year, and the Administration wanted the status quo. The Commissioners and the Police Chief also wanted the status quo.

First Lieutenant Priscilla Kozac's crime files disappeared. This time, **Oz** had nothing to do with it. Washington returned to normalcy, still infected with Potomac Fever.

◆   ◆   ◆

Leith Ohmstead and Cody Dittus rested and enjoyed a two-month vacation. A grateful Oz flew in cargo-carrying helicopters. Within days, Leith and Cody were enjoying their beautiful tree-bordered swimming pool. From the air it lay hidden within the patio timberland. Jabal, who swam like a fish, was suddenly gone. A whirlybird took him away before dawn. Soon after, Hidey Hole's satellite antennae picked up an international story: President Sadah Diyarbar had been critically hurt by his cousin, the powerful Druid Kahn Membossie. Diyarbar lived, and still rules. But, a fleeing Membossie was found at a desert oasis. He had been savagely knifed, and his neck had been shattered by heavy blows.

Jabal, the jackal, returned to Hidey Hole to convalesce. His wounds had been stitched, but his bandages were numerous. Healthy, he healed fast.

A suspicious Leith and Cody said little. Infallibly curious, Leith finally said one word, "Membossie?"

Jabal thought a moment. "He fought well, Sahib. America,...and Oz, can deal with Diyarbar more easily, now." The subject never came up again.

◆   ◆   ◆

After several months Leith and Cody were as "restive" as Jabal. They were pacing like caged lions. Even Jabal was getting into trouble: He was learning to like American beer. He was a shame to his forebearers.

One evening all three Ozmen were startled by the approach of a howling turbine. An attack helicopter, one of the newest and fastest, zoomed over the patio landing pad, turned, and quickly dropped to earth.

Out sprang Senator Charter Saladin who had signaled the pilot <u>not</u> to stop the engine. The foursome adjourned to the lodge.

"Gentlemen, Holcombe Broderick is at his home waiting to brief you. We've got serious problems."

The Oz trio looked at one another. Leith said, "Those problems must carry a high rating for the U.S. Army to allow use of their new attack helicopter. Why the rush?"

"Leith, Cody, there's a powerful consortium—worth BILLIONS—who are taking over the Big Three. There will be <u>no more</u> American auto manufacturers. Before spring, all trucks and cars will be under the control of Far East tycoons. The consortium involves Japan, Korea, Viet Nam, Singapore, Malaysia, Thailand, Hong Kong, and China. It's the East against the West and, with those eastern governments supplying financial support, we will be unable to compete economically. They can ruin the American Republic!"

Cody Dittus said, "Our leaders would never allow that. It would create a depression, vast unemployment, and likely destroy our system of government."

Charter Saladin laughed. "Ordinarily, you'd be right about our leaders not allowing a takeover. Yet, so far we've been able to trace a dozen of our best congressmen and senators who are members of the consortium's Board of Directors. And they're making no effort to hide their alliance."

"Whatever happened to patriotism? To God and country?" asked Leith.

Charter Saladin paused, then answered faintly, "Holcombe Broderick and I have been asking the same question: We believe the only game played today is 'Money and Power'. Nothing else seems to matter.

"Patriotism has been going, going. And now, it is gone!"

Leith Ohmstead acted quickly. "Cody, get our tote bags and guns. Everyone on the copter. We must confer with House Speaker Broderick and find out what's happening. He may require us to do some 'unannounced visiting'."

The agents of Oz packed quickly, then strapped on their guns as they raced to the waiting whirlybird. Senator Saladan was already on board. Suddenly, Ohmstead realized that there were only the three of them. Looking back, Leith saw a dejected, sulking British-trained, Mid-East warrior.

Ohmstead grinned and shouted, **"Hey, Jabal! Coming?"**

THE END

978-0-595-35935-6
0-595-35935-3

www.ingramcontent.com/pod-product-compliance
Lightning Source LLC
Chambersburg PA
CBHW030256290526
45785CB00001B/112